Praise for the previous editions
of
Understanding Arabs
and Margaret Nydell

D0092461

For 15 years, Margaret Nydell's *Understanding Arabs* has been used by countless Americans preparing to work or live in the Arab World. It is a unique source; there is nothing like it. Written with wit as well as seriousness, it provides a sound cultural appreciation as well as basic data on the region. A new appendix, "Muslims and Arabs in the West," constitutes a major innovation in the third edition. But her personal message regarding the tragic events of September 11 should be required reading by all who make decisions or write commentary on the Arab world.

—MAX L. GROSS
Joint Military Intelligence College

This is an important and fascinating book, especially for Americans in the crucial time in U.S.–Arab relations. Dr. Nydell presents a timely, lucid, and engaging guide to the values and cultures of the Arab World, based on her many years of working and living there and on her training as a professional linguist. This candid and wonderfully readable book captures the contrasts and the characteristics of this great civilization and brings them vividly to life for a Western audience.

—KARIN RYDING, PH.D.
SULTAN QABOOS BIN SAID PROFESSOR OF ARABIC
Chair of the Department of Arabic Language
Georgetown University

Ever wonder what the Arabs are thinking? *Understanding Arabs* offers both an analysis and a perspective that are in great demand. This book covers what the media typically overlook and what is *necessary* to make some sense of what is going on. We have relied on this source of cultural information for many years. I have found no other book in English to be so useful.

—COLONEL TERRENCE M. POTTER
US Military Academy

Middle East specialists have long relied on their worn copies of *Understanding Arabs* for insights about Arab social behavior. Following September 11, a third edition of this classic could not be more timely. A whole generation of U.S. diplomats were introduced to the subject by Dr. Nydell...in the 1970s and 1980s. In this concise and practical guide, she shares her wealth of scholarly and real-world experience, and she does so without the psycho-babble that too often dominates the other surveys of the subject.

—AMBASSADOR DAVID L. MACK, VICE PRESIDENT
Middle East Institute, Washington, D.C.

Among other things, the events of September 11 dramatized our ignorance as Americans about Arabs and Islam. This book helps to fill that void by exploring the enormous misconceptions that we hold about each other. In this work...Nydell explores both the background and context for our mutual misunderstandings. She discusses beliefs and values, relationships between men and women, etiquette and social structure, communication styles, religion, the Arabic language, and both the similarities and differences among the various Arab nations. As a result, we not only recognize the basis for misunderstanding but also the need for increased information and communication...A must read book for all!

—ALVINO E. FANTINI, FORMER PRESIDENT, SIETAR INTERNATIONAL
Senior Faculty, School for International Training
Brattleboro, Vermont

UNDERSTANDING
ARABS

UNDERSTANDING ARABS

A GUIDE FOR MODERN TIMES

Fourth Edition

Margaret K. Nydell

INTERCULTURAL PRESS
an imprint of Nicholas Brealey Publishing

BOSTON • LONDON

First published by Intercultural Press, a division of Nicholas Brealey Publishing, in 2006.

Intercultural Press, Inc.,
a division of Nicholas Brealey Publishing
20 Park Plaza, Suite 11154
Boston, MA 02116 USA
Information: 617-523-3801
Fax: 617-523-3708

Nicholas Brealey Publishing
3-5 Spafield Street, Clekenwell
London, EC1R 4QB, UK
Tel: +44-(0)-207-239-0360
Fax: +44-(0)-207-239-0370

www.nicholasbrealey.com

Printed in the United States of America

15   14   13   12   11   9   10   11   12   13

ISBN-13: 978-1-931930-25-3
ISBN-10: 1–931930–25–2
Library of Congress Cataloging-in-Publication Data

Nydell, Margaret K. (Margaret Kleffner)
  Understanding Arabs: A Guide for Modern Times / Margaret K. Nydell.– 4th ed.
    p. cm.
  Includes bibliographical references.
  ISBN 1-931930-25-2
  1. Arabs. I. Title.
  DS36.77.N93 2006
  909'.04927–dc22

                          2006019008

Cover Design: Rara Avis Graphic Design
Text Design: Alisa Andreola/Dartmouth Publishing, Inc.

Contents

A Message from the Author

In the late morning of 11 September 2001, I walked from the Georgetown University campus in Washington, D.C., and crossed the Key Bridge into Virginia. I found many buildings evacuated, public transportation stopped, and all roads going past the Pentagon blocked off. I finally found a taxi, and the driver assured me that he would help me get home to Crystal City by skirting around the Pentagon area and going far into Virginia. He did so, brilliantly, using small residential streets, until I was close enough to walk home. It took over an hour. He was Pakistani and, of course, Muslim. He was near tears (I was crying openly). He did not want to take any money. He said he was going to do this all day as a public service. I gave him money anyway and told him that if he didn't want to take it, he could donate it to Zakat charity (Islamic alms).

The shock of September 11 brought all Americans together in a moment of clarity—we are one nation. I hope this clarity will persist and will encourage us to seek greater understanding of other cultures. America is part of the world. We are all one family now. We are all in it together.

The terrorist attacks on the World Trade Center and the Pentagon on 11 September left Americans and millions of others around the world bewildered as well as shocked and angry. Who could have committed such an atrocity? As the smoke cleared, a Saudi Arab, Osama Bin Laden, became identified as the chief perpetrator, commanding a network called Al Qaeda, which were previously unknown to the general public. Its known members and accomplices are mostly Arabs and were all Muslims.[*]

People all over the world asked why. Why the United States? What could have motivated this act? The media, impelled as always to provide instant answers, came up with a variety of theories of varying degrees of merit. Some of them were based on popular misconceptions about Muslims, notably:

- This is a religion- and culture-based clash—the "clash of civilizations" theory. The Bin Laden group is characterized as representative of the thinking of the majority of Muslims.

- The attackers (and others who "hate America") are envious of the American way of life. They want to change American values and eliminate American freedoms.

- These particular attackers were motivated by visions of rewards in Paradise because for them this was a Jihad (a so-called Holy War) against unbelievers.

All of these explanations are without merit. They do not conform to the facts. They confuse the motives of this particular terrorist group with the prevailing discontent in the Islamic world. But the Al Qaeda group did not come out of nothing; it is an aberrant, cultlike faction that grew out of the Mideast milieu. This terrorist act, although rooted in political grievances, was an expression of the group's anger, through terrorist violence, for its own sake.

Statements such as "They hate American freedom" and "They want to destroy America" do not satisfy for long—they are impossibly vague. As time passes, people have begun to identify reasons that make more sense. We must dig deeper, because unless the terrorists are all crazy or all evil, there must be better reasons. If the three statements above were true, they would lead us first to despair, then to defiance, and ultimately back to despair.

Perhaps the reasons include things we don't understand or even know about. For example, resentments against the United States in particular

---

*Al Qaeda arose from a puritanical version of Islam, Wahhabism, which is followed officially only in Saudi Arabia. It was the prevailing interpretation of Islam among the Taliban group. The Wahhabi version of Islam forbids, for example, theaters and churches. It forbids the marking of graves. No alcohol or pork products may be imported. Publications are censored. Government-appointed officials enforce the law that requires all commercial establishments to close during prayer time. Wahhabis require women to cover their faces. Only Saudi Arabia has all these restrictions. An alternative term for Wahhabi is *Salafi*.

have grown out of a context with which few Americans are familiar. The resentments are not primarily against American wealth and power as such. Rather, the people in the Middle East are profoundly angry at how they *perceive* America using its wealth and power when dealing with other countries and cultures.

Perceptions become realities to the people who hold them, and people who lack cross-cultural experience can easily misunderstand the attitudes and behaviors they confront. Americans, for example, are notoriously ill-informed about the Mideast. In turn, the average Mideastern individual may be keenly interested in American political policies but actually knows very little about Western societies. Each side has enormous misconceptions about the other.

Language is a huge barrier. If we accept the premise that all people express themselves more accurately and candidly in their own language, then we should be skeptical about statements being reported from conversations with foreigners, filtered through English or other languages. Unfortunately, too many of our Mideast experts and reporters do not speak the local languages (imagine an expert on the U.S. who did not speak English). Thus they have severely limited access to information, and they may gravitate toward people with whom they can communicate easily, people who sometimes misrepresent the thinking of the general populace.

There are many arguments that can be made on both sides, but one thing is certain: the language barrier accounts for much of the misunderstanding. In the forty years I have been listening to political discussions in Arabic, among Arabs who were talking to one another and not to me, I have never heard resentment expressed about anything American except for foreign policy. Middle Easterners in general care only about American activities that negatively affect their own lives. Consider the explanations offered by the terrorist leaders and others we have associated with terrorist movements. We must not ignore what they are saying; we must try to understand their statements, recognizing that this does not require agreeing with them.

- Bin Laden: "They violate our land and occupy it and steal the Muslims' possessions, and when faced with resistance, they call it terrorism.... What America is tasting now is something insignificant compared with what we have tasted for scores of years. Our nation has been tasting this humiliation and this degradation for more than eighty years."[†]

- Muhammad Omar, leader of the Taliban: "America has created the evil that is attacking it...the U.S. should step back and review its policy."
- A spokesman, Muslim Brotherhood (Egypt): "We want to understand, are you Americans in favor of human rights and freedom? Or is that the privilege of some people and not others?"
- Ayatollah Sayyed Ali Khamenei, religious authority in Iran: "We are neither with you nor with the terrorists.... They [America] expect the entire world to help them because their interests demand it. Do they ever care about others' interests? These are the characteristics that make America so hated in the world."

None of these statements expresses threats that any group or faction is setting out to conquer the United States, force it to change its society, or impose its own ways of thinking on us. As far as I know, there have been no such statements. The September attacks were not aimed at targets like the Statue of Liberty, a cathedral, or a packed baseball stadium, but at structures that symbolize U.S. economic and military power.

How do Americans respond to this type of criticism? Righteous indignation is natural but not very productive over time. We need to examine the terrorists' statements and try to understand the context out of which they come. It is not appeasement to search for knowledge we do not currently have. How can such acts be prevented from happening again if the *real reasons* for the acts are left undiscovered—or worse, ignored? In my opinion one of the most tragic aspects of this trauma has been that thousands of families are bereaved, forever, and they do not know why this happened to them. Perhaps this book can help.

Understanding Arabs provides background and context for increasing cultural awareness, but it was first written years before the problem of world terrorism assumed its present proportions. It was written primarily

---

†Few Americans can hear this and know what happened in 1920. (See Chapter 12, page 125)

as a guide for Westerners, particularly Americans. To make the book more relevant to the current situation and to broaden the intended audience, I offer here some salient points that I believe must be considered as the world's people decide how as nations they will cope with this emergent threat. My purpose is to list what I believe to be objective facts rather than to interject recommendations or to suggest specific solutions.

- Mainstream Muslims do not approve of this terrorist group's acts. In fact they are horrified. The decision to engage in terrorism was the response of a singularly misguided cult-mentality group. Terrorism is in no way supported by the doctrines of the Islamic religion, which has always placed emphasis on human relationships and social justice. (There is much material on this topic, some of it available on the Internet.)

- Al Qaeda group members disguised themselves as immigrants, thus taking advantage of the good reputation Middle Eastern immigrants have earned. As a group, the immigrants are known to be industrious and family-centered. The terrorists betrayed these people. They posed as immigrants who wanted to share in the bounties of the West, but from the very beginning the terrorists had an entirely different agenda.

- Mainstream Muslims do not want to change Western (or other non-Muslim) cultures. Many Muslims do not want Western values to enter their own societies, but providing their own lives are not affected, Muslims (and Middle Easterners in general) are not concerned with how Westerners and others structure their own lives. The vast majority do not resent Western prosperity and freedom; in fact, millions of them immigrate to the West because they admire many of the social values and want to participate in a Western way of life. They want their children to grow up free and with the possibility of prosperity.

- We must not allow a cult to represent an entire religion. The bombing of abortion clinics is not justified by mainstream Christian faith. Sectarian violence in Ireland does not represent mainstream Protestantism or Catholicism.

- Muslims, Arabs, and other Middle Easterners do not blame Americans as individuals. Their assumption, right or wrong, is that the people of the United States cannot be held personally responsible because they are generally unaware of their government's policies. Americans are known to other nations as being uninformed about their country's foreign policy. (Less obvious to Middle Easterners is the fact that many Americans, at least prior to 11 September, also didn't care.) Unlike the terrorists' sympathizers, most Middle Easterners have genuinely grieved for innocent lives lost in this or in any violent warlike act. They are like people everywhere.

- The 11 September attack was not a real Jihad. The term *Jihad*, as used in mainstream Islam, is misunderstood. Its primary meaning is not "Holy War," although that has become its meaning in Western languages. Most pertinent here, a true Jihad must be a response to an overt attack or threat made by non-Muslims toward the Muslim community. *Muslims may not initiate a Jihad.* The terrorists have interpreted Western, and most recently U.S. political power in the Middle East, as an attack on their people.

- The terrorists are trying to promote enmity between Islam and Christianity. They are misusing the term *Jihad* just as they misuse terms like *Crusade, infidel,* and *unbeliever.* The term Jihad has become politicized and is constantly being invoked and misused for political purposes. During the war between Iraq and Iran, for example, each declared a Jihad against the other.

- The Qur'an and other Muslim sacred scriptures, like those of other religions, are long, complex, and open to wide-ranging interpretations. Emphasis on details such as presumed rewards in Paradise for people who die in a Jihad are, frankly, irrelevant and insulting to most educated Muslims. Muslims are not religiously motivated in any way to harm or kill non-Muslims. As with any body of sacred scripture, a selective choice of quotes can "prove" anything, including completely opposite ideas.

- Focusing on Al Qaeda and Islamic terrorists is too narrow a goal. It will not end the threat. These terrorists are short-term enemies, current targets against whom the United States now wages war. But even if they are eliminated, *the root causes of resentment will continue to exist.* The U.S. must reverse the negative perceptions about itself, and this cannot be done by force. No security is effective enough to prevent an attack by a person who is willing to commit suicide. Long-term strategic thinking is needed.

Sweeping statements that are frightening but do not suggest a remedy are not a solution. What use are statements such as "All humanity is at risk" and "You will never take down this great nation" and "What the United States has done to attract violent attacks is to be strong, wealthy, and successful"? If Americans blindly declare that the terrorists hate them for their benevolence, successes, and innocence, where does it lead? It does not help in framing an appropriate response. If the United States and the Western world continue to ignore accusations, especially those they do not fully understand, they do so at their own peril. What brings forth statements that America is "morally corrupt and hypocritical"? Why is America accused of "supporting state-sponsored terrorism"? Why is there cheering when someone says "Americans never see the blood"? These are the types of statements that must be thoughtfully considered if there is to be any hope of a just and lasting peace.

* * *

Thousands of innocent citizens have died. More may follow. What should be done?

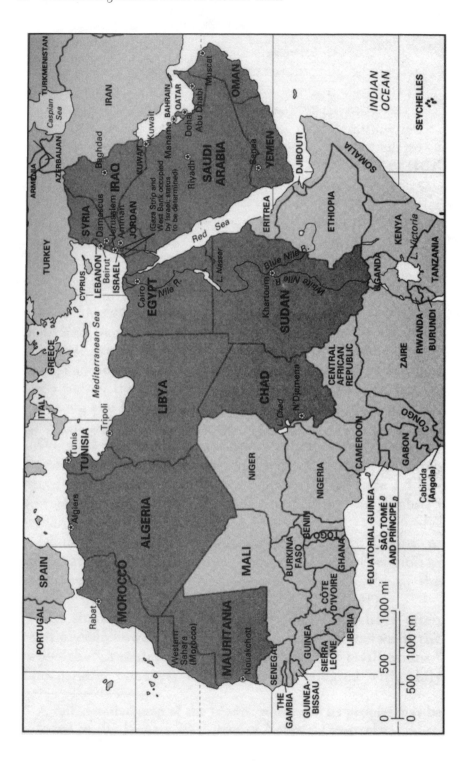

Preface

Understanding Arabs: A Guide for Modern Times is a handbook, intended to be read, easily and quickly, by people who are not specialists in Middle East studies. The purpose of this book is to assist outsiders, especially Westerners in America and Europe, to *understand* modern-day Arabs. This includes looking at the thought patterns, social relationships, and ways of life of urban Arabs in the twenty-first century. The majority of today's Arabs, the people we are likely to encounter in the media or in person, are mostly middle class (or slightly above or below), not exotic Bedouins from the desert. It is time to get away from "the Bedouin ethos."*

It is essential that we look at Arabs realistically as they are *today*, and not attempt to describe and explain them in terms of Middle East history that goes back centuries. Ancient and Medieval history cannot be used to provide *reasons* for the present-day nature of Arab society—there have been too many changes in the last one hundred years, particularly in the last sixty. I think we have heard quite enough about pre-Islamic Arabia, the Muslim conquests, the eleventh-century Assassins, the twelfth- and thirteenth-century Golden Age, the harems, the House of War, the dragomans in Ottoman times, and the like.

Most of us are aware of the degree to which different national and

---

*The Bedouin ethos is the basis for the code of chivalry brought to Europe in Crusader and post-Crusader times. It is no more relevant to the lives of modern Arabs than the Christian code of chivalry is to the lives of modern Westerners. Modern Arab society is not tied to the Bedouin ethos.

cultural groups stereotype each other, at a distance or in person-to-person relations. When Westerners and Arabs interact, especially if neither understands the other, they often come away with impressions that are mutually negative.

Similarly, the Israeli/Palestinian conflict is about Israelis and Palestinians of today, who are not the same people referred to in the Bible as Hebrews and Ishmaelites (Arabians). Many Israelis are of European and other non-Semitic origins, and the Palestinians are *Arabs* but not *Arabians* from the Arabian Peninsula;† they are descended from indigenous populations such as Canaanites, Moabites, and Phoenicians. The current conflict is political, a clash over land, and has its origins entirely in the twentieth century.

It is important to understand that the conflict is *not* religious; Islam is far closer to Judaism than is Christianity. Muslims accept all of the Jewish prophets and many of their religious practices. Muslims have no historical grievance against Jews and did not engage in periodic massacres as happened repeatedly in Europe, causing many Jews to flee south. However, after sixty years of bitter conflict, the religion of Judaism and the political ideology of Zionism have become mixed, by both sides. Still, I have never heard an Arab or a Muslim say anything negative about Jews as people *except in the context of Israel.*

The shared origins of Christianity and Islam have often been over-shadowed by the historical conflicts between the two religions—the Crusader mentality, the clash of civilizations. Both religions have a concept of Holy War—Crusade and Jihad. Conflicts have accentuated the differences and polarized the West and the Middle East, obscuring the shared beliefs of the three great interrelated monotheistic faiths: Judaism, Christianity, and Islam.

A word about the title: *Arab* is a very general term, something like the word *European.* People in these groups have much in common, but there are distinct regional differences. The term *Arab* is useful, though, in contexts such as the Arab League, the Arab world, and pan-Arabism. Arab refers not to ethnicity, but to *all Arabic-speaking people.*

We must not confuse Arabs with Muslims. There are 17 Arabs countries

---

†The distinction between Arabs and Arabians is crucial. Confusing these groups leads to statements like "Jews...were settled in the country a thousand years before the coming of the Arabs [Arabians] in A.D. 634."[1]

referred to here (it is a matter of definition; there are 22 members of the Arab League). Muslims are a majority in 55 countries. There are about 300 million Arabs, 5 percent of whom are Christian or other religions. There are 1.5 billion Muslims in the world.‡ Islam is the world's fastest-growing religion. Owing primarily to immigration, Islam has become the second-largest religion in both the United States and Europe.§

Understanding Arabs deals with the Arab countries in the Middle East and North Africa. It does *not* discuss the primarily Muslim but non-Arab populations in Turkey (where the people speak a language of Mongolian origin) or the Middle Eastern countries in which people speak Aryan languages, which are part of the Indo-European language family—Iran (Persia), Afghanistan, the Kurds, and Pakistan.

Foreigners find very little material available to help them understand modern Arab society. Not much has been written on the subject of Arab cultural and social practices, either in Arabic or in Western languages. A great deal of the material that exists is over thirty years old and appears dated to anyone who is familiar with Arab society today.# Some observations made only twenty years ago are no longer applicable. Many foreign writers and reporters have very limited contact with Arabs, often only colleagues in their profession (the military, the media, banking officials) and people who speak English. In recent years changes in education, housing, health, technology, and the media have had a marked effect on attitudes and customs.

The most serious deficiency in research about Arab society is the lack of attention given to the large majority of urban, educated (often Western-educated) Arabs. Researchers, especially anthropologists, have mostly focused on village life and nomadic groups and on the study of traditional, sometimes quaint, social patterns. Interesting as these studies are, they offer little directly applicable information for Westerners who will, for the

---

‡ A full, detailed map of the Islamic world and its peoples may be found in the January 2002 issue of *National Geographic.*

§ *Islam* is the name of the religion; the adjective is *Islamic.* A Muslim is a *person* who practices Islam.

The well-known book *The Arab Mind* by Raphael Patai[2] was based on his residence in Jerusalem in the 1930s and 1940s, and his acquaintances during that era. He lived in the U.S. after 1947, and was a "frequent visitor" to the Jerusalem area. The book was outdated when it was published in 1973. It has continued to be republished, most recently in 2002, *unchanged.* It is heavily based on the Bedouin ethos, and much other information is inaccurate. It should be read, if at all, with skepticism.

most part, encounter Arabs who are well educated, well traveled, and sophisticated. Keep in mind that the large majority of the people (more than 95 percent) are never mentioned in the news, because they are getting on with their lives and do not engage in newsworthy activities.

This book is an attempt to fill that gap. It focuses on the middle and upper classes—businessmen and -women, bureaucrats, managers, scientists, professors, military officers, lawyers, banking officials and intellectuals—and the ways in which they interact with foreigners and with each other. In most Arab countries the urban educated people differ considerably from rural or tradition-oriented social groups; indeed, some types of behavior required by the norms of one group are considered obsolete by another. At the same time, many basic traditions and customs still determine the way of life of all Arabs and affect their goals, values, and codes of accepted behavior. The many similarities among social groups and among the various Arab countries still outweigh the differences, so valid generalizations are possible. Any significant differences among groups will be pointed out.ǀǀ

Scholars have varying opinions about the sociological effort to characterize groups of people as the same, different, ahead, or behind. Multiculturalists say that all cultural practices are equally valid, so attempts at comparisons can be a form of racism. Other scholars are quick to criticize certain cultures, quick to draw their own conclusions, especially when compared to, in this case, the West. We hear of "cultural stagnation" and "cultural failure" and the justifications for creating such labels—it's amazing how observers, from historians to reporters to government advisors, are never lacking in confidence when it comes to explaining what the Arabs think. These opinions are often based on erudite references to events back through several centuries, and they come to sweeping conclusions such as "The social basis of the Arab-Islamic hatred is mingled both with fanaticism and feelings of inferiority toward the West.... the greatest sin of the West is to place the individual and the rule of reason at the center."[3] My goal, in contrast, is to present what most

---

ǀǀThe term *Arab* is so broadly used that many people wrongly assume that they are all one block of people. It is confusing, for example, to read about the "Janjaweed Arab militias" in south Sudan. They are called Arabs because they share language and religion, but they have no other similarities, ethnically or culturally, with Arabs of the Middle East.

Arabs believe and leave it at that.

I hope that this book will help alleviate stereotyping in two ways: (1) by explaining some of the behavioral characteristics of Arabs in terms of cultural background, thereby deepening the reader's understanding and helping to avoid negative interpretations, and (2) by serving as a guide to cross-cultural interaction with Arabs, which will help people avoid inadvertent insults and errors of etiquette, and help them make a favorable impression.

It is important that Westerners who interact with Arabs be aware of the particular characteristics of Arab etiquette and patterns of behavior and thought, since the differences may be quite subtle and, initially, hard to identify. It is easy to be lulled into the security of assuming that the superficial similarities of appearance, dress, and lifestyle among educated Arabs mean that they are "just like us." One is more likely to remain alert for different social proprieties when seated in a tent or a mud-floor village house; it is not so easy to remember the differences when seated in the living room of a modern home, surrounded by Western-style furnishings and English-speaking Arabs.

Any attempt to describe the motives and values of an entire people is challenging. On the one hand, it leads to generalizations that are not true in all cases, and, on the other, it necessarily involves the observer's perspectives and interpretations and leads to emphasizing some traits over others. I hope to present a balanced view, one that is generally descriptive of Arabs throughout the entire cultural area of the Arab world. Most of the material in this book, including anecdotes (I have hundreds), comes from my own personal experiences and from interviews with others. These interviews have taken place in virtually all of the Arab countries—in North Africa, the Levant, the Fertile Crescent, and the Arabian Peninsula.

American college students return from a stay in the Arab world enthusiastic, even effusive, in their praise of the Arab people they have come to know and are anxious to find a way to go back. "They are so friendly…they were so nice to me…everyone was helpful…people in public would say 'Welcome' in English…I loved sitting in a café playing backgammon with Syrians and Iraqis"—not what we would expect based on the media image.

There are many delightful surprises that await foreigners as they come to know more—the hospitality, the wonderful food, the kindness to children and elderly people, the large, loving families. But this is not a book for tourist agencies. We also need to look at the problem areas, as many of them as possible, in order for this book to be helpful. Many factors can lead to mistaken interpretations, on both sides, and perhaps *lead to serious errors in judgment.*

The Arabs have been subjected to so much direct or indirect criticism by the West that they are very sensitive to a Westerner's statements about them. I have made an effort here to be fair, honest, and at the same time, sympathetic to the Arab way of life, especially when contrasting Arab and Western cultural behavior. Value judgments do not belong here; there is no assumption that one cultural approach is better than another.

Note: Arabic words may be written in English in their conventional spelling, or spelled in a way that is closer to the actual Arabic pronunciation. Both ways are fine; it depends on your purpose. We see variant spellings: *Moslem/Muslim, Mohammed/Muhammad, Koran/Qur'an,* and names with *Abdul/Abdel.* You will also see the prefix *Al-* or *El-,* which means "the" and is often included in names.

Finally, the word *Shiite* in English was coined so we could add *–s* and make it look like an English plural. In Arabic, the singular is *Shii* and the plural is *Shia—Shia* is the term used in this book.

Introduction:
Patterns of Change

Arab society has been subjected to enormous pressures from the outside world, particularly since the Second World War. Social change is evident everywhere because the effects of economic modernization and political experimentation have been felt in all areas of life. Even for nomads and residents of remote villages, the traditional way of life is disappearing.

Modernization

Most social change has come through the adoption of Western technology, consumer products, healthcare systems, financial structures, educational concepts, and political ideas. These changes, necessarily, are controversial but inevitable and are present to varying degrees in all of the Arab countries.

The Arab nations have experienced an influx of foreign advisers, managers, businesspeople, teachers, engineers, healthcare and military personnel, diplomats, politicians, and tourists. Through personal contact and increased media exposure, Arabs have been learning how outsiders live. Thousands of Arab students have been educated in the West and have returned with changed habits and attitudes. The spread of the Internet has had a major impact as well.

1

Tens of thousands of Westerners live, or have lived, in the Arab world, and most of them loved the experience. Many stay on for years and have a wide circle of Arab friends. They comment that human relations seem deeper, and friendships, even business transactions, feel more personal and meaningful than in Western societies.

Arab governments are building schools, hospitals, housing units, airports, and industrial complexes so fast that entire cities and towns change their appearance in a few years. It is easy to feel lost in some Arab cities if you have been away only a year or two. Modern hotels are found in any large city; the streets and roads are full of cars; and the telephone, fax, and Internet services are often overtaxed. Imported consumer products are abundant in most Arab countries, ranging from white wedding dresses to goods in supermarkets. While these are surface changes, they also symbolize deeper shifts in values.

Overall rates of literacy have skyrocketed since the 1960s. In the last 40 years the number of educated people doubled in some countries and increased ten times or more in others. Literacy in the Arab countries is an average of 68 percent, and literacy in the states of the Arabian Peninsula rose from less than 10 percent to an average of 86 percent by 2003. Among those living in urban areas, it has reached 80 percent or more almost everywhere. The highest rates of literacy are in Saudi Arabia (94 percent), Jordan (91 percent), Bahrain (89 percent), Lebanon (86 percent), Qatar (85 percent), and Kuwait (83 percent). Since 1970, women's literacy expanded threefold and girls' primary enrollment more than doubled.

The rise in literacy is due to a phenomenal growth in public education, which is free and mandatory in all Arab countries.* In Saudi Arabia enrollment in primary schools more than quadrupled since 1980. In Kuwait there were 3,600 students in schools in 1945 (primary and secondary), 270,000 in 1994, and 400,000 in 2001.[1] In Saudi Arabia literacy rates were 15 percent for men and 2 percent for women in 1970; and a startling 82 percent for men and 68 percent for women in 2000.[2, 3]

Education at the university level is growing even faster, sometimes doubling or tripling in one or two decades. The following are the percentages of eligible students enrolled at the university level in their home countries.

---

*Except Saudi Arabia.

Percentage Enrolled in University Education[4, 5]

	1980	2001
Jordan	13	31
Saudi Arabia	7	22
Tunisia	5	23
Oman	0	7

	1985	2001
Libya	9	58
Lebanon	28	45

Arab women are becoming more educated and active professionally. In 1973 only 7 percent of women were employed in the workforce.[6] Currently the average is 21 percent. Arab women are definitely aware of the fact that this percentage is low compared with many regions of the world. The industrial world, by comparison, averages from 40 to 50 percent of female employment.

Percentage of Women in the Workforce 2004[7]

	Percentage 2004
Algeria	12
Bahrain	22
Egypt	22
Iraq	18–19†
Jordan	21
Kuwait	25
Lebanon	28
Libya	21
Morocco	25
Oman	18
Saudi Arabia	11
Sudan	28
Syria	21
Tunisia	24
United Arab Emirates (UAE)	12
Yemen	27

†It was 40 percent in Iraq in the early 1980s.

Improved health care is changing the quality and length of life. The increase in the number of physicians per 1,000 people has completely transformed the healthcare situation.

Number of Physicians per 1000 People[8, 9]

	1980	2003
Jordan	0.8	205
Oman	0.5	137
Syria	0.4	142
UAE	1.1	177

The number of hospitals and clinics has increased at the same rate.

Life expectancy in the Arab countries has risen dramatically. These are examples of what happened in fifty years.

Life Expectancy[10]

	1955	2005
Morocco	43	69
Egypt	42	69
Kuwait	55	77
Saudi Arabia	34	73

This increased longevity is reflected in population statistics. Since the 1950s, the average rate of population growth has ranged between 2.5 to 3 percent, as high as anywhere in the world. In the four years between 1986 and 1990, the overall Arab population grew by 5 to 7 percent (8 percent in the UAE and 10 percent in Oman); it has now leveled out to about 2 to 3 percent per year.[11]

In recent years Gaza, Yemen, and Oman had the highest rates of natural growth (not counting migration) in the world, with 3.8, 3.4 and 3.3 percent per year, respectively. Libya, Iraq, and Syria grew at the rate of 2.4 to 2.8 percent, also extremely high rates. This compares with a world rate of 1.14. The rate is 0.92 in the U.S., 1.4 in India, 0.39 in France, and 0.08 in Japan.[12]

By 2000, 30 to 40 percent of the entire Arab population was *age 14 or under*. The World Bank estimates that the population of the Middle East as a whole (including non-Arabs) will increase from 448 million to 650 million by 2050.[13]

All over the Arab world, the population has been shifting from farms and villages to large urban centers, most dramatically during the period from the end of the Second World War through 1980. The magnitude of urbanization is illustrated by comparing urbanization rates in recent years. Some countries are among the most urbanized in the world.

Percentage Urbanized[14, 15]

	1970	1995	2001
Saudi Arabia	49	83	87
Libya	45	85	88
Jordan	51	71	79
Tunisia	43	62	66
UAE	57	84	87

By 2020, 70 percent of all the people in the Middle East will live in cities, an addition of 86 million people.[16]†

Urbanization brings its own problems. Except in the Gulf countries, governments face housing shortages, overuse of municipal services (Amman, Jordan, has water only a few hours per day, public transportation is almost impossible in Cairo, everywhere traffic is ten times more than the roads were designed for), and overburdened social services, from schools to healthcare centers to job centers. In the poorer countries, unauthorized housing proliferates (notably Casablanca, Algiers, Cairo); in fact, 20 percent of Cairo's population live in illegal housing. And occasional political crises contribute to problems—at the end of 1990, after the invasion of Kuwait, 4 to 5 million people left the Gulf region.[17]

Internet access illustrates the current situation well. Only 1.6 percent of the overall Arab population has access. More recent data show that in 2004 the number of users per 1,000 people was between 250 and 300 in parts of the Arabian Gulf, more than 100 in Lebanon, in the 60s in Saudi Arabia, in the 50s in Jordan and Tunisia, and in the 30s, 20s or fewer in Libya, Syria, Algeria, Egypt, and Morocco. This is compared with 550 people per 1,000 in the U.S., and 400 to 500+ in the developed world.[18]

---

†Some of the less urbanized countries include Egypt (43 percent), Sudan (37 percent), and Yemen (25 percent).

Some of the other major social changes and trends in the Arab world include the following:

- Family planning is promoted and increasingly practiced in most Arab countries, and it is accepted as permissible by most Islamic jurists.

- People have far more exposure to newspapers, television, radio, computers, and the Internet.

- Entertainment outside the home and family is growing more popular.

- More people travel, work, and study abroad.

- Parents are finding that they have less control over their children's choice of career and lifestyle.

- More people are working for large, impersonal organizations and industries.

- Business organizations are increasingly involved in international trade.

- Political awareness and participation have increased significantly.

- Educational and professional opportunities for women have completely changed family life.

The Arab Human Development Reports

The publication of the *Arab Human Development Report* in 2002 was the first of its kind, a major event in Arab self-appraisal. It was written by a group of Arab intellectuals from the 22 countries in the Arab League and funded by the Arab Fund for Economic and Social Development, which is part of the United Nations. The report was notable for its frankness in pointing out the region's lack of freedom, economic development, and achievements in science and technology,§ as well as gender inequality, and the high rate of illiteracy. The report was updated for 2003, and the report for 2004 came out in April 2005. The most recent report stated that "there is a serious failing in the Arab world, and this is located specifically in the political sphere."[19] It called for greater political freedom, a sharing of absolute ruling power, and a curtailment of cor-

---

§It is refreshing to see a frank analysis of the current situation without reference to the glories of the Golden Age of Islamic civilization in medieval times. It is important to acknowledge these contributions, but it is also time to move on.

ruption. It also expressed complete acceptance of "liberal democratic ideals" and a distrust of the current U.S. administration's sincerity in promoting Arab welfare and commitment to broad goals of democratization, because of its alliances with certain Arab governments.[20]

The report also mentioned that because of poor economic conditions, the Arab world has lost 25 percent of its university graduates to emigration, and 15,000 medical doctors emigrated between 1998 and 2000.

The Effects of Change

The disruptive effects of the sudden introduction of foreign practices and concepts on traditional societies are well known, and the Arabs have not been spared. The social strains among groups of people who represent different levels of education and Western exposure can be intense, the mutual frustrations existing to a degree that can hardly be imagined by Westerners.

Both modernist and traditionalist ways of thinking are present at the same time in modern Arab society, forming a dualism. Modern science and technology are taught side by side with traditional law and religious subjects.

Arabs, particularly the younger generations, are *very attracted to* and *appreciative of* American culture and its products, including entertainment, music, clothing, and liberal ideals such as freedom and equal opportunity. The generation gap, which is widening, is excruciatingly painful for some communities and families—some of the younger people are liberal and influenced by the West, while others have become more conservative and religious. All this affects family decisions—a Westernized Arab once equated the feelings of an Arab father whose son refuses to accept the family's choice of a bride with the feelings of a Western father who discovers that his son is on drugs.

A common theme of Arab writers and journalists is the necessity for scrutinizing Western innovations, adopting those aspects that are beneficial to their societies (for example, scientific and technical knowledge) and rejecting those that are harmful (such as a lessening concern for family cohesion or social morality).

Arabs have long been concerned about the Westernization that is often a part of modernization. They want to modernize, but not at the expense of certain traditions. It is a mistake to assume that Arabs aspire to create societies and governments identical to Western models. Many Americans, in particular, find it surprising that most foreigners are not interested in the way Americans do things, in personal life or in society. Arabs often disapprove of what they hear about American and European social practices and moral standards (understood correctly or not), but they have no interest in changing the Western way of life. They just don't want it imposed on them.

The issue for Arabs is not whether they want modernization. The momentum cannot be stopped now. The issue is *whether they can adopt Western technology without adopting the Western values and social practices that go with it* and thereby retain cherished traditional values.

Speaking as a Westerner, I find it hard to envision a modern society (a self-sustaining, competitive, industrial and technological society) unless it is open, with industry privatized, individual initiative rewarded, and free markets established as part of a global economy. A government cannot forbid its citizens to hear and consider such options. Many of these issues cannot be answered by a religion, any religion.

The Muslim View

It is important to realize that interpretations of Islamic practices vary widely. Many of the customs that distinguish Middle East countries stem from *local cultural practices* (family relationships, women's role in society, people's manner of dress, child-rearing practices, female circumcision), *not religion*. Because Sunni Islam has no organized hierarchy and no central authority, decisions by religious scholars often vary as well.

Educated people want modernization and change, but as stated earlier, they also want to keep much of what they consider their Islamic lifestyle. The idea is not to replace Islam, but to renew it, in order to face the new conditions of modern life. But this is more easily said than done, particularly in the face of the renewed emphasis on Islam.

All over the Arab world and the entire Middle East, religious studies have increased in universities, as has the publication of religious tracts, and more religious orations are heard in public. This has been going on for a long time — the number of religious broadcasts and Islamic newspapers and books tripled in the 1980s alone.[21]

There has also been a steady increase in Islamic-oriented organizations, laws, social welfare services, educational institutes, youth centers, publishers, and even Islamic banks. Many tradition-oriented Muslims have entered politics. A more visible Islamic dimension has become a part of everyday life.

Determining how to confront changes will be difficult indeed — heated discussions about various solutions will go on forever. The resurgence of conservative religion further supports the views of the traditionalists, who oppose any reinterpretations of Islam, and this group contains many government authorities, military officers, teachers, journalists, and intellectuals. *But traditionalists are not fundamentalists* if we use the term *fundamentalist* to mean "militant Islamist." Traditionalists want to maintain cultural and religious authenticity; they are exactly like traditionalists in other religions. The Muslim traditionalist view is that while Islam must accommodate modernity, modernity must also accommodate Islam.[22]

Muslims are determined to accommodate change in their own way. They believe they can contribute to the changing world, to a possible new global order. The West excels at progress through the development of technology, and Islam can provide a humanizing factor — morality. The goal is a universally *moral and materially advanced* global world order. Many non-Westerners believe that the Western exercise of world power lacks a strong underpinning of morality that leads to preferences for special interests, without consideration of whether the policies are "right" or "wrong" for all people.

Benazir Bhutto characterized two groups of Muslims — reactionary and progressive:

> *I would describe Islam in two main categories: reactionary Islam and progressive Islam. We can have a reactionary interpretation of Islam, which upholds the status quo, or we can have a progressive interpretation of Islam, which tries to move with a changing world.*[23]

There has long been discussion about how Islamic education could or should differ from Western education, and this subject is continuously discussed in the media. Of particular concern is how science and technology relate to traditional Islamic values and ways of looking at the world, and how these can be retained. Many Muslim commentators believe that Western education relies too exclusively on process, without the spiritual dimension. They contend that the search for knowledge about the world constantly changes, but values do not change.

Muslims believe that textbooks should be prepared so that they reflect the Islamic outlook even as they present pertinent modern theories and discoveries. One educator suggested, for example, that, in the natural sciences, the word nature could be replaced with God so that it is clear that God is the source of natural growth and development, of the properties of chemicals, of the laws of physics and astronomy, and the like. Historical events are to be evaluated not for military or political significance but by their success in furthering the spiritual aims of humanity; for example, an agnostic society that amassed a great empire would not be judged as "successful."[24]

It seems to me that evangelical Christians would find very little to differ with in the above statement.

The relationship between Islam and science is uncertain and attracts many opinions. Some assert that "Islamic science" does not exist, because Islam does not encourage free, creative inquiry, while others are confident that the two can be reconciled.[25] Some Muslims find modern Western science lacking in that it asks "what" and "how" but not "*why*," the latter bringing in a religious/philosophical dimension. For example, Seyyed Hossein Nasr, a noted American-Iranian specialist in Islamic philosophy, states that Islamic science must differ from modern science by setting ethical limits and remaking a science entwined with Islamic ontology and philosophy, which would result in holistic vision of knowledge. He is countered by Pervez Hoodbhoy, a Pakistani physicist, who writes that the idea of an Islamic science must be abandoned, as it is a delusion, and Muslim societies must accelerate the learning of modern science in order to be competitive. Much was written on this subject in the late 1970s and 1980s, and it is well reviewed at some Internet sites.[26]

Muslim intellectuals everywhere are actively seeking Islamic alternatives for their societies. In many countries young people belong to informal groups in which the role and contributions of Islam to modern society are avidly discussed. For example, at a meeting of the Current Religious Affairs Consultation held in Istanbul in 2002, a group of religious scholars issued this statement:

Social changes which have been expedited by the developments in scientific and technological areas have deeply influenced the traditional understanding of the religion and in turn necessitate new discussions over many issues....[The issues include] traditional and modern approaches in understanding, the interpretation of religious texts and its reflections on society, [and] religious discussions regarding women's problems in the modern world.[27]

Facing the Future

Outside pressure toward change is glaringly visible in the changes in the Arab countries' architecture and city planning. Skyscrapers and air conditioning have replaced thick-walled traditional houses that were designed to condition the air themselves by means of a wind tower. Many crowded "old city" districts, with twisted lanes and jumbled markets and houses, have been destroyed; those that are left are in stark contrast with the newer parts of cities, built with wide streets on a city-block plan. Unfortunately, some modern housing does not address the needs of families and communities: there is no daily gathering place for women or separate living and entertainment areas for men and women. In most Arab cities, it is difficult nowadays for members of an extended family to find housing in one place or even in one area.

Many young people in particular agonize about their identity (family? nation? Arab region? religious group or secular?) and what constitutes appropriate lifestyle choices, a dilemma that is simply unknown among Westerners. Balancing between the modern and the authentic traditional way of life is a concern among Arabs in all levels in society.

Westerners may perceive a dual personality present in many educated Arabs, who have the ability to synthesize two diverse ways of thinking and appreciate both. Few of us in the West have to contend with a dualism of this kind.

It is clear that a great deal of confusion and upheaval is still to be experienced. The ambivalence toward, or rejection of, liberal social change, particularly if it contradicts traditional social values, can be better understood by considering the questions it raises in the mind of an Arab: How do you compare the relative value of a communications satellite with the wisdom of a village elder? What good is a son who is a computer expert but lacks filial respect? How do you cope with a highly educated daughter who announces that she never intends to marry?

This is the context in which Westerners encounter Arabs today. This is the background for Arabs' choices and aspirations.

Beliefs and Values

When we set ourselves the task of coming to a better understanding of groups of people and their culture, it is useful to begin by identifying their most basic beliefs and values. It is these beliefs and values that determine their outlook on life and govern their social behavior. We have to make broad generalizations in order to compare groups of people — here, Arabs and Westerners. Bear in mind that this generalizing can never apply to all individuals in a group; the differences among Arabs of the 17 nations described here are numerous, although all have an Arab identity.

Westerners tend to believe, for instance, that the individual is the focal point of social existence, that laws apply equally to everyone, that people have a right to certain kinds of privacy, and that the environment can be controlled by humans through technological means. These beliefs have a strong influence on what Westerners think about the world around them and how they behave toward each other.

Arabs characteristically believe that many, if not most, things in life are controlled, ultimately, by fate rather than by humans; that everyone loves children; that wisdom increases with age; and that the inherent personalities of men and women are vastly different. These beliefs play a powerful role in determining the nature of Arab culture.

One might wonder whether there is, in fact, such a thing as Arab culture, given the diversity and spread of the Arab region. Looking at a map, one realizes how much is encompassed by the phrase "the Arab world." The Arab countries cover considerable territory, almost all of it desert or wilderness; if the uninhabitable land were removed, the Arab world would be *very small* for its 300 million people. Much of the inhabited land is along coasts and rivers. Sudan is larger than Western Europe, yet its population is 35 million (as compared with 706 million in Western Europe); Saudi Arabia is bigger than Texas and Alaska combined, yet has only 25 million people. Egypt, with 76 million people, is 95 percent desert.* One writer has stated, "A true map of the Arab world would show it as an archipelago: a scattering of fertile islands through a void of sand and sea. The Arabic word for desert is *sahara* and it both divides and joins."[2]

The differences among Arabs in different regions are immediately obvious—they have different foods, manner of dress, housing, decorative arts, and architectural styles. The political diversity is also notable; governmental systems include monarchies, military governments, and socialist republics.

But despite these differences, the Arabs are more homogenous than Westerners in their outlook on life. All Arabs share basic beliefs and values that cross national and class boundaries. Social attitudes have remained relatively constant because Arab society is conservative and demands conformity from its members. Arabs' beliefs are influenced by Islam, even if they are not Muslims (many family and social practices are cultural, some are pre-Islamic); child-rearing practices are nearly identical; and the family structure is essentially the same. Arabs are not as mobile as people in the West, and they have a high regard for tradition. Some features shared by all Arab groups are: the role of the family, class structure, religious and political behavior, patterns of living, standards of social morality, the presence of change, and the impact of economic development on people's lives.[3]

Initially, foreigners may feel that Arabs are difficult to understand, or that sometimes their behavior patterns are not what was expected. In fact, though, their behavior is very comprehensible, even predictable. For the most part it conforms to certain patterns that make Arabs consistent in their reactions to other people.

---

*Like many Arab countries, Egypt is large; statistics on population density reflect that. In terms of total area, Egypt's population density is 77 persons per square kilometer. If considering only the habitable area, it is 1670 persons per square kilometer.[1]

It is important for a foreigner to be aware of these cultural patterns, to distinguish them from individual traits. By becoming aware of patterns, one can achieve a better understanding of what to expect and thereby cope more easily. The following lists of Arab values, religious attitudes, and self-perceptions are central to the fundamental patterns of Arab culture and will be examined in detail in subsequent chapters.

Basic Arab Values

- It is important to behave at all times in a way that will create a good impression on others.
- A person's dignity, honor, and reputation are of paramount importance, and no effort should be spared to protect them. Honor (or shame) is often viewed as collective, pertaining to the entire family or group.
- Loyalty to one's family takes precedence over personal preferences.
- Social class and family background are the major determining factors of personal status, followed by individual character and achievement.
- Social morality standards should be maintained, through laws if necessary.

Basic Arab Religious Attitudes

- Everyone believes in God, acknowledges His power, and has a religious affiliation.
- Humans cannot control all events; some things depend on God's will, that is, fate.
- Piety is one of the most admirable characteristics in a person.
- There should be no separation between church and state; religion should be taught in schools and promoted by governments (this is the Islamic view, not necessarily shared by Arab Christians).
- Established religious beliefs and practices are sacrosanct. Liberal interpretations or indiscriminate imitations of Western

culture can lead to social disorder, lower moral standards, and a weakening of traditional family ties, so they must be rejected.*

Basic Arab Self-Perceptions

- Arabs are generous, humanitarian, polite, and loyal. Arabs see these traits as characteristic of themselves and as distinguishing them from some other groups.

- Arabs have a rich cultural heritage, as illustrated by their contributions to religion, philosophy, literature, medicine, architecture, art, mathematics, and the natural sciences (some of which were made by non-Arabs living within the Islamic empire). Most of these outstanding accomplishments are largely unknown and unappreciated in the West.

- Although there are many differences among Arab countries, the Arabs are a clearly defined cultural group and perceive themselves to be members of the Arab Nation (al-umma al-'arabiyya).

- The Arab peoples see themselves as having been victimized and exploited by the West. For them, the experience of the Palestinians represents the most painful and obvious example. Arabs are misunderstood and wrongly characterized by most Westerners. Many people in the West are anti-Arab and anti-Muslim. Most Westerners do not distinguish between Arabs and Muslims.

---

*Often cited are the West's tolerance of youthful rebellion, alcohol, drugs, pornography, homosexuality, unchaperoned dating, and the rate of illegitimate births (currently one in three in the U.S.)[4]. Half a million children are in foster care. Surveys indicate that the dominant perception in Arab and Muslim countries is that religion and family are not important in America. They assume that such practices, tolerated as part of individual freedom, are in fact condoned by Westerners. Arabs value social morality far more than individual choice.

Friends and Strangers

Relationships are very personalized in the Arab culture. Friendships start and develop quickly. But the Arab concept of friendship, with its rights and duties, is quite different from that in the West.

The Concept of Friendship

Westerners, especially Americans, usually think of a friend as someone whose company they enjoy. A friend can be asked for a favor or for help if necessary, but it is considered poor form to cultivate a friendship primarily for what can be gained from that person or his or her position. Among Arabs, also, a friend is someone whose company one enjoys. *However, equally important to the relationship is the duty of a friend to give help and do favors to the best of his or her ability.*

Differences in expectations can lead to misunderstandings and, for both parties, a feeling of being let down. The Westerner feels set up to do favors, and the Arab concludes that no Westerner can be a true friend. In order to avoid such feelings, we must bear in mind what is meant by both sides when one person calls another friend.

Reciprocal Favors

For an Arab, good manners require that one never openly refuse a request from a friend. This does not mean that the favor must actually be done, but rather that the response must not be stated as a direct no. If a friend asks you for a favor, do it if you can—this keeps the friendship flourishing. If it is unreasonable, illegal, or too difficult, the correct form is to listen carefully and suggest that while you are doubtful about the outcome, you will at least try to help. Later, you express your regrets and offer instead to do something else in the future. In this way you have not openly refused a favor, and your face-to-face encounters have remained pleasant.

I once talked to an Egyptian university student who told me that he was very disappointed in his American professor. The professor had gratefully accepted many favors while he was getting settled in Egypt, including assistance in finding a maid and buying furniture. When the Egyptian asked him to use his influence in helping him obtain a graduate fellowship in the United States, the professor told him that there was no point in trying because his grades were not high enough to be competitive. The Egyptian took this as a personal affront and felt bitter that the professor did not care about him enough to help him work toward a better future. The more appropriate response by the professor would have been to make helpful gestures; for example, helping the student obtain information about fellowships, assisting him with applications, and offering encouragement—even if he was not optimistic about the outcome.

In Western culture actions are far more important and more valued than words. In the Arab culture, *an oral promise has its own value* as a response. If an action does not follow, the other person cannot be held entirely responsible for a failure.

If you fail to carry out a request, you will notice that no matter how hopeful your Arab friend was that you would succeed, he or she will probably accept your regrets graciously without asking precisely why the favor could not be done (which could embarrass you and possibly force you to admit a failure). You should be willing to show the same forbearance and understanding in inquiring about one of your requests. Noncommittal answers probably mean there is no hope. This is one of the most frustrating cultural patterns Westerners confront in the Arab world. You must learn to work with this idea rather than fighting against it.

When Arabs say yes to your request, they are not necessarily certain that the action will or can be carried out. Etiquette demands that your request have a positive response. The result is a separate matter. A positive response to a request is a declaration of intention and an expression of goodwill—no more than that. *Yes* should not always be taken literally. You will hear phrases such as Inshallah (If God wills) used in connection with promised actions. This is called for culturally, and it sometimes results in lending a further degree of uncertainty to the situation.

It is more polite on both sides to express goodwill rather than to criticize a person's ideas or to refuse a request bluntly. Arabs are responding to a different culturally defined concept of politeness; it does not mean that they are "lying" or that they are not dependable. This is a subtle point, and it depends on the situation.*

Sometimes an Arab asks another person for something and then adds the phrase, "Do this for my sake." This phrasing sounds odd to a foreigner, especially if the persons involved do not know each other well, because it appears to imply a very close friendship. In fact the expression means that the person requesting the action is acknowledging that he will consider himself indebted to return the favor in the future. "For my sake" is very effective in Arab culture when added to a request.

An Arab expects loyalty from anyone who is considered a friend. The friend is therefore not justified in becoming indignant when asked for favors, since it should be understood from the beginning that giving and receiving favors is an inherent part of the relationship. Arabs will not form or perpetuate a friendship unless they also like and respect you; their friendship is not as calculated or self-serving as it may appear. The practice of cultivating a person only in order to use him or her is no more acceptable among Arabs than it is among Westerners.

Introductions

Arabs quickly determine another person's social status and connections when they meet. They will, in addition, normally give more information about themselves than Westerners will. They may indulge in a little (or a lot of) self-praise and praise of their relatives and family, and they may present a detailed account of their social connections. When Westerners meet someone for the first time, they tend to confine personal information to generalities about their education, profession, and interests.

---

*This is from a recent recording made of a Qatari woman's speech: "There is no polite flattery or indirectness—I liked this in Europe. They tell the truth when they talk. If someone likes something, he tells you *Yes*. If he doesn't like it, he says *No*. I might get irritated, but it's the truth."[1]

To Arabs, information about family and social connections is important, possibly even more important than the information about themselves. Family information is also what they want from you. They may find your response so inadequate that they wonder if you are hiding something, while your impression is that much of what they say is too detailed and largely irrelevant. Both parties give the information they think the other wants to know.

Your Arab friends' discourse about their influence network is not bragging, and it is not irrelevant. This information may turn out to be highly useful if you are ever in need of high-level personal contacts, and you should appreciate the offer of potential assistance from insiders in the community. Listen carefully to what they have to say.

Visiting Patterns

Arabs feel that good friends should see each other often, at least every few days, and they offer many invitations to each other. Westerners who have Arab friends sometimes feel overwhelmed by the frequent contact and wonder if they will ever have any privacy. There is no concept of privacy among Arabs. In translation, the Arabic word that comes closest to *privacy* means "loneliness"!

A British resident in Beirut once complained that he and his wife had almost no time to be alone—Arab friends and neighbors kept dropping in unexpectedly and often stayed late. He said, "I have one friend who telephoned and said, 'I haven't seen you anywhere. Where have you been for the last three days?'"

By far the most popular form of entertainment in the Arab World is conversation. Arabs enjoy long discussions over shared meals or many cups of coffee or tea. You will be expected to reciprocate invitations, although you do not have to keep pace precisely with the number you receive. If you plead for privacy or become too slack in socializing, people will wonder if they have offended you, if you don't like them, or if you are sick. You can say that you have been very busy, but resorting to this too often without sufficient explanation may be taken as an affront. "Perhaps," your friends may think, "you are just too busy for us."

I once experienced a classic example of the Arab (and especially Egyptian) love of companionship in Cairo. After about three hours at a party where I was surrounded by loud music and louder voices, I stepped onto the balcony for a moment of quiet and fresh air. One of the women noticed and followed immediately, asking, "Is anything wrong? Are you angry at someone?"

A young Arab American was quoted as saying:

In the United States...you can have more personal space, I guess is about the best way to put it. You have privacy when you want privacy. And in Arab society they don't really understand the idea that you want to be alone. That means that you're mad, you're angry at something, or you're upset and you should have somebody with you."[2]

People want to be surrounded by others when they are sick in the hospital or in a state of mourning, times when a Westerner might prefer to be alone. All hospital rooms have facilities for relatives, and a patient cannot possibly keep them out, even if he or she wanted to. Arabs feel terribly lonely in a new place where they don't know anyone; a comfortable security has been lost. This is a description of an Arab woman who had just arrived in England, written by her daughter:

She hated the cold weather and the rain and she complained she could scarcely keep the house warm. She was lonely and longed for company. In the Arab world, you were never alone for a moment. Your neighbors or friends were always there to call on every day and, in any case, there was the family around you at all times.[3]

If you are not willing to increase the frequency or intensity of your personal contacts, you may hurt your friends' feelings and damage the relationship. Ritual and essentially meaningless expressions used in Western greeting and leave-taking, such as "We've got to get together sometime," may well be taken literally, and you have approximately a one-week grace period in which to follow up with an invitation before your sincerity is questioned.

Some Westerners, as they learn about the intricate and time-consuming relationships that develop among friends, decide they would rather keep acquaintances at a distance. If you accept no favors, you will eventually be asked for none, and you will have much more time to yourself, but you will soon find that you have no Arab friends. Arab friends are generous with their time and efforts to help you, are willing to inconvenience themselves for you, and are concerned about your welfare. They will go to great lengths to be loyal and dependable. If you spend much time in an Arab country, it would be a great personal loss if you develop no Arab friendships.

Business Friendships

In business relationships, personal contacts are much valued and quickly established. Arabs do not fit easily into impersonal roles, such as the "business colleague" role (with no private socializing offered or expected) or the "supervisor/ employee" roles (where there may be cordial relations during work hours but where personal concerns are not discussed). For Arabs, all acquaintances are potential friends.

A good personal relationship is the most important single factor in doing business successfully with Arabs. A little light conversation before beginning a business discussion can be extremely effective in setting the right tone. Usually Arabs set aside a few minutes at the beginning of a meeting to inquire about each other's health and recent activities. If you are paying a business call on an Arab, it is best to let your host guide the conversation in this regard—if he is in a hurry, he may bring up the matter of business almost immediately; if not, you can tell by a lull in the conversational amenities when it is time to bring up the purpose of your visit. If an Arab is paying a call on you, don't be in such a rush to discuss business that you appear brusque.

The manager of the sales office of a British industrial equipment firm based in Kuwait told me about his initial inability to select effective salesmen. He learned that the best salesmen were not necessarily the most knowledgeable, eager, or efficient but were instead those who were relaxed, personable, and patient enough to establish friendly personal relations with their clients.

You will find it useful to become widely acquainted in business circles, and if you learn to mix business with pleasure, you will soon see how the latter helps the former proceed. *In the end personal contacts lead to more efficiency than following rules and regulations.* This is proven over and over again, when a quick telephone call to the right person cuts through lengthy procedures and seemingly insurmountable obstacles.

Office Relations

When Westerners work with the same people every day in an office, they sometimes become too casual about greetings. Arabs are conscientious about greeting everyone they see with "Good morning" or "Good afternoon" if it is the first encounter of the day, and they will go out of their way to say "Welcome back" when you return after an absence. Some Westerners omit greetings altogether, especially if they are distracted or hurried, and Arab coworkers invariably take notice. They usually understand and are not personally offended, but they interpret it as a lack of good manners.

An American nurse at a hospital in Taif, Saudi Arabia, had an enlightening experience on one occasion when she telephoned her Saudi supervisor to report arrangements for an emergency drill. She was enumerating the steps being taken when the Saudi said, "That's fine, but just a moment—first of all, how are you today?"

If you bring food or snacks into the office, it is a good idea to bring enough to share with everyone. Arabs place great value on hospitality and would be surprised if you ate or drank alone, without at least making an offer to share with everyone. The offer is a ritual, and if it is obviously your lunch or just enough food for yourself, it is usually politely refused; it depends on the situation.

Remember to inquire about business colleagues and coworkers if they have been sick, and ask about their personal concerns from time to time. Arabs do mention what is happening in their lives, usually good things like impending trips, weddings, and graduations. You do not need to devote much time to this; it is the gesture that counts.

In Arab offices supervisors and managers are expected to give praise to their employees from time to time, to reassure them that their work is noticed and appreciated. Direct praise, such as "You are an excellent employee and a real asset to this office," may be a little embarrassing to a Westerner, but Arabs give it frequently. You may hear "I think you are a wonderful person, and I am so glad you are my friend" or "You are so intelligent and knowledgeable; I really admire you." Statements like these are meant sincerely and are very common.

I was once visiting an American engineering office in Riyadh and fell into conversation with a Jordanian translator. I asked him how he liked his work. He answered in Arabic so that the Americans would not understand, "I've been working here for four years. I like it fine, but I wish they would tell me when my work is good, not just when they find something wrong." Some Westerners assume that employees know they are appreciated simply because they are kept on the job, whereas Arab employees (and friends, for that matter) expect and want praise when they feel they have earned it. Even when the Westerner does offer praise, it may be insufficient in quantity or quality for the Arab counterpart.

Criticism

Arab employees usually feel that criticism of their work, if it is phrased too bluntly, is a personal insult. The foreign supervisor is well advised to take care when giving criticism. It should be indirect and include praise of any good points first, accompanied by assurances of high regard for the individual. To preserve the person's dignity, avoid criticism in front of others, unless an intermediary is used (see below for further discussion of intermediaries). The concept of constructive criticism truly cannot be translated into Arabic—forthright criticism is almost always taken as personal and destructive.

The need for care in criticism is well illustrated by an incident that occurred in an office in Amman. An American supervisor was discussing a draft report at some length with his Jordanian employee. He asked him to rewrite more than half of it, adding, "You must have entirely misunderstood what I wanted." The Jordanian was deeply hurt and said to one of the other employees, "I wonder why he doesn't like me." A far better approach would have been, "You are doing excellent work here, and this is a good report. We need to revise a few things, however; let's look at this again and work through it together, so we can make it even better."

I remember overhearing a dramatic confrontation in an office in Tunis, when an American supervisor reprimanded a Tunisian employee because he continually arrived late. This was done in front of other employees, some of whom were his subordinates. The Tunisian flared up in anger and responded, "I am from a good family! I know myself and my position in society!" Clearly he felt that his honor had been threatened and was not at all concerned with addressing the issue at hand.

Intermediaries

The designation of one person to act as an intermediary between two other persons is very common in Arab society. Personal influence is helpful in getting decisions made and things done, so people often ask someone with influence to represent them (in Arabic this process is called *wasta*).

If you are a manager, you may find that some employees prefer to deal with you through another person, especially if that person knows you well. An intermediary may serve as a representative of someone with a request or as a negotiator between two parties in a dispute.

Mediation or representation through a third party also saves face in the event that a request is not granted, and it gives the petitioner confidence that maximum influence has been brought to bear. You may want to initiate this yourself if an unpleasant confrontation with someone appears necessary. But because you, as an outsider, could easily make a mistake in selecting an intermediary, it is best to consult with other Arab employees (of a higher rank than the person with whom you have a conflict).

Foreign companies have local employees on their staff who maintain liaison with government offices and help obtain permits and clearances. The better acquainted the employee is with government officials, the faster the work will be done and the better the service will be. Arab "government relations" employees are indispensable; no foreigner could hope to be as effective with highly placed officials.

You will observe the wide use of intermediaries in Arab political disputes. Mediators, such as those who undertake shuttle diplomacy, are often essential in establishing the personal contact that makes consensus possible. Their success depends on the quality of the personal relationship they establish with the parties involved. If mediators are recognized by both parties as being honorable and trustworthy, they have already come a long way in solving the problem. That is why some negotiators and diplomats are far more effective than others; personalities and perceptions, not issues, determine their relative success.

An outstanding example of diplomatic success due, in large part, to personality may be seen in Henry Kissinger's achievements when he served as a negotiator between the leaders of Syria, Egypt, and Israel after the 1973 War. He established personal friendships with the individuals involved; Anwar Sadat's remark that "Dr. Henry is my friend" is very revealing. These friendships contributed greatly to Kissinger's ability to discuss complicated issues and keep a dialogue going, something no one had managed to do before.

On the political level, you will constantly see situations in which an individual Arab leader attempts to mediate disputes among other Arab governments.

Private and Public Manners

In the Arab way of thinking, people are clearly divided into friends and strangers. The manners required when dealing with these two groups are very different. With friends and personal acquaintances, it is essential to be polite, honest, generous, and helpful at all times. When dealing with strangers, "public manners" are applied and do not call for the same kind of considerateness.

It is accepted practice to do such things as crowd into lines, push, drive aggressively, and overcharge tourists. If you are a stranger to the person or persons you are dealing with, then they will respond to you as they do to any stranger. Resenting this public behavior will not help you function better in Arab societies, and judging individuals as ill-mannered because of it will inhibit the development of needed relationships.

All over the Arab world people drive fast, cross lanes without looking, turn corners from the wrong lane, and honk their horns impatiently. Yet, if you catch a driver's eye or ask his or her permission, the driver will graciously motion for you to pull ahead or will give you the right-of-way.

While shopping in a tourist shop in Damascus, I watched a busload of tourists buy items at extremely high prices. When they were gone, I chatted with the shopkeeper for a few minutes and then bought some things. After I had left, a small boy came running after me—the shop owner had sent him to return a few more pennies in change.

Whenever I am in a crowded airport line, I try to make light conversation with the people around me. Never has anyone with whom I talked tried to push in front of me; in fact, they often motion for me to precede them.

Personal contact makes all the difference. If you feel jostled while you are waiting in line, the gentle announcement "I was here first" or "Please wait in line" will usually produce an apology, and the person will at least stand behind you. Keep calm, avoid scenes, and remember that none of the behavior is directed at you personally.

3

Emotion and Logic

How people deal with emotion or what value they place on objective versus subjective behavior is culturally conditioned. *While objectivity is given considerable emphasis in Western culture, the opposite is true in Arab culture.* But whatever you encounter, there are always reasons; no behavior is random.

Objectivity and Subjectivity

Westerners are taught that objectivity, the examination of facts in a logical way without the intrusion of emotional bias, is the mature and constructive approach to human affairs. One of the results of this belief is that in Western culture, subjectivity—a willingness to allow personal feelings and emotions to influence one's view of events—represents immaturity. Arabs believe differently. They place a high value on the display of emotion, sometimes to the embarrassment or discomfort of foreigners. It is not uncommon to hear Westerners label this behavior as immature, imposing their own values on what they have observed.

A British office manager in Saudi Arabia once described to me his problems with a Palestinian employee. "He is too sensitive, too emotional about everything," he said. "The first thing he should do is grow

27

up." While Westerners label Arabs as too emotional, Arabs may find Westerners cold and inscrutable.

Arabs consciously reserve the right to look at the world in a subjective way, particularly if a more objective assessment of a situation would bring to mind a too-painful truth. There is nothing to gain, for example, by pointing out Israel's brilliant achievements in land reclamation or in comparing the quality of Arab-made consumer items with imported ones. Such comments will generally not lead to a substantive discussion of how Arabs could benefit by imitating others; more likely, Arab listeners will become angry and defensive, insisting that the situation is not as you describe it and bringing up issues such as Israeli occupation of Arab lands or the moral deterioration of technological societies. They would have to do this, because you have offended their pride.

Fatalism

Fatalism, or a belief that people are powerless to control events, is part of traditional Arab culture. It has been much overemphasized by Westerners, however, and is far more prevalent among traditional, uneducated Arabs than it is among the educated elite today. Nevertheless, it still needs to be considered, since it is often encountered in one form or another.

For Arabs, fatalism is based on the belief that God has direct and ultimate control of all that happens. If something goes wrong, people can absolve themselves of blame or can justify doing nothing to make improvements or changes by assigning the cause to God's will. Indeed, too much self-confidence about controlling events is considered a sign of arrogance tinged with blasphemy. The legacy of fatalism in Arab thought is most apparent in the ritual phrase "Inshallah," noted in Chapter 2.

Western thought has essentially rejected fatalism. Although God is believed by many Westerners to intervene in human affairs, Greek logic, the humanism of the Enlightenment, and cause-and-effect empiricism have inclined the West to view humans as having the ability to control their environment and destiny.

What Is Reality?

Reality is what you perceive—if you believe something exists, it is real to you. If you select or rearrange facts and if you repeat these to yourself often enough, they eventually become reality.

The difference between Westerners and Arabs arises not from the fact that this selection takes place, but from the manner in which each makes the selection. Arabs are more likely to allow subjective perceptions to determine what is real and to direct their actions. This is a common source of frustration for Westerners, who often fail to understand why people in the Middle East act as they do. This is not to say that Arabs cannot be objective — they can. But there is often a difference in outward behavior.

If Arabs feel that something threatens their personal dignity, they may be obliged to deny it, even in the face of facts to the contrary. A Westerner can point out flaws in their arguments, but that is not the point. If they do not want to accept the facts, they will reject them and proceed according to their own view of the situation. Arabs will rarely admit to errors openly if doing so will cause them to lose face. *To Arabs, honor is more important than facts.*

Any Arab would understand what is happening, and would never suggest that the other person is lying. Nor would he insist on proving the facts and thus humiliate the other person ("lying" is a common Western accusation).

An American woman in Tunis realized, when she was packing to leave, that some of her clothes and a suitcase were missing. She confronted the maid, who insisted that she had no idea where they could be. When the American found some of her clothes under a mattress, she called the company's Tunisian security officer. They went to the maid's house and found more missing items. The maid was adamant that she could not account for the items being in her home. The security officer said that he felt the matter should not be reported to the police; the maid's humiliation in front of her neighbors was sufficient punishment.

An American diplomat recounted an incident he had observed in Jerusalem. An Israeli entered a small Arab-owned cafe and asked for some watermelon, pointing at it and using the Hebrew word. The Arab proprietor responded that it should be called by the Arabic name, but the Israeli insisted on the Hebrew name. The Arab took offense at this point. He paused, shrugged, and instead of serving his customer, said, "There isn't any!"

At a conference held to discuss Arab and American cultures, Dr. Laura Nader related this incident:

The mistake people in one culture often make in dealing with another culture is to transfer their functions to the other culture's

> *functions. A political scientist, for example, went to the Middle East to do some research one summer and to analyze Egyptian newspapers. When he came back, he said to me, "But they are all just full of emotions. There is no data in these newspapers." I said, "What makes you think there should be?"* [1]

Another way of influencing the perception of reality is by the choice of descriptive words and names. The Arabs are very careful in naming or referring to places, people, and events; slogans and labels are popular and provide an insight into how things are viewed. The Arabs realize that *names have a powerful effect on perception.*

There is a big psychological gap between opposing labels like "Palestine/Israel," "the West Bank/Judea and Samaria," and "freedom fighters ("hero martyrs" if they are killed)/ terrorists." The 1967 Arab-Israeli War is called in Arabic the War of the Setback—in other words, it was not a "defeat." The 1973 War is called the War of Ramadan or the Sixth of October War, not the Yom Kippur War.

Be conscious of names and labels—they matter a great deal to the Arabs. If you attend carefully to what you hear in conversations with Arabs and what is written in their newspapers, you will note how precisely they select descriptive words and phrases. You may find yourself being corrected by Arab acquaintances ("It is the Arabian Gulf, not the Persian Gulf," for example), and you will soon learn which terms are acceptable and which are not.

The Human Dimension

Arabs look at life in a personalized way. They are concerned about people and feelings and place emphasis on human factors when they make decisions or analyze events. They feel that Westerners are too prone to look at events in an abstract or theoretical way and that most Westerners lack sensitivity toward people.

In the Arab World, a manager or official is always willing to reconsider a decision, regulation, or problem in view of someone's personal situation. Any regulation can be modified or avoided by someone who is sufficiently persuasive, particularly if the request is justified on the grounds of unusual personal need. This is unlike most Western societies, which emphasize the equal application of laws to all citizens. *In the Arab culture, people are more important than rules.*

T. E. Lawrence stated it succinctly: "Arabs believe in persons, not in institutions."[2] They have a long tradition of personal appeal to authorities for exceptions to rules. This is commonly seen when they attempt to obtain special permits, exemptions from fees, acceptance into a school when preconditions are not met, or employment when qualifications are inadequate. They do not accept predetermined standards if these standards are a personal inconvenience.

Arabs place great value on personal interviews and on giving people the opportunity to state their case. They are not comfortable filling out forms or dealing with an organization impersonally. They want to know the name of the top person who makes the final decision and are always confident that the rejection of a request may be reversed if top-level personal contact can be made. Frequently, that is exactly what happens.

Persuasion

Arabs and Westerners place a different value on certain types of statements, which may lead to decreased effectiveness on both sides when they negotiate with each other. Arabs respond much more readily to personalized arguments than to attempts to impose "logical" conclusions. When you are trying to make a persuasive case in your discussions with Arabs, you will find it helpful to supplement your arguments with personal comments. You can refer to your friendship with each other or emphasize the effect approval or disapproval of the action will have on other people.

In the Middle East, negotiation and persuasion have been developed into a fine art. Participants in negotiations enjoy long, spirited discussions and are usually not in any hurry to conclude them. Speakers feel free to add to their points of argument by demonstrating their verbal cleverness, using their personal charm, applying personal pressure, and engaging in personal appeals for consideration of their point of view.

The display of emotion also plays its part; indeed, one of the most commonly misunderstood aspects of Arab communication involves their "display" of anger. Arabs are not usually as angry as they appear to be. Raising the voice, repeating points, even pounding the table for emphasis may sound angry, but in the speaker's mind, they merely indicate sincerity. A Westerner overhearing such a conversation (especially if it is in Arabic) may wrongly conclude that an argument is taking place. *Emotion connotes deep and sincere concern for the substance of the discussion.*

Foreigners often miss the emotional dimension in their cross-cultural transactions with Arabs. A British businessman once found that he and his wife were denied reservations on a plane because the Arab ticketing official took offense at the manner in which he was addressed. The fact that seats were available was not an effective counterargument. But when the Arab official noticed that the businessman's wife had begun to cry, he gave way and provided them with seats.

Arabs usually include human elements in their arguments. In arguing the Palestine issue, for instance, they have often placed the greatest emphasis on the suffering of individuals rather than on points of law or a recital of historical events. This is beginning to change, however, with a growing awareness of how to relate effectively to the way Westerners think and argue.

Getting Personal

The concept of what constitutes personal behavior or a personal question is culturally determined, and there are marked differences between Westerners and Arabs. This is a subject that is rarely discussed openly, since how one defines what is personal or private seems so natural to each group. On the whole, Westerners feel that Arabs become too personal, too soon.

Personal Questions

Arabs like to discuss money and may ask what you paid for things or what your salary is (this is more common among less Westernized people). If you don't wish to give out the information, consider responding without answering. You can speak on the subject of money in general—how hard it is to stay ahead, high prices, inflation. After a few minutes of this, the listener will realize that you do not intend to give a substantive answer. This is the way Arabs would respond if they were asked a question they did not really want to answer.

If you are unmarried or if you are married and childless, or have no sons, Arabs may openly ask why. They consider it unusual for an adult to be unmarried, since marriage is arranged for most people by their families and, in any event, is expected of everyone. People want children, especially sons, to enhance their prestige and assure them of care in their old age.

Unmarried people may well find themselves subjected to well-intentioned matchmaking efforts on the part of Arab friends. If you wish to avoid being "matched," you may have to resort to making up a fictitious long-distance romance! You might say, "I am engaged and we're working out the plans. I hope it won't be long now." Statements such as "I'm not married because I haven't found the right person yet" or "I don't want to get married" make little sense to many Arabs.

When you explain why you don't have children, or more children, don't say "We don't want any more children" (impossible to believe) or "We can't afford more" (also doubtful). A more acceptable answer is "We would like more children, and if God wills, we will have more."

Questions that Arabs consider too personal are those pertaining to women in the family (if asked by a man). It is best to ask about "the family," not a person's wife, sister, or grown daughter.

Sensitive Subjects

There are two subjects that Arabs favor in social conversation—religion and politics—and both can be sensitive.

Muslims enjoy discussing religion with non-Muslim Westerners because of their curiosity about Western religious beliefs and because they feel motivated to share information about Islam with friends as a favor to them. They are secure in their belief about the completeness of Islam, since it is accepted as the third and final refinement of the two previously revealed religions, Judaism and Christianity. They like to teach about Islam, which eventually leads to the question: why don't you consider conversion? A Westerner may feel uncomfortable and wonder how to give a gracious refusal. The simplest, most gracious, and most acceptable answer is to state that you appreciate the information and respect Islam highly as a religion but that you cannot consider conversion because it would offend your family. Another option is to assure people that you are a serious, committed Christian (if this is the case). There is a widespread perception that most Westerners are not religious; if you are, people will be very impressed.

Arabs like to talk politics with Westerners and readily bring up controversial issues like the Palestine issue and the legacy of colonialism and

imperialism. Yet they are not prepared for frank statements of disagreement with their positions on these questions or even inadvertent comments that sound negative toward their point of view or supportive of the
opposing side of the argument. The safest response, if you cannot agree
fully, is to confine yourself to platitudes and wait for the subject to
change, expressing your concern for the victims of war and your hope for
a lasting peace. *A frank, two-sided discussion is usually not constructive if
the subject is an emotional one,* and you may find that Arabs remember
only the statements you made in support of the other side.

You will be able to tell when you have brought up a sensitive subject
by the way your Arab friend evades a direct answer to your questions. If
you receive evasive answers, don't press further; there is a reason why the
person does not want to pursue the subject.

It is useful to introduce other topics into the conversation if you can,
to change the subject. These are suggested topics that most people love
to discuss:

- The Golden Age of the Arabs and their contributions in the
  Middle Ages
- The culturally required traits of an "ideal person"
- The experience of making the Hajj (pilgrimage)
- The person's extended family
- The Arabic language, its literature, and poetry

Social Distance

Arab and Western cultures differ in the amount of touching they feel
comfortable with in interpersonal relations and in the physical distance
they maintain when conversing. These norms are largely unconscious,
so both Arabs and Westerners may feel uncomfortable without knowing
exactly why.

In general Arabs tend to stand and sit closer and to touch other people (of the same sex) more than Westerners do. It is common to see two
men or two women holding hands as they walk down a street, which is
simply a sign of friendship. You must be prepared for the possibility that
an Arab will take your hand, especially when crossing the street. After
shaking hands in greeting, Arabs may continue to hold your hand while

talking—if the conversation is expected to be brief. They will then shake it again when saying good-bye. Kissing on both cheeks is a common form of greeting (again, only with members of the same sex), as is embracing. It is also common to touch someone repeatedly during a conversation, often to emphasize a point. Children, especially if they are blond, should be prepared to have their heads rubbed by well-meaning adults.

Arab culture does not have the same concept of public and private space as do Western cultures. Westerners, in a sense, carry a little bubble of private space around with them. Arabs, on the other hand, are not uncomfortable when they are close to or touching strangers.

Westerners are accustomed to standing in an elevator in such a way that maximum space is maintained between people. In the Arab World it is common for a person to board an elevator and stand close beside you rather than moving to the opposite corner. When an Arab boards a bus or selects a seat on a bench, he often sits beside someone rather than going to an empty seat or leaving a space between himself and others. To give a typical example, this tendency was particularly annoying to an American who was standing on a street corner in Beirut waiting for a friend. He had a good view of the intersecting streets until a Lebanese man came to the corner and, apparently also waiting for someone, stood directly in front of him.

When Arabs and Westerners are talking, they may both continually shift position, in a kind of unconscious dance, as the Arab approaches and the Westerner backs away, each trying to maintain a comfortable distance. For Arabs the space that is comfortable for ordinary social conversation is approximately the same as that which Westerners reserve for intimate conversation.

Anthropologist Edward T. Hall was the first to write about the concept of personal space in his classic book *The Hidden Dimension*, never since equaled:

> *For the Arab, there is no such thing as an intrusion in public. Public means public. In the Western world, the person is synonymous with an individual inside a skin. And in northern Europe generally, the skin and even the clothes may be inviolate. You need permission to touch either if you are a stranger...For the Arab, the location of the person in relation to the body is quite different. The*

person exists somewhere down inside the body.... Tucking the ego down inside the body shell not only would permit higher popula-tion densities but would explain why it is that Arab communica-tions are stepped up as much as they are when compared to north-ern European communication patterns. Not only is the sheer noise level much higher, but the piercing look of the eyes, the touch of the hands, and the mutual bathing in the warm moist breath during conversation represent stepped-up sensory inputs to a level which many Europeans find unbearably intense.[1]

You do not need to adopt Arab touching patterns, of course; just be aware that they are different from your own and accept them as natural and normal. Note: in Saudi Arabia and the Arabian Peninsula countries, touch-ing other people is not nearly so common and can even be offensive.

Gestures

Arabs make liberal use of gestures when they talk, especially if they are enthusiastic about what they are saying. Hand and facial gestures are thus an important part of Arab communication. If you are able to recognize them, you will be able to get the full meaning of what is being said to you.

Listed here are some of the most common gestures used in Arab countries. There are variations among countries, but most are in wide use. Men use gestures more than women do, and less educated people use them more than the educated do. You should not try to use these ges-tures (foreigners often use gestures in the wrong place or situation), but you should learn to recognize them.

- Moving the head slightly back and raising the eyebrows=no. Moving the head back and chin upward=no. Moving the chin back slightly and making a clicking sound with the tongue=no.
- After shaking hands, placing the right hand to the heart or chest=greeting someone with respect or sincerity.
- Holding the right hand out, palm downward, and moving it as if scooping something away from you=go away.
- Holding the right hand out, palm upward, and opening and closing it=come here.

- Holding the right hand out, palm upward, then closing the hand halfway and holding it=give it to me.
- Holding the right hand out, palm downward, and moving it up and down slowly=quiet down.
- Holding the right hand out, palm upward, and touching the thumb and tips of fingers together and moving the hand up and down=calm down; be patient; slowly.
- Holding the right forefinger up and moving it from left to right quickly several times (the "windshield wiper")=no; never.
- Holding the right hand out, palm downward, then quickly twisting the hand to show the palm upward=what? why?

Names

In many Western societies, one indication of the closeness of a personal relationship is the use of first names. In Arab society the first name is used immediately, even if it is preceded by "Miss," "Mrs.," or "Mr." Arabs do not refer to people by their third, or "last," name. Arab names, for both men and women, consist of a first name (the person's own), the father's name and the paternal grandfather's name, followed by a family name (in countries where family names are used). In other words an Arab's name is simply a string of names listing ancestors on the father's side. A Western example might be John (given name) Robert (his father) William (his grandfather) Jones.

Because names reflect genealogy on the father's side, women have masculine names after their first name. Some people include *ibn/bin* (son of) or *bint* (daughter of) between the ancestral names. This practice is common in the Arabian Peninsula; for example, Abdel-Aziz ibn Saud (son of Saud), the founder of the Kingdom of Saudi Arabia and Khalifa bin Zayed, the ruler of the UAE. In North Africa the word *ben* or *ould* is used to mean "son of"; *bou* (father of) is also a common element of a family name. Examples are political figures such as Abdelaziz Bouteflika, the president of Algeria; Maaouya Ould Sid Ahmed Taya, the president of Mauritania; and Zayn Al-Abdin Ben Ali, the president of Tunisia.

Because a person's first name is the only one that is really his or hers, Arabs use it from the moment they are introduced. A Western man can expect to be called "Mr. Bill" or "Mr. John." If he is married, his wife would be called "Mrs. Mary," or possibly "Mrs. Bill." An unmarried woman would be "Miss Mary." First names are also used with titles such as "Doctor" and "Professor."*

A person may retain several names for legal purposes but will often omit them in daily use. A man named Ahmad Abdallah Ali Muhammad, for example, would be commonly known as Ahmad Abdallah; if he has a family or tribal name, let's say Al-Harithi, he would be known as Ahmad Abdallah Al-Harithi or possibly Ahmad Al-Harithi. Similarly, a woman whose full name is Zeinab Abdallah Ali Muhammad Al-Harithi may be known as Zeinab Abdallah or Zeinab Al-Harithi. People are not always consistent when reciting their names on different occasions.

When a genealogical name becomes too long (after four or five generations), some of the older names will be dropped. The only pattern that is really consistent is that the father's name will be retained along with the family name, if there is one. It is entirely possible that full brothers and sisters may be registered with different combinations of names.

In Arabian Peninsula countries telephone books list people under their family names. In some Arab countries, however, the telephone book lists people under their first names, because the first name is the only one that can be depended on to be consistently present (and telephone books don't work well; they are rarely consulted). Some business organizations find it easier to keep payroll records by first name.

A family or tribal name identifies a large extended family or group whose members still consider themselves tied by bonds of kinship and honor. A family name may be geographical (Hijazi, "from Hijaz"; Halaby, "from Aleppo"); denote an occupation (Haddad, "smith"; Najjar, "carpenter"); be descriptive (Al-Ahmar, "red"; Al-Tawil, "tall"); denote tribe (Al-Harithi; Quraishi); or sound like a personal name because it is the name of a common ancestor (Abdel-Aziz; Ibrahim).

An Arab Muslim woman does not change her name after marriage, since she does not take her husband's genealogy. Arabs are very proud of their mother's family and want her to retain the name and refer to it. Only informally is a wife called "Mrs." with her husband's first or last name.

---

* The headline in *The Washington Post* on April 10, 2003, was "Hussein's Baghdad Falls." Arabs unused to the Western naming system would not understand who this referred to.

When people have children, an informal but very pleasing and polite way to address the parents is by the name of the oldest son or oldest child: *abu* (father of) or *umm* (mother of) the child; for example, Umm Ahmad (mother of Ahmad). These terms of address are considered respectful, and *umm* is especially useful when talking to a woman because it provides a less personal way of addressing her.

Arabs do not name their sons after the father, but naming a child after his paternal grandfather is common. You will meet many men whose first and third names are the same.

Titles are used more widely in Arabic than in English. Anyone with an M.D. or Ph.D. degree must be addressed as "Dr." ("Duktor" for a man, "Duktora" for a woman). It is important to find out any titles a person may have; omitting the title can be insulting. "Sheikh" is a respectful title for a wealthy, influential, or elderly man. Government ministers are called "Ma'ali," and senior officials are given the honorary title "Sa'ada" before their other titles and name. Most Arab names have a meaning and can be clues to certain facts about a person. Many names indicate religion or country of origin. Because the exchange of personal information is so important, some people introduce themselves with various long combinations of names, especially if their first and last names are ambiguous (used by more than one group).

It is useful for foreigners to be able to place people, at least partially, upon hearing their names. Here are a few guidelines:

- If a name sounds Western (George, Antoine, Mary), it marks a Christian.

- If a name is that of a well-known figure in Islamic history (Muhammad, Bilal, Salah-Eddeen, Fatima, Ayesha), it marks a Muslim.

- Most hyphenated names using "Abdel-" are Muslim. The name means "Servant (Slave) of God," and the second part is one of the attributes of God (Abdallah, "Servant of Allah"; Abdel-Rahman, "Servant of the Merciful"; Abdel-Karim, "Servant of the Generous"). There are a few Christian names on this pattern (Abdel-Malak, "Servant of the Angel"; Abdel-Massih, "Servant of the Messiah"), but over 90 percent of the time you can assume that a person with this type of name is

Muslim. Of the ninety-nine Muslim attributes for God (the All-Powerful, All-Knowing, All-Compassionate, All-Wise, etc.), most are currently in use as names.

- Names containing the word *deen* (religion) are Muslim (Sharaf-Eddeen, "The Honor of Religion"; Badr-Eddeen, "The Moon of Religion"; Salah-Eddeen, "The Rightness of Religion").

- Many names are simply descriptive adjectives (Aziz, "powerful"; Said, "happy"; Amin, "faithful"; Hasan, "good"). Such descriptive names do not mark religion.

- Names that derive from both the Qur'an and the Bible (Ibrahim, "Abraham"; Sulaiman, "Solomon"; Daoud, "David"; Yousef, "Joseph") do not distinguish whether the person is Muslim, Christian, or Jewish. Isa (Eisa), "Jesus," is a common name among Muslims.

Men and Women

In Arab society the nature of interaction between men and women depends on the situation. Continual interaction is expected at work or in professional situations (although it remains reserved by Western standards, and in Saudi Arabia is actually restricted), but social interaction is very carefully controlled. The degree of control differs among Arab countries, depending on their relative conservatism, but nowhere is it as free and casual as in Western societies.

Social Interaction

The maintenance of family honor is one of the highest values in Arab society. Many Westerners fail to understand that, because misbehavior by women is believed to do more damage to family honor than misbehavior by men, clearly defined patterns of behavior have been developed to protect women (in the traditional view) and help them avoid situations that may give rise to false impressions or unfounded gossip. Women interact freely only with other women and close male relatives.

Arab men and women are careful about appearances when they meet. They avoid situations where they would be alone together, even for a short time. It is improper to be in a room together with the door closed, to go out on a date as a couple, or to travel together, even on a short daytime trip. Guarding a woman's image is neither a personal nor a family choice; it is imposed by the culture, just as chaperones were once required in Western society. The point is not the woman's character, or what did or did not happen — the point is how it looks.

Shared activities take place with other people present. At mixed social events women are accompanied by their husbands or male relatives. In Saudi Arabia "religious police" often question couples who are at a restaurant or in a car together and ask for proof that they are married.

Foreigners must be aware of the restrictions that pertain to contact between Arab men and women and then consider their own appearance in front of others. *Arabs quickly gain a negative impression if you behave with too much (presumed) familiarity toward a person of the opposite sex.* They will interpret your behavior on their own terms and may conclude that you are a person of low moral standards. If an embarrassing incident involves a Western man and an Arab woman, they may feel that the Westerner insulted the woman's honor, thereby threatening the honor of her family.

A Western man can feel free to greet an Arab woman at a social gathering (though it is not a common practice in Saudi Arabia), but their subsequent discussion should include other people rather than just the two of them. A married Western woman may greet and visit with Arab men, provided she is accompanied by her husband. If a woman is unmarried or if her husband is not present, she should be more reserved.

In many Arab countries, men and women separate into their own conversation groups shortly after arrival at a social gathering; this depends on the customs of a given area. In Saudi Arabia women are often excluded from social gatherings altogether, or they may be more restricted in their behavior when they are included. It is important to point out that social separation is not practiced merely because it is required by custom; it is often preferred by both men and women because they feel more comfortable. Westerners can expect to spend much of their social time in all-male or all-female groups.

Western men and women should also give thought to their appearance in front of others when they interact among themselves. Behavior such as overly enthusiastic greetings, animated and joking conversations, and casual invitations to lunch are easily misinterpreted by Arabs and reinforce their stereotype of the morally lax Westerner.

Displaying Intimacy

The public display of intimacy between men and women is strictly forbidden by the Arab social code, including holding hands or linking arms or any gesture of affection such as kissing or prolonged touching. Such actions, even between husband and wife, are highly embarrassing to Arab observers. A married couple was once asked to leave a theater in Cairo because they were seen holding hands.

This type of behavior is a particularly serious offense in Saudi Arabia, and incidents of problems and misunderstandings are frequent. One such incident occurred when an American woman was observed getting into a car with an American man, sliding over to his side, and kissing him on the cheek. A captain of the Saudi National Guard, who happened to see this, demanded proof that they were married. They were, but not to each other. The woman was deported, and the man, who compounded his problem by being argumentative, was sent to jail. Even behavior such as holding hands (especially among young people in the less traditional countries) is still viewed by most people with disapproval.

The Status of Women

The degree to which women have been integrated into the workforce and circulate freely in public varies among the Arab countries. In Morocco, Tunisia, Egypt, Lebanon, Syria, Jordan and Iraq, educated women have been active at all levels of society. Women have been heads of state in four non-Arab Islamic countries: Pakistan, Bangladesh, Indonesia, and Turkey.

In the Arabian Gulf states fewer women have jobs outside the home (few need the income), but there is a huge push from those governments to encourage women's education and participation in the workplace. Saudi Arabia is a special case — women are becoming well educated, but few are present in the workplace. Those who do work, are mainly in the professions, in all-female environments; an exception is made for the medical professions. All Arab governments now support efforts to increase women's educational opportunities.

In the area of domestic law Arab women have traditionally not fared so well. Weighing Islamic law (*Sharia*) against current Western criteria of what constitutes women's equality has become very controversial. An impassioned discussion of this issue is ongoing virtually everywhere. Traditional Islamic law restricts the rights of women, and this seems to many people to be seriously outdated. The various points of view rest on interpretations of the Qur'an, which, like any holy book, can be obscure and unclear. Like the Bible, the Qur'an is a product of its times, and it does not reflect modern concepts on issues such as slavery, women's rights, and the morality of slaughtering enemies.

"Women's issues are moving to center-stage in the Arab world. The process might not be as rapid as some may wish, but it is happening," reported Amr Moussa, secretary general of the Arab League, at the Third Annual Arab International Women's Forum.[1] On a similar note, Wadouda Badran, secretary general of the Arab Women's Organization, stated, "Nobody ever said that the change is going to happen overnight. At least we have the commitment of the governments that they want to work in this direction."[2]

Some Arab countries have been notable for decades for improving the status of women. In 1956 the Tunisian president, Habib Bourguiba, instituted laws improving the legal status of women; he was proud to be known as the "Liberator of Women." Iraq revised personal status laws regarding marriage, child custody, and inheritance in 1959. Several countries have outlawed polygamy, and more are under pressure to do so. Morocco, Egypt (the president's wife chairs the Egyptian National Council for Women), Jordan (Queen Rania is working in the cause of women's rights), Yemen, the Gulf states (the ruler's wife in Qatar is promoting women's rights and education)—all have recently passed laws affirming women's rights. Because the laws are subject to change (forward or backward), the role of women in Arab society and in Islam is by no means static or fixed, even in Saudi Arabia.[3]

Women's Right to Vote

In most Arab countries women have the right to vote. Progress in this sphere is evident, and any differences among Arab countries are social, certainly not related to Islam. Below is a summary of the current situation. In Saudi Arabia and the UAE, women still do not have the right to vote, but the pressure is growing. There was, for example, a large protest demonstration in Kuwait in March 2005, which resulted in women gaining the right to vote (it was the parliament, not the ruler, who opposed it).

Date Women's Suffrage Granted[4]	
Iraq	1948
Syria	1949/1953
Lebanon	1952
Egypt	1956
Tunisia	1957/1959
Algeria	1962
Morocco	1963
Libya	1964
Sudan	1964
Jordan	1974
Yemen	1993
Oman	1994
Qatar	1998/2003
Bahrain	2001/2002
Kuwait	2005

Women in Government Positions

Arab women are increasingly represented at various levels of their governments. In the Iraq elections of 2005, political parties were required to field enough female candidates to ensure that they would make up a least one quarter of the National Assembly. Nearly one-third of the winning candidates on the Shia parliamentary list were women.[5]

Arab Women in Government in 2004[6]	
Algeria	5 ministers, 52 parliament
Bahrain	1 minister, 6 parliament
Egypt	2 ministers, 23 parliament
Iraq[7]	6 ministers, 86 parliament
Jordan	3 ministers, 13 parliament
Kuwait	0
Lebanon	2 ministers, 3 parliament
Libya	0
Morocco	2 ministers, 38 parliament
Oman	1 minister, 10 parliament

Qatar	1 minister
Saudi Arabia	0
Syria	2 ministers, 30 parliament
Tunisia	1 minister, 21 parliament
UAE	0
Yemen	1 minister, 4 parliament

Several Arab governments have set up a gender allocation in their parliaments. Algeria, for example, reserves a minimum of 20 percent of its parliamentary seats for women; the Iraq interim government reserves 25 percent; Morocco, 10 percent; and Tunisia, 20 percent.

In December 2004 a conference was held in Cairo sponsored by the International Institute for Democracy and Electoral Assistance (International IDEA), where representatives of fourteen countries discussed gender quotas for women in Arab governments.[8]

Women's Power in the Family

In traditional Arab society, men and women have well-defined spheres of activity and decision making. Do not assume that because Arab women are not highly visible in public, their influence is similarly restricted in private life.

Inside the family, women have a good deal of power. They usually have the decisive voice in matters relating to household expenditures, the upbringing and education of children, and sometimes the arrangement of marriages. Men are responsible for providing the family's material welfare; even if a woman has her own money, she need not contribute to family expenses. Many women *do* have their own money, and many own property. Islamic law states clearly that they retain sole control of their money and inheritance after marriage.

The older a woman becomes, the more status and power she accrues. Men owe great respect to their mothers all their lives, and must make every effort to obey their mother's wishes, including her whims. All older women in the family are treated with deference, but the mother of sons gains even more status.

Arab women generally wear clothing that is at least knee-length, with sleeves that cover at least half of their arms. The practice of wearing more conservative, floor-length, long-sleeved clothing is increasing, not decreasing (as it once was), even in modern cities like Cairo and Amman.

The Headscarf and the Veil

The wearing of the Hejab (the headscarf) is, of course, controversial. Everyone who visits the Arab world on a regular basis can't help but notice that the number of women wearing the Hejab has increased enormously in the last twenty years. It began with the Islamic revival in the 1980s and 1990s, and has gradually and steadily spread throughout society.

Most Westerners see the Hejab as a symbol of women's oppression, but not all Muslims agree. It may only be a sign that the wearer is conservative, with no political significance attached. She is (theoretically) making a free choice, since the Hejab is *not required by the Islamic religion*. However, there is growing social pressure from family or friends to wear the head covering (on the other hand, some families are distressed that their daughters are doing so).

Some observers believe that the voluntary wearing of headscarves is a manifestation (in a person or in the whole society) of a growing sense of pan-Arab Muslim identity. Some say that it may also have political significance. Women often say that by masking their sexuality, they are far freer in their movements in society—the headscarf deters unwelcome attentions from men because they see it and respect it. Some women wear headscarves that are chic, expensive, and highly decorated.

Covering the hair should not be referred to as "veiling," since that requires that the face be covered. Most women in conservative countries such as all those of the Arabian Peninsula, as well as some parts of North Africa, do veil their faces, wholly or partially. At the other end of the spectrum, Tunisia forbids the veil.

The Qur'an itself says nothing about veiling or, for that matter, secluding women from men in a separate part of the house. These were later developments and did not become widespread in the Islamic empire until three or four generations after the death of Muhammad. The custom of veiling and secluding women came into the Muslim world from Persia and Byzantium, where women had long been treated in this way.[9]*

---

*Restricting women from public view is an example of a two-sided argument, and it is irrelevant because it refers to a time long ago. "In the Middle Ages the position was reversed: then the Muslims were horrified to see the way Western Christians treated their women in the Crusader states, and Christian scholars denounced Islam for giving too much power to menials like slaves and women."[10]

The Qur'an is far more protective of women's rights and status than is the case with more recent social practices. It contains only three verses referring to women's modesty, none of which mentions hair.[11] Here are the two most cited (the third refers to the Prophet's wives who generally conversed with people from behind a curtain):

O Prophet, tell thy wives and daughters that they should cast their outer garments over their persons when abroad, that is most convenient, that they should be known and not molested. (33:59)

Say to the believing men that they should lower their gaze and guard their modesty…. And say to the believing women that they should lower their gaze and guard their modesty; that they should not display their beauty and ornaments except what must appear thereof; that they should draw their veils over their bosoms and not display their beauty except to their husbands, their fathers…(it goes on to list male relatives, small children, etc.) (24: 30-31).

While some Arab Muslim women see the Hejab as a religious, cultural, or political statement, other women strongly disagree and disapprove. At one French-owned textile factory in Morocco, more than 95 percent of the 2500 female workers cover their hair; ten years ago, only 20 percent did.[12]

Polygamy

The issue of polygamy in Arab countries is overemphasized in the West, where many people think it is a common practice and is widely condoned. In fact, though, polygamy is severely restricted and is allowed only under certain conditions in most Arab countries. About 1 or 2 percent of married men have more than one wife. As women's rights are more restricted in the Arabian Peninsula, polygamy is more common there.†

---

†Current statistics are hard to come by. Various sources give the rate of polygamy in the 1960s as 2 percent in Lebanon, 4 percent in Syria, and 8 percent in Jordan and Egypt. The rate was 2 percent in Algeria in 1955, 2 percent in Baghdad in the 1970s, and 3 percent in Morocco in 2004. Polygamy is far more prevalent in West Africa—in 1994, the latest year statistics are available, the rate was 45-55 percent in the Sahel region (southern fringe of the Sahara Desert) of Africa, and 25 to 35 percent in West, Central, and East Africa.[13] Yet polygamy is still associated in the minds of Westerners with Middle Eastern Arabs.

Nowadays almost nobody can afford the cost of maintaining more than one family, so polygamy is practiced only by the very rich or by villagers and peasants, who need help with labor and do not incur large expenses.

Polygamy was sanctioned in the seventh century, after a series of battles in which many men were killed and many widows and orphans were left behind. The following verse from the Qur'an refers to the aftermath of these battles:

If you fear that you will not act justly towards the orphans, marry such women as seem good to you, two, three, four; but if you fear that you will not be able to deal justly (with them), then only one, or what your right hands own. That will be more suitable to prevent you from doing injustice. (4:3)

Most modern commentators take this verse to mean that polygamy is restricted to certain circumstances and monogamy is encouraged, because it is difficult to treat all wives equally in every respect. "What your right hands own" refers to slaves or captives, common in the seventh century. The Qur'an continues:

You will not be able to be fair and just between your wives, even if it is your ardent desire. (4:129)

This is, at best, ambiguous, and it is easy to see how the verses could have multiple interpretations.

It is unfortunate that we see so many references in Western magazines and newspapers to polygamy, making it look commonplace.‡ Polygamy is *highly* controversial, and mainstream Muslims realize that it has outlived its time and purpose. Polygamy was decreasing markedly for

---

‡A case in point is Bernard Lewis' article "Targeted by a History of Hatred: The United States is now the unquestioned leader of the free world, also known as infidels," which appeared in *The Washington Post* on September 10, 2002.[14] The subject was his explanation of Muslims' (referring to all of them) hating the United States and hating the West for centuries. It goes on to state that hatred has been growing, and "one reason for the contempt with which they regard us" is due to "what they perceive as the rampant immorality and degeneracy of the American way" (the reference to "they" is unclear). Then polygamy is mentioned as a factor to explain contempt toward Christianity and, more generally, toward the West. There follows a quote from "a recent Arabic newspaper article in defense of polygamy." The quote is explicit, detailed, and to Western ears offensive, yet the source is left vague and the author gives the impression that polygamy is part of the modern Arab way of life, when 98 percent of Arab men are monogamous. I mention this because I think that including this without any qualifications reinforces a stereotype about Middle Eastern Arabs and Muslims and may strengthen a negative image.

years, although with the recent rise of religious conservatism we may see it increase once again. It is no surprise that Osama Bin Laden is said to have married 11 to 16 women, although only (!) four at a time.

Traditional Gender Roles

Westerners see, hear, or read about Muslim women and perceive it as the subjugation of women in Islamic society as a whole. This is a valid criticism, and many people in the West and the Middle East believe that redress is urgently needed. Nevertheless, even if we Westerners disagree with the status quo (and most of us do), we must at least try to *understand* the traditional view and not be too quick to judge and condemn motives and cultural practices.

Unlike Western assumptions about Arab society, tradition-oriented Arab men and women do not view social customs and restrictions as repressive but as *an appropriate acknowledgement of the nature of women.* They do not see this as cruel, nor do they despise women. They sincerely see the restrictions as providing protection for women so that they need not be subjected to the stress, competition, temptations, and possible indignities found in outside society. Most Arab women, even now, feel satisfied that the present social system provides them with security, protection, and respect.

Middle East gender roles have traditionally been governed by a patriarchal kinship system that had already existed in the regions to which Islam spread. Many of the variations in the status of women are due to local traditions and social customs (such as covering the entire face). Men are expected to provide for their families; women, to bear and raise children; children, to honor and respect their parents and grow up to fulfill their adult roles (which includes marriage).[15] It is important for an outsider to keep these points of view in mind when analyzing and discussing the status of Arab women. A woman recently elected to Iraq's National Assembly stated, "To tell you the truth, I am not a feminist. I don't want to commit the same mistakes Western women have committed. I like that family should be the major principle for women here."[16]

Western Women

Western women find that they do not quite fit into Arab society; they are not accorded all the rights of men but they are not considered bound by all the restrictions of Arab women either.

Western women are expected to behave with propriety, but they are not required to be as conservative as Arab women in dress or in public behavior. They need not veil in Saudi Arabia, for example, but must wear conservative dress in all Arab countries. They may go shopping, attend public activities, or travel alone. The respectability of a Western woman will be judged by *the way she is groomed and dressed.*

Arabs accept professional Western women and admire them for their accomplishments. Well-educated women find that their opinions are taken seriously, and they are often invited to all-male professional gatherings. Women have had great success as diplomats in the region. When a woman has a work-related reason to call on someone or to be present at any event, she is usually welcomed, and men are comfortable with her presence.

Social Formalities and Etiquette

Social formalities and rules of etiquette are extremely important in Arab society. *Good manners constitute the most salient factor in evaluating a person's character.*

Hospitality

Arabs are generous in the hospitality they offer to friends and strangers alike, and they admire and value the same in others. *Generosity to guests is essential for a good reputation.* It is a serious insult to characterize someone as stingy or inhospitable.

Arabs assume the role of host or hostess whenever the situation calls for it—in their office, home, or shop. Sometimes people say "Welcome to my country" (in English) when they see a foreigner on the street or in a shop, thus assuming the role of host to a guest. Arabs are always willing to help a foreigner, again, because they take on the role of host. If you ask directions, some people may insist on accompanying you to your destination.

A guest in someone's home or in the workplace never stays long without being offered something to drink, and it is assumed that the guest will accept and drink at least a small quantity as an expression of friendship or esteem. When you are served a beverage, accept and hold the cup or glass with your right hand.

No matter how much coffee or tea you have had elsewhere, never decline this offer (some shops and business offices have employees whose sole duty is to serve beverages to guests). You will notice that while a Westerner would likely ask guests, "Would you care for coffee or tea?" using an intonation pattern that suggests that the guest may or may not want any refreshment, a Middle Easterner would ask, "What would you like — coffee or tea?" simply giving the guests a choice. If someone comes to a home or place of business while food is being served, the people eating always offer to share the food. Usually an unexpected guest declines, but the gesture must be made.

The phrase *Ahlan wa Sahlan* or *Marhaba* (Welcome) is used when a guest arrives, and it is repeated several times during a visit. A guest is often given a seat of honor (this is particularly common as a gesture to a foreigner), and solicitous inquiries are made about the guest's comfort during the visit. Sometimes you may feel uncomfortable because you are getting so much attention.

Regardless of pressing circumstances, an Arab would never consider refusing entrance to a guest, even if he or she is unexpected and the visit inconvenient. The only excusable circumstance would be if a woman (or women) were at home alone when a man dropped by — and then it would be the visitor who would refuse to enter, even if his prospective host were expected back very soon.

Arabs are proud of their tradition of hospitality and have many anecdotes illustrating it. A favorite is the story of the Bedouin who killed his last camel (or sheep) to feed his guest. The word for "generous, hospitable" in Arabic is *kareem*, and this concept is so highly valued that its meanings extend to "distinguished, noble-minded, noble-hearted, honorable, respectable" (there are 25 meanings in the dictionary).

In turn, Arabs expect to be received with hospitality when they are guests, and your personal image and status will be affected by people's perceptions of your hospitality.

The most important components of hospitality are welcoming a guest (including using the word Welcome), offering the guest a seat (in many Arab homes, there is a special room set aside for receiving guests, called the "salon"), and offering something to drink. As a host, stay with your guests as much as possible, excusing yourself for brief absences from

the room only as necessary. This is a description of Arab hospitality written by an Arab woman:

> For Arabs, hospitality lies at the heart of who we are. How well one
> treats his guests is a direct measurement of what kind of a person
> she or he is. Hospitality is among the most highly admired of
> virtues. Indeed, families judge themselves and each other according
> to the amount of generosity they bestow upon their guests when
> they entertain. Whether one's guests are relatives, friends, neigh-
> bors, or relative strangers, they are welcomed into the home and to
> the dinner table with much the same kindness and generosity.[1]

A guest does not see the rest of the house and meets only the family
members who are presented. Privacy *within* a family is not valued, but
privacy from *the outside* is essential. Most houses are behind tall walls.

Hospitality extends to the public sphere, too. In Tunis, Cairo, Beirut,
and Amman I have asked for directions and been escorted to my destination though in each instance it was a long walk and a considerable inconvenience for my guide. When thanking someone for such a favor, you
will hear the response, "No thanks are needed for a duty." No task is too
burdensome for a hospitable host.

Time and Appointments

Among Arabs time is not as fixed and rigidly segmented as it tends to be
among Westerners. It flows from past to present to future, and Arabs flow
with it. Social occasions and appointments need not have fixed beginnings or endings. Arabs are thus much more relaxed about the timing of
events than they are about other aspects of their lives. Nevertheless, these
attitudes are beginning to change as people respond to the demands of
economic and technological development and modernization.

Some Arabs are careful to arrive on time (and are impatient with
those who do not), and some are habitually late, especially for social
events. Given these attitudes, a person who arrives late and has kept you
waiting may not realize that you have been inconvenienced and expect
an apology.

Frequently, an Arab shopkeeper or someone in a service trade fails to have something finished by a promised time. This also pertains to public services (such as getting a telephone connected), personal services, bus and train departures, customer services (where standing in long lines can be expected), and bureaucratic procedures. Be flexible; everyone expects delays. You will appear unreasonably impatient and demanding if you insist on having things finished at a precise time.

If you invite people for dinner or a social event, do not expect all of your guests to arrive on time. A dinner should be served rather late, and social plans should always be flexible enough to accommodate latecomers.

The Arabic word (and sentence) *Ma'alish* represents an entire way of looking at life and its frustrations. It means "Never mind" or "It doesn't matter" or "Excuse me—it's not that serious." You will hear this said frequently when someone has had a delay, a disappointment, or an unfortunate experience. Rather than give in to pointless anger, Arabs often react to impersonally caused adversity with resignation and, to some extent, an acceptance of their fate.

Discussing Business

Arabs mistrust people who do not appear to be sincere or who fail to demonstrate an interest in them personally or in their country. They also don't like to be hurried or to feel they are being pressured into a business agreement. If they like you, they will agree to try to work out an arrangement or a compromise; if they do not like you, they will probably stop listening. *Arabs evaluate the source of a statement or proposal as much as the content.*

Initial reactions by your Arab counterparts to your suggestions, ideas, and proposals can be quite misleading if taken at face value. Arabs are not likely to criticize openly but are more likely to hint that changes are needed or to give more subtle indications that the proposal is unacceptable—by inaction, for instance. They may promise to be in touch but fail to do so, or they might offer a radical counterproposal that may constitute a position from which compromise is expected. Don't take flattery and praise too seriously. It will more likely be adherence to good manners than an indicator of potential success in the business transaction. Some decisions simply require consultation with superiors (if you are not dealing with the top person). A noncommittal reaction to a proposal does not mean it has been rejected, nor does it guarantee ultimate acceptance.

Only time will tell the outcome, with success dependent, more often than not, on patience and the cultivation of good personal relations.

Despite the frustration you may feel as the result of delays, *if you press for a specific time by which you want a decision, you may actually harm your chances of success.* Your counterpart may perceive it as an insult, especially if the person is a high-ranking manager or executive.

The vice president of an American engineering company was meeting with a high-level Saudi official in the Ministry of Planning in Riyadh. The company's local representative had been trying for several weeks to obtain approval of one of the company's proposals. The vice president decided at the meeting to request that the ministry give them a definite answer during the week he was to be in town. The Saudi looked surprised and appeared irritated, then answered that he could not guarantee action within that time period. The proposal was never approved.

If a decision is coming slowly, it may mean that the proposal needs to be reassessed. Do not expect to conclude all of your business at once, especially if several decisions are required. Patience and repeated visits are called for. Arabs have plenty of time, and they see little need to accommodate foreigners who are in a hurry and trying to pressure them.

Sharing Meals

Arabs enjoy inviting guests to their home for meals; you will probably be a guest at meals many times. Sharing food together provides an Arab host and hostess with a perfect opportunity to display their generosity and demonstrate their personal regard for you.

It is not an Arab custom to send written invitations or to request confirmation of acceptance. Invitations are usually verbal and often spontaneous.

If it is your first invitation, check with others for the time meals are usually served and for the time you are expected to arrive. Westerners often arrive too early and assume the meal will be served earlier than is customary. In most Arab countries (but not all), a large midday meal is served between 2:00 and 3:00 P.M., and a supper (with guests) is served about 10:00 or 11:00 P.M. Guests should arrive about two hours before the meal, since most of the conversation takes place before the meal, not after it. If the dinner is formal and official, you may be expected to arrive at the specified time, and you can expect the meal to end within an hour or two.

Arabs serve a great quantity of food when they entertain—indeed, they are famous for their munificence and very proud of it. They do not try to calculate the amount of food actually needed; on the contrary, the intention is to present abundant food, which displays generosity and esteem for the guests. (The leftover food does not go to waste; it is consumed by the family or by servants for several days afterward.)

Most foreigners who have experienced Arab meals have their favorite hospitality stories. For example, I was told about a banquet once given by a wealthy merchant in Qatar who was known for his largesse. After several courses the guests were served an entire sheep—one per person!

You can expect to be offered second and third helpings of food, and you should make the gesture of accepting at least once. Encouraging guests to eat is part of an Arab host or hostess's duty and is required for good manners. This encouragement to eat more is called 'uzooma in Arabic, and the more traditional the host, the more insistently it is done. Guests often begin with a ritual refusal and allow themselves to be won over by the host's insistence. You will hear, for example,

"No, thanks."

"Oh, but you must!"

"No, I really couldn't!"

"You don't like the food!"

"Oh, but I do!"

"Well then, have some more!"

Water is often not served until after a meal is finished; some people consider it unhealthy to eat and drink at the same time. In any case Arab food is rarely "hot," although it may be highly seasoned.

A guest is expected to express admiration and gratitude for the food. Because you are trying to be polite, you will probably overeat. Many people eat sparingly on the day they are invited out to dinner because they know how much food will be served that evening.

When you have eaten enough, you may refuse more by saying, *"Alhamdu lillah"* ("Thanks be to God"). When the meal is over and you are about to leave the table, it is customary to say, *"Dayman"* ("Always")

or "*Sufra dayma*" ("May your table always be thus") to the host and hostess. The most common responses are "*Ti'eesh*" ("May you live") and "*Bil hana wa shifa*" ("To your happiness and health").

After a meal, tea or coffee will be served, usually presweetened. Conversation continues for a while longer, perhaps an hour, and then guests prepare to leave. In some countries, bringing a tray of ice water around is a sign that dinner is over and the guests are free to leave. In the Arabian Peninsula countries, incense or cologne may be passed around just before the guests depart. When guests announce their intention to leave, the host and hostess usually exclaim, "Stay a while — it's still early!" This offer is ritual; you may stay a few more minutes, but the expression need not be taken literally, and it does not mean that you will give offense by leaving. Generally, you can follow the example of other guests, except that many Arabs prefer to stay out very late, so you may still be the first to leave. In most Arab countries you do not have to stay after midnight.

When you are invited to a meal, it is appropriate, although not required, to bring a small gift; flowers and candy are the most common.

If you invite Arabs to your home, consider adopting some of their mealtime customs; it will improve their impression of you. In the countries of the Arabian Peninsula, women rarely go out socially. When you invite a man and his wife to your home, the wife may not appear. It depends largely on whether the couple is accustomed to socializing with foreigners and on who else will be there. It is considerate, when a man is inviting a couple, to say, "My wife invites your wife" and to volunteer information about who else is invited. This helps the husband decide whether he wishes his wife to meet the other guests, and it assures him that other women will be present. Don't be surprised if some guests do not come, or if someone arrives with a friend or two.

Always serve plenty of food, with two or three main meat dishes; otherwise you may give the impression of being stingy. I once heard an Egyptian describe a dinner at an American's home where the guests were served one large steak apiece. "They counted the steaks, and they even counted the potatoes," he said. "We were served baked potatoes — one per person!"

If you serve buffet style rather than a sit-down dinner with courses, your eating schedule will be more flexible and the visual impression of the amount of food served will be enhanced. Give thought to your menu, considering which foods are eaten locally and which are not. Serve foods in fairly simple, easily recognizable form, so guests won't wonder what they are eating in a foreigner's home. Arabs usually do not care for sweetened meats or for sweet salads with the main meal.

Muslims are forbidden to eat pork. Some foreigners serve pork (as one of the choices at a buffet) and label it; this is not advisable, since it can be disconcerting to Muslim guests, who may wonder if the pork has touched any of the rest of the food.

The consumption of alcohol is also forbidden for Muslims. Do not use it in your cooking unless you either label it or mention it. If you cook with wine or other alcohol, you will limit the dishes available to your Muslim guests—it does not matter that the alcohol may have evaporated during cooking. If you wish to serve wine or alcoholic beverages, have nonalcoholic drinks available too.

Be sure to offer your guests second and third helpings of food. Although you don't have to insist vigorously, you should make the gesture. Serve coffee and tea at the end of a meal.

Smoking

The overwhelming majority of Arab adults smoke, although women seldom smoke in public. Smoking is considered an integral part of adult behavior and constitutes, to some extent, the expression of an individual's "coming of age." Arab men, in particular, view smoking as a right, not a privilege. Do not be surprised if you see people disregarding "no smoking" signs in airplanes, waiting rooms, or elevators.

Arabs are rarely aware that smoking may be offensive to some Westerners. You can ask someone to refrain from smoking by explaining that it bothers you, but he may light up again after a few minutes. If you press the point too strongly, you will appear unreasonable. If possible, have a place available where people are welcome to smoke; it will help them relax.

Rules of Etiquette

Listed below are some of the basic rules of etiquette in Arab culture:

- It is important to sit properly. Slouching, draping the legs over the arm of a chair, or otherwise sitting carelessly when talking with someone communicates a lack of respect for that person. Legs are never crossed on top of a desk or table when talking with someone.

- When standing and talking with someone, it is considered disrespectful to lean against the wall or keep one's hands in one's pockets.

- Sitting in a manner that allows the sole of one's shoe to face another person is an insult.

- In many countries and homes, a guest removes his or her shoes at the door. You can tell if this is required, first, by watching others and also if there is a pile of shoes at the door. This is especially common in the Arabian Peninsula, which is one reason that slip-on sandals are usually worn. Removing your shoes is a sign of respect; it is also required in a mosque.

- Failure to shake hands when meeting or bidding someone good-bye is considered rude. When a Western man is introduced to an Arab woman, it is the woman's choice whether to shake hands or not; she should be allowed to make the first move. (Pious Muslims may decline to shake hands with a woman; this is not an insult.)

- Casual dress at social events, many of which call for rather formal dress (a suit and tie for men, a dress, high heels, and jewelry for women), may be taken as a lack of respect for the hosts. There are, of course, some occasions for which casual dress is appropriate. Notice how others are dressed.

- One who lights a cigarette in a group must be prepared to offer cigarettes to everyone.

- Men stand when a woman enters a room; everyone stands when new guests arrive at a social gathering and when an elderly or high-ranking person enters or leaves.

- Men allow women to precede them through doorways, and men offer their seats to women if no others are available.

- It is customary to usher elderly people to the front of any line or to offer to stand in their place. Elderly people should be greeted first.

- When saying good-bye to guests, a gracious host accompanies them to the outer gate, or to their car, or at least as far as the elevator in a high-rise building.
- If a guest admires something small and portable, an Arab may insist that it be taken as a gift. Guests need to be careful about expressing admiration for small, expensive items.
- In many countries gifts are given and accepted with both hands and are not opened in the presence of the donor.
- In some social situations, especially in public places or when very traditional Arabs are present, it may be considered inappropriate for women to smoke or to drink alcoholic beverages.
- When eating with Arabs, especially when taking food from communal dishes, guests should not use the left hand (it is considered unclean). This is overemphasized, though; it does not pertain if you have your own plate and are eating with a knife and fork.
- At a restaurant, Arabs will almost always insist on paying, especially if there are not many people in the party or if it is a business-related occasion. Giving in graciously after a ritual offer to pay and then returning the favor later is an appropriate response.
- Arabs have definite ideas about what constitutes proper masculine and feminine behavior and appearance. They do not approve of long hair on men or mannish dress and comportment by women.
- Family disagreements and disputes in front of others or within hearing of others are avoided.
- People should not be photographed without their permission.
- Staring at other people is not usually considered rude or an invasion of privacy by Arabs (especially when the object is a fascinating foreigner). Moving away is the best defense.
- When eating out with a large group of people where everyone is paying his or her own share, it is best to let one person pay and be reimbursed later. Arabs find the public calculation and division of a restaurant bill embarrassing.

- Most Arabs do not like to touch or be in the presence of house-hold animals, especially dogs. Pets should be kept out of sight when Arab guests are present.

It is impossible, of course, to learn all the rules of a culture. The safest course of action is to imitate. In a social situation with Arabs, *never be the first one to do anything!* In some situations, such as in the presence of royalty, it is incorrect to cross your legs; in some situations, in the presence of royalty or a high-ranking older man, for instance, it is incorrect to smoke.

The Social Structure

Arab society is structured into social classes, and individuals inherit the social class of their family. The governments of Libya and the former South Yemen have tried experimenting with classless societies, but this has not affected basic attitudes.

Social Classes

In most Arab countries there are three social classes. The upper class includes royalty (in some countries), large and influential families, and some wealthy people, depending on their family background. The middle class is composed of government employees, military officers, teachers, and moderately prosperous merchants and landowners. Peasant farmers and the urban and village poor make up the lower class. Nomadic Bedouins do not really fit into any of these classes; they are mostly independent of society and are admired for their preservation of Arab traditions.

The relative degree of privilege among the classes and the differences in their attitude and way of life vary from country to country. Some countries are wealthy and underpopulated, with a large privileged class; others are poor and overpopulated, with a high percentage of peasants and manual laborers.

There is usually very little tension among social classes. Arabs accept the social class into which they were born, and there is relatively little effort on the part of individuals to rise from one class to another. In any case it would be difficult for a person to change social class, since it is determined almost entirely by family origin. One can improve one's status through professional position and power, educational attainment, or acquired wealth, but the person's origins will be remembered. A family of the lower class could not really expect social acceptance in the upper class for two or three generations. Similarly, an upper-class family that squandered its wealth or influence would not be relegated to lower-class status for some time.

Foreign residents of Arab countries automatically accrue most of the status and privileges of the upper class. This is due to their professional standing, their level of education, and their income.

Image and Upper-Class Behavior

Certain kinds of behavior are expected of people in the upper class who wish to maintain their status and good public image. Some activities are not acceptable in public and, if seen, cause shock and surprise.

If you know the basic norms of upper-class behavior, you will be free to decide the extent to which you are willing to conform. While you risk giving a negative impression by breaking a rule, doing so will not necessarily be offensive. You may simply be viewed as eccentric or as having poor judgment.

No upper-class person engages in manual labor in front of others. Arabs are surprised when they see Westerners washing their cars or sweeping the sidewalk. While upper-class Arabs may do some menial chores inside their homes, they do not do them in public or in front of others.

A white-collar or desk job in an office is much desired by Arabs because of the status it confers. There is an enormous difference between working with the hands and working as a clerk. Arabs who have white-collar jobs will resent being asked to do something they consider beneath their status. If, in an office situation, your requests are not being carried out, you may find that you have been asking a person to do something that is demeaning or threatening to his or her dignity. And not wishing to offend you, the employee would be hesitant to tell you.

An Egyptian interpreter in an American-managed hospital once told me that she was insulted when a Western doctor asked her to bring him a glass of water. She felt that her dignity had been threatened and that she had been treated like the "tea boy" who took orders for drinks.

Manual work is acceptable if it can be classified as a hobby—for example, sewing, painting, or craftwork. Refinishing furniture might get by as a hobby (though it would probably raise eyebrows), but repairing cars is out. If you decide to paint the exterior of your house or to refinish the floors yourself, expect to be the subject of conversation.

Upper-class Arabs are careful about their dress and appearance whenever they are in public, because the way a person dresses indicates his or her wealth and social standing. Arab children are often dressed in expensive clothes, and women wear a lot of jewelry, especially gold. The men are partial to expensive watches, cuff links, pens, and cigarette lighters. Looking their best and dressing well are essential to Arabs' self-respect, and they are surprised when they see well-to-do foreigners wearing casual or old clothes (faded jeans, a tattered T-shirt). Why would a person dress poorly when he or she can afford better?

Usually upper-class Arabs do not socialize with people from other classes, at least not in each other's homes. They may enjoy cordial relations with the corner grocer and newsstand vendor, but, like most Westerners, they would not suggest a dinner or an evening's entertainment together. (A possible exception is a big occasion like the celebration of a wedding.)

When you plan social events, do not mix people from different social classes. You can invite anyone from any class to your home, and the gesture will be much appreciated, but to invite a company director and your local baker at the same time would embarrass both parties.

Dealing with Service People

Westerners living in an Arab country usually have one or more household servants. You may feel free to establish a personal relationship with your servants; they appreciate the kindness and consideration they have come to expect from Westerners—"Please" and "Thank you" are never out of place. You may, in fact, work right alongside the servant, but you will notice that the relationship changes if Arab guests are present. The servant will then want to do all the work alone so as not to tarnish your social image. If a glass of water is spilled, for example, you should call the servant to clean up, rather than be seen doing it yourself. Inviting your servant to join you and your guests at tea or at a meal would be inappropriate and very embarrassing for everyone.

Servants expect you to assume some responsibility for them; you may, for example, be asked to pay medical expenses and to help out financially in family emergencies. Give at least something as a token of concern, then ask around to find out how much is reasonable for the situation. If you feel that the expense is too high for you to cover completely, you can offer to lend the money and deduct it from the person's salary over a period of time. Be generous with surplus food and with household items or clothing you no longer need, and remember that extra money is expected on holidays. All of this is in keeping with the cultural and religious requirement to be generous with charity.

Make the acquaintance of shopkeepers, doormen, and errand boys. Such acquaintances are best made by exchanging a few words of Arabic and showing them that you like and respect them.

If you become friendly with people who have relatively little money, limit the frequency of your social visits. They may be obliged to spend more than they can afford to receive you properly, and the problem is far too embarrassing to discuss or even admit. It is enjoyable to visit villagers or the home of a taxi driver or shopkeeper, but if you plan to make it a habit, bring gifts with you or find other ways to compensate your hosts.

The Role of the Family

Arab society is built around the extended family system. Individuals feel a strong affiliation with all of their relatives—aunts, uncles, and cousins—not just with their immediate family. The degree to which all blood relationships are encompassed by a family unit varies among families, but most Arabs have over a hundred "fairly close" relatives.

Family Loyalty and Obligations

Family loyalty and obligations take precedence over loyalty to friends or the demands of a job. Relatives are expected to help each other, including giving financial assistance if necessary. Family affiliation provides security and assures one that he or she will never be entirely without resources, emotional or material. Only the most rash or foolhardy person would risk being censured or disowned by his or her family. Family support is indispensable in an unpredictable world; the family is a person's ultimate refuge.

Members of a family are expected to support each other in disputes with outsiders. Regardless of personal antipathy among relatives, they must defend each other's honor, counter criticism, and display group cohesion, if only for the sake of appearances. Internal family disputes rarely get to the point of open, public conflict.

Membership in a well-known and influential family ensures social acceptance and is often crucial to members in obtaining a good education, finding a good job, or succeeding in business. Arabs are very proud of their family connections and lineage.

The reputation of any member of a family group reflects on all of the other members. One person's indiscreet behavior or poor judgment can damage his or her relatives' pride, social influence, and marriage opportunities. For this reason family honor is the greatest source of pressure on an individual to conform to accepted behavior patterns, and one is constantly reminded of his or her responsibility for upholding that honor.

The family is the foundation of Middle Eastern society, and family security is essential. The peace and security offered by a stable family unit is greatly valued and seen as essential for the spiritual growth of its members. A harmonious social order is created by the existence of extended families. Strong families create strong communities and underpin social order.

An employer must be understanding if an employee is late or absent because of family obligations. *It is unreasonable to expect an Arab employee to give priority to the demands of a job if they conflict with family duties.*

The description of Syrian society found in the book *Syria: A Country Study*, is applicable to Arab societies in general.

Syrians highly value family solidarity and, consequently, obedience of children to the wishes of their parents. Being a good family member includes automatic loyalty to kinsmen as well. Syrians employed in modern bureaucratic positions, such as government officials, therefore find impersonal impartiality difficult to attain because of a conflict with the deeply held value of family solidarity.

There is no similarly ingrained feeling of duty toward a job, an employer, a coworker, or even a friend. A widespread conviction exists that the only reliable people are one's kinsmen. An office-holder tends to select his kinsmen as fellow workers or subordinates because of a sense of responsibility for them and because of the feeling of trust between them. Commercial establishments are largely family operations staffed by the offspring and relatives of the owner. Cooperation among business firms may be determined by the presence or absence of kinship ties between the heads of firms. When two young men become very close friends, they often enhance their relationship by accepting one another as "brothers," thus placing each in a position of special responsibility toward the other. There is no real basis for a close relationship except ties of kinship.[1]

Relations among Family Members

An Arab man is recognized as the head of his immediate family, and his role and influence are overt. His wife also has a clearly defined sphere of influence, but it exists largely behind the scenes. Although an Arab woman is careful to show deference to her husband in public, she may not always accord him the same submissiveness in private.

In matters where opinions among family members differ, much consultation and negotiation take place before decisions are made. If a compromise cannot be reached, however, the husband, father, or older men in the family prevail.

Status in a family increases as a person grows older, and most families have patriarchs or matriarchs whose opinions are given considerable weight in family matters. Children are taught profound respect for adults, a pattern that is pervasive in Arab society at all ages. It is common, for example, for adults to refrain from smoking in front of their parents or older relatives.

Responsibility for other members of the family rests heavily on older men in the extended family and on older sons in the immediate family. Children are their parents' "social security," and grown sons, in particular, are responsible for the support of their parents. In the absence of the father, brothers are responsible for their unmarried sisters.

Members of a family are very dependent on each other emotionally, and these ties continue throughout a person's life. Some people feel closer to their brothers and sisters and confide in them more than they do their spouses. A directive written for social workers in the Muslim Arab world stated:

The family's involvement in individual helping may be considerable, and could make the social worker's task more complex. In Muslim Arab communities, many are raised to consider the family unit as a continual source of support. Extended family members may be highly valued as well. They may be expected to be involved and may be consulted in times of crisis. When a family member experiences a problem, the person's restoration may be of concern to many other members...although Muslim Arab peoples may value privacy and guard it vehemently, their personal privacy within the family is virtually non-existent. Decisions regarding health care are made by the family group and are not the responsibility of the individual.[2]

In the UAE, a conference was held on the subject, "Role of the Family and Welfare of the Elderly," in which the ruler's wife stated:

We believe our sons and daughters are responsible towards God and our nation, for their parents when they grow old. We believe that undertaking this responsibility is...one of the essential anchors of our society.... We have noticed, regretfully, some family members who do not care for the elderly. These contravene our values and traditions. We hope this seminar will help in fighting these trends and suggest necessary legislation to punish those who are responsible for contravening our values and traditions.[3]

In the traditional Arab family, the roles of the mother and the father are quite different as they relate to their children. The mother is seen as a source of emotional support and steadfast loving-kindness. She is patient, forgiving, and prone to indulge and spoil her children, especially her sons. The father, while seen as a source of love, may display affection less overtly; he is also the source of authority and punishment. Some Arab fathers feel that their status in the family is best maintained by cultivating awe and even a degree of fear in other members of the family, but this is quite rare.

In most Arab families the parents maintain very close contact with their own parents and with their brothers and sisters. For this reason Arab children grow up experiencing constant interaction with older relatives, including their grandparents, who often live in the same home. This contributes to the passing on of social values from one generation to another, as the influence of the older relatives is continually present. Relatively few Arab teenagers and young adults rebel against family values and desires, certainly not to the extent common in Western societies. Even people who affect modern tastes in dress, reading material, and entertainment subscribe to prevailing social values and expect their own family lives to be very similar to that of their parents. Many Arab families living in the West gather together every weekend if possible.

Marriage

Most Arabs still prefer family-arranged marriages. Though marriage customs are changing in some modern circles, couples still seek family approval of the person they have chosen. This is essential as an act of respect toward their parents, and people rarely marry in defiance of their families.

Many Arabs feel that because marriage is such a major decision, it is considered prudent to leave it to the family's discretion rather than to choose someone solely on the basis of emotion or ideas of romance. In almost all Arab countries and social groups, however, the prospective bride and bridegroom have the opportunity to meet, visit, and become acquainted—and to accept or reject a proposal of marriage. The degree to which the individuals are consulted will vary according to how traditional or modern the family is.

Among Muslim Arabs, especially in rural and traditional communities and in the Arabian Peninsula, the preferred pattern of marriage is to a first or second cousin. In fact, marriage to relatives is on the rise. On average, about a third of all marriages are between cousins or someone in the same kin group (the global average is about 20 percent).[4] Estimates vary, though, between 20 percent and 50 percent, higher in the Arabian Peninsula. There are good reasons for this. Since an important part of a marriage arrangement is the investigation into the social and financial standing of the proposed candidates, it is reassuring to marry someone whose background, character, and financial position are well known. Marriage to a cousin also ensures that money, in the form of a dowry or inheritance, stays within the family.

Marrying within the family is the principal means of reinforcing kinship solidarity (this is one reason many Arabs do not give their first loyalty to their nation and remain kin- or clan-oriented; even heads of state often place other loyalties ahead of national interests). Marrying a cousin acts as a protection for the wife, who has better relations with her in-laws and can win their support in time of need. Daughters who marry relatives will be better able to care for elderly parents who are also kin to the husband.

If the bride is outside the family, potentially her husband may develop more solidarity with her family and lessen his loyalty to his own. Genetic problems occur in about 10 percent of these marriages.[5]

In contrast with Western customs, Arab couples do not enter marriage with idealistic or exaggerated romantic expectations. True, they are seeking companionship and love, but equally important, they want financial security, social status, and children. These goals are realistic and are usually attained. Arab marriages are, on the whole, very stable and characterized by mutual respect. Having a happy family life is considered a paramount goal in the Arab world.

Divorce

Most Arab Christians belong to denominations which do not permit divorce. Among Muslims, divorce is permitted and carefully regulated by religious law. Divorce is common enough that it does not carry a social stigma for the individuals involved, and people who have been divorced are eligible for remarriage. There is probably not as much personal pain associated with divorce if the marriage was arranged; obtaining a divorce is not an admission of mistaken judgment or an implied statement of personal failure, as it is sometimes viewed in Western society.

Although a Muslim man may divorce his wife if he wishes, he risks severe damage to his social image if he is arbitrary or hasty about his decision. The process in traditional Islam is quite simple: he merely recites the formula for divorce ("I divorce you") in front of witnesses. If he says the formula once or twice, the couple can still be reconciled; if he repeats it a third time, it is binding. Almost every Middle Eastern country has modified this formula and requires court proceedings, stipulating the wife's rights to alimony and child support. A woman has more difficulty in initiating divorce proceedings, but usually she is successful on grounds of childlessness, desertion, or nonsupport. A woman must go through court proceedings in order to divorce her husband. In Jordan, Syria, and Morocco, she may write into her marriage contract the right to initiate divorce. Such protections are increasing.

When a Muslim woman is divorced, her husband must pay a divorce settlement, which is included in every marriage contract and is usually a very large sum of money. In addition she is entitled to financial support for herself for at least three months (a waiting period to determine that she is not pregnant) and more if she needs it, as well as support for her minor children while they are in her custody. Additional conditions can be written into a marriage contract.

A few Arab countries follow Islamic law entirely in matters of divorce; most have supplemented it. Laws pertaining to divorce have been widely discussed, and changes are constantly being proposed. For example, the custody of children is theoretically determined by Islamic law. They are to stay with their mothers to a certain age (approximately seven years for boys and nine years for girls, though it differs slightly among countries), and then they may go to their fathers. This shift is not always automatic, however, and may be ruled upon by a court or religious judge, according to the circumstances of the case.

Child-Rearing Practices

Arabs dearly love children, and both men and women express that love openly. Arab children grow up surrounded by adoring relatives who share in child rearing by feeding, caring for, and even disciplining each other's children. Because so many people have cared for them and served as authority figures and because the practice is so universal, Arabs are remarkably homogeneous in their experience of childhood. Arab children learn the same values in much the same way; their upbringing is not as arbitrarily dependent on the approach of their particular parents as it is in Western societies.

In traditional Arab culture there has always been a marked preference for boys over girls because men contribute more to the family's influence in the community. Arab children are provided different role models for personality development. Boys are expected to be aggressive and decisive; girls are expected to be more passive. This attitude toward boys and girls is starting to change now that women are being educated and becoming wage earners. Many Arab couples practice birth control and limit the size of their families to two or three children, even if they are all girls.

Some educated or liberal-thinking Arabs find the pressure from the family to conform to rigid social standards to be oppressive. Much of what has been written on the subject of Arab character and personality development is extremely negative, particularly statements made by Arabs themselves.* Clearly many Arabs feel resentful of the requirements

---

*See, for example, the description of child-rearing practices in Sharabi and Ani (1977), 240-56, or almost any-where in Hamady (1960).

imposed by their families and by society and believe that conformity leads to the development of undesirable personal traits.

Most Arabs feel that while their childhood was, in many ways, a time of stringent training, it was also a time of indulgence and openly expressed love, especially from their mothers. Failure to conform is punished, but methods of discipline are usually not harsh.

In Arab culture the most important requirement for a "good" child is respectful behavior in front of adults. Unlike Westerners, all adults may share in correcting a child, because parents know that all adults have the same values. Children grow up without confusion about social requirements. Children must greet adults with a handshake, stay to converse for a few minutes if asked, and refrain from interrupting or talking back. Children often help to serve guests and thus learn the requirements of hospitality early. Westerners who want their children to make a good impression on Arab guests might wish to keep these customs in mind.

Among Arabs it is an extremely important responsibility to bring children up so that they will reflect well on the family. It is an insult to accuse someone of not being well raised. Children's character and success in life reflect directly on their parents. Arabs tend to give parents much of the credit for their children's successes and much of the blame for their failures. Parents readily make sacrifices for their children's welfare; they expect these efforts to be acknowledged and their parental influence to continue throughout the child's lifetime.

Many Western parents begin training their children at an early age to become independent and self-reliant. They give the children token jobs and regular allowance money and frequently encourage them to make their own decisions. This training helps children avoid being dependent on their parents after they have reached adulthood.

Arab parents, on the other hand, welcome their children's dependence. Mothers, especially, try to keep their children tied to them emotionally. Young people continue to live at home until they are married. It is customary for the parents of a newly married couple to furnish the couple's home entirely and to continue to help them financially.

Talking about Your Family

Given this emphasis on family background and honor, you may want to carefully consider the impression you will make when giving information to Arabs about your family relationships. Saying the wrong thing can affect your image and status.

Arabs are very surprised if someone talks about poverty and disadvantages experienced in early life. Rather than admiring one's success in overcoming such circumstances, they wonder why anyone would admit to humble origins when it need not be known.

If your father held a low-status job; if you have relatives, especially female relatives, who have disgraced the family; or if you have elderly relatives in a nursing home (which Arabs find shocking), there is nothing to be gained by talking about it. If you dislike your parents or any close relatives, keep your thoughts to yourself. On the other hand, if you are from a prominent family or are related to a well-known person, letting people know this information can work to your advantage.

In sum, if you do not have positive things to say about your family, things that will incline Arabs to admiration, it is best to avoid the subject.

9

Religion and Society

Arabs identify strongly with their religious groups, whether they are Muslim or Christian and whether they participate in religious observances or not. A foreigner must be aware of the pervasive role of religion in Arab life in order to avoid causing offense by injudicious statements or actions.

Religious Affiliation

Religious affiliation is essential for every person in Arab society. There is no place for an atheist or an agnostic. If you have no religious affiliation or are an atheist, this should not be mentioned. Shock and amazement would be the reaction of most Arabs, along with a loss of respect for you. Arabs place great value on piety and respect anyone who sincerely practices his or her religion, no matter what that religion is.

Religious Practices

An Arab's religion affects his or her whole way of life on a daily basis. Religion is taught in the schools, the language is full of religious expressions, and people practice their religion openly, almost obtrusively, expressing it in numerous ways: decorations on cars and in homes; jewelry in the form of gold crosses, miniature Qur'ans, or pendants inscribed with Qur'anic verses; and religious names.

The Qur'an provides an all-encompassing code of interpersonal relations, beyond ethical teachings and exhortations to faith. Much of the Qur'an was revealed when the Prophet Muhammad was administering a community, so much of it deals with forming a just society, government, economic principles, laws, schools and conducting business. It is a religious text and a legal code, all in one.

Muslims say the Qur'anic formula, "In the name of God, the Merciful, the Compassionate" (*Bismillah Ar-Rahman Ar-Raheem*), whenever they are setting out on a trip, about to undertake a dangerous task, or beginning a speech. This formula is printed at the top of business letterheads and included at the beginning of reports and personal letters—it even appears on business receipts.

For both Muslims and Christians, marriage and divorce are controlled by religious law. In some countries there is no such thing as a civil marriage; it must be performed by a religious official. For Muslims inheritance is also controlled by religious law, and in conservative countries religious law partially determines methods of criminal punishment.

The practice of "Islamic banking" is gaining in popularity. The Islamic religion forbids lending money at a fixed rate of interest, viewing it as unfair and exploitative. Islamic banks, therefore, place investors' money in "shared risk" partnership accounts, with rates of return varying according to profits (or losses) on investments.

Marriage across religious lines is rare, although the Islamic religion permits a Muslim man to marry a Jewish or Christian woman without requiring that his wife convert. A Muslim woman, however, must marry a Muslim man; in this way the children are assured of being Muslim (children are considered to have the religion of their father).

Never make critical remarks about any religious practice. *In Arab culture all religions and their practices are treated with respect.* If you are a Christian foreigner and ask Christian Arabs about accompanying them to church services, they will be very pleased. Non-Muslims do not attend Islamic religious services, however, and you should not enter a mosque until you have checked whether it is permitted, which varies from country to country and even from mosque to mosque.

The Religion of Islam

To understand Arab culture it is essential that you become familiar with Islamic history and doctrine. If you do, you will gain insights that few Westerners have, and your efforts will be greatly appreciated.

The Islamic religion had its origin in northern Arabia in the seventh century A.D. The doctrines of Islam are based on revelations from God to His last prophet, Muhammad, over a period of twenty-two years. The revelations were preserved and incorporated into the holy book of the Muslims, the Qur'an.*

The God Muslims worship is the same God Jews and Christians worship (*Allah* is simply the Arabic word for *God*; Arab Christians pray to Allah). Islam is defined as a return to the faith of Abraham, the prophet who made a covenant with God.

The Qur'an contains doctrines that guide Muslims to correct behavior so that they will find salvation on the Day of Judgment, narrative stories illustrating God's benevolence and power, and social regulations for the Muslim community. It is the single most important guiding force for Muslims and touches on virtually every aspect of their lives.

The word *Islam* means "submission" (to the will of God), and *Muslim* (also spelled "Moslem," which is more familiar to Westerners but not as close to the Arabic pronunciation) means "one who submits." The doctrines of the Islamic religion are viewed as a summation and completion of previous revelations to Jewish and Christian prophets. Islam shares many doctrines with Judaism and Christianity, and Jews and Christians are known as "People of the Book" (the Scriptures).

Shortly after the advent of Islam, the Arabs began an energetic conquest of surrounding territory and eventually expanded their empire from Spain to India. The widespread conversion to Islam by the people in the Middle East and North Africa accounts for the fact that today over 90 percent of all Arabs are Muslims.

Most Muslim Arabs are *Sunni* (also called "orthodox"), and they constitute 85 percent of Muslims. Fifteen percent are *Shia* and are found in Lebanon, Iraq, and the Arabian Gulf (Iran, the most important Shia country, is not Arab). The separation of the Muslims into two groups stems from a dispute over the proper succession of authority (the "caliphate") after the death of the Prophet Muhammad. Sunnis and Shia

---

*The Qur'an is the most read, recited, memorized, debated, analyzed, and venerated book in the annals of history.[1]

differ today in some of their religious practices and emphases on certain doctrines, but both groups recognize each other as Muslims.

Muslim society is governed by the *Sharia,* or Islamic law, which is based on the Qur'an and the *Sunnah,* which originated during the years when Muhammad was governing the Muslim community in Medina and Mecca. The Sunnah is the description of the acts and sayings of the Prophet and incorporates the *Hadith* (traditions of the Prophet). Islamic jurists also use *ijma'* (consensus) and *qiyas* (reasoning by analogy) when interpreting and applying Islamic law.

The application of Islamic law differs by country and local interpretation of the Qur'an and Sharia law. Some countries (Saudi Arabia, Libya, Sudan) follow it almost exclusively in domestic and criminal law, but most have modified or supplemented it. Islamic jurists are faced with new issues on which there has not been final agreement or consistency. Birth control, for instance, which is permitted in most Islamic countries, is openly promoted by some and discouraged by others. In Pakistan and Bangladesh (Muslim, non-Arab countries), for example, birth control is a huge social taboo based on their interpretation of religious principles. There are many Islamic conferences where issues such as population control, women's dress, capital punishment, nuclear and biological warfare, terrorism, human rights, and societal pluralism are discussed. There is, however, no binding central authority to enforce agreed-upon decisions.

The basic tenets of the Islamic faith are known as the five "pillars," the primary obligations for Muslims:

Reciting the Declaration of Faith ("There is no God but God and Muhammad is the Messenger [Prophet] of God"). The recitation of this declaration with sincere intention in front of two male Muslim witnesses is sufficient for a person to become a Muslim.

Arabs, Muslims and Christians alike, intersperse their ordinary conversations with references to the will of God (see "Social Greetings" in the Appendix). To make a good impression, you are advised to do the same. Using Arabic religious expressions acts as a formal acknowledgment of the importance of religious faith in their society.

Praying five times daily. The five prayers are said at dawn, noon, afternoon, sunset, and night, and their times differ slightly every day. Muslims are reminded to pray through a prayer call broadcast from the minaret of a mosque. A Muslim prays facing in the direction of the Kaaba in Mecca. The weekly communal prayer service is the noon prayer in the mosque on Fridays, generally attended by men (women may go but it is not as common, nor is it expected). The Friday prayer also includes a sermon. Prayer is regulated by ritual washing beforehand and a predetermined number of prostrations and recitations, depending on the time of day. The prayer ritual includes standing, bowing, touching the forehead to the floor (which is covered with a prayer mat, rug, or other clean surface), sitting back, and holding the hands in cupped position, all while reciting sacred verses. Muslims may pray in a mosque, in their home or office, or in public places. Avoid staring at, walking in front of, or interrupting a person during prayer.

The Call to Prayer, broadcast five times a day, contains the following phrases, the repetition of which varies slightly depending on the time of day:

God is Great.

I testify that there is no god but God.

I testify that Muhammad is God's messenger.

Come to prayer.

Come to success.

God is Great.

There is no god but God.

If you learn the Call in Arabic, it will add to your pleasure in hearing it (many Westerners become so accustomed to the Call that they miss it when they leave). The first statement, *Allahu Akbar* (God is Great), is much used in Islam in other contexts as well. It is, in fact, "the dominant cultural chord of Islam, the declaration that punctuates all life, the reason to believe, the motive for action, inspiration for soldier and revolutionary, consolation for the oppressed."[2]

Giving alms (charity) to the needy. Muslims are required to give as Zakat (a religious offering) 2 1/2 percent of their net annual income (after basic family expenses) for the welfare of the community in general and for the poor in particular. Some people assess themselves annually and give the money to a government or community entity; others distribute charity throughout the year.

If you are asked for alms by a beggar, it is best to give a token amount. Even if you give nothing, avoid saying no, which is very rude. Instead, say "Allah ya'teek" (God give you); at least you have given the person a blessing. There is a very strong emphasis on charity in Islam; it is hugely important. Muslims see Islam as the religion of social justice.

Fasting during the month of Ramadan. Ramadan is the ninth month of the Islamic lunar calendar year (which is eleven days short of 365, so religious holidays move forward every year). During Ramadan, Muslims do not eat, drink, or smoke between sunrise and sunset. The purpose of fasting is to experience hunger and deprivation and to perform an act of self-discipline, humility, and faith. The Ramadan fast is not required of persons whose health may be endangered, and travelers are also excused; however, anyone who is excused must make up the missed fast days later when health and circumstances permit. Ramadan brings with it a holiday atmosphere, as people gather with family and friends to break the fast at elaborate meals every evening. Work hours are shortened, shops change their opening and closing hours, and most activities take place in the early morning or late at night.

Be considerate of people who are fasting during Ramadan by refraining from eating, drinking, or smoking in public places during the fasting hours. To express good wishes to someone before or during Ramadan, you say, *"Ramadan Kareem"* ("Gracious Ramadan"), to which the response is *"Allahu Akram"* ("God is more gracious").

Performing a pilgrimage to Mecca at least once during one's lifetime if finances permit. The Hajj is the peak religious experience for many Muslims. In the twelfth month of the Islamic year, Muslims from all over the world gather in Saudi Arabia to perform several separate activities, which are carried out at different sites in the Mecca and Medina area over a period of six days. The Hajj commemorates the life of the patriarch Abraham.

Pilgrims, men and women, wear white garments to symbolize their state of purity and their equality in the sight of God. At the end of the Hajj period is a holiday during which all families who can afford it sacrifice a sheep (or other animal) and, after taking enough for one meal, share the rest of it with the poor. The sacrifice relates to Abraham's test of faith—he was willing to sacrifice his son but was instructed to sacrifice a ram instead. Sharing on this holiday is such an important gesture that each year many governments send surplus sacrificial meat to refugees and to the poor in low-income Muslim countries around the world.

When someone is departing for the pilgrimage, the appropriate blessing is *Hajj Mabroor* (Reverent Pilgrimage). When someone returns, offer congratulations and add the title *Hajj* (*Hajja* for a woman) to the person's name (except in Saudi Arabia, where the title is not used).

The Qur'an and the Bible

Much of the content of the Qur'an is similar (though not identical) to the teachings and stories found in the Old and New Testaments of the Bible. Islamic doctrine accepts the previous revelations to biblical prophets as valid, but states, as the Bible does, that the people continually strayed from these teachings. Correct guidance had to be repeated through different prophets, one after the other. By the seventh century, doctrines and practices again had to be corrected through the revelations to Muhammad, who is known as the last, or "seal," of the prophets.

The Qur'an is divided into 114 chapters, arranged in order of length, longest to shortest (with a few exceptions). The chapters are not in chronological order, although the reader can identify whether a chapter was revealed in Mecca (earlier) or Medina (later). Each chapter is made up of verses. If you decide to read the Qur'an in translation, it is a good idea to obtain a list of the chapters in chronological order and read through them in that order so that the development of thought and teachings becomes clear.†

Most of the chapters in the Qur'an are in cadenced, rhymed verse, while some (particularly the later Medinan ones) are in prose. The sustained rhythm of the recited Qur'an, combined with the beauty of its content, accounts for its great esthetic and poetic effect when heard in Arabic. The Qur'an is considered the epitome of Arabic writing style, and when it is recited aloud, it can move listeners to tears. The elegance and beauty of the Qur'an are taken as proof of its divine origin—no human being could expect to produce anything so magnificent.

The three most often cited characteristics of the Qur'an are these: it is inimitable, it is eternal (it always existed but was not manifested until the seventh century), and it is in Arabic (the Arabic version is the direct Word of God, so translations of the Qur'an into other languages are not used for prayer). Verses from the Qur'an are much used for decoration.

It is common for Muslims to memorize the Qur'an, or large portions of it; a person who can recite the Qur'an is called a Hafiz. Reading and reciting the Qur'an was once the traditional form of education, and often the only education many people received. In most Arab schools today memorization of Qur'anic passages is included in the curriculum. The word *Qur'an* means "recitation" in Arabic.

The Qur'an and the Bible have much in common:

- The necessity of faith

- Reward for good actions and punishment for evil actions on the Day of Judgment

- The concept of Heaven (Paradise) and Hell

- The existence of angels who communicate between God and man

- The existence of Satan (*Shaytan* in Arabic)

- The recognition of numerous prophets.‡

---

†A list of Qur'anic chapters in chronological order may be found in Richard Bell's *Introduction to the Qur'an* (1953). It is also available on the Internet.

‡The Qur'an recognizes eighteen Old Testament figures as prophets (among them Adam, Noah, Abraham, Ishmael, Isaac, Jacob, Moses, Joseph, Job) and three New Testament figures (Zachariah, John the Baptist, and Jesus), and it mentions four prophets who do not appear in the Bible. Of all these prophets, five are considered the most important. In order of chronology these are Noah, Abraham, Moses, Jesus, and Muhammad.

- The prohibition of the consumption of pork and the flesh of animals not slaughtered in a ritual manner, which is very similar to kosher dietary law in the Old Testament

- The teaching that Jesus was born of a virgin; Mary is called "Miriam" in Arabic (the theme is the same, although details differ)

- The teaching that Jesus worked miracles, including curing the sick and raising the dead

There are some notable differences between the Qur'an and the Bible as well:

- Islam does not recognize the concept of intercession between God and man; all prayers must be made to God directly. Jesus is recognized as one of the most important prophets, but the Christian concept of his intercession for man's sins is not accepted.

- Islam teaches that Jesus was not crucified; instead, a person made to look like him was miraculously substituted in his place on the cross; God would not allow such an event to happen to one of His prophets.

- Islam does not accept the doctrine of Jesus' resurrection and divinity.

- Islam is uncompromisingly monotheistic and rejects the Christian concept of the Trinity.

Some of the biblical stories that are retold in the Qur'an (in a shortened version) include the following:

- The story of the Creation
- The story of Adam and Eve
- The story of Cain and Abel
- The story of Noah and the Flood

- The story of the covenant of Abraham and his willingness to sacrifice his son as a test of faith§
- The story of Lot and the destruction of the evil cities
- The story of Joseph (told in much detail)
- The story of David and Goliath
- The story of Solomon and the Queen of Sheba
- The story of the afflictions of Job
- The story of the birth of Jesus||

Muslims feel an affinity with the Jewish and Christian religions and find it unfortunate that so few Westerners understand how similar the Islamic religion is to their own. Islam is a continuation of the other two religions, and Muslims view it as the completed true faith.

Passages from the Qur'an

Selected passages from the Qur'an are presented here to give the reader an idea of the tone and content of the book (from *The Koran Interpreted*, by A. J. Arberry, 1955). Titles of chapters refer to key words in that chapter, not to content.

Chapter 1: The Opening
In the Name of God, the Merciful, the Compassionate.
Praise belongs to God, the Lord of all Being
the All-merciful, the All-compassionate
the Master of the Day of Judgment.
Thee only we serve; to Thee alone we pray for help.
Guide us in the straight path,
the path of those whom Thou hast blessed,
not of those against whom Thou art wrathful,
nor of those who are astray.

---

§Islam holds that Abraham was ordered to sacrifice Ishmael, whereas the Bible states that it was Isaac. Abraham is recognized as the ancestor of the Arabs through Ishmael.

||In the Qur'anic version, Jesus was born at the foot of a palm tree in the desert and saved his unmarried mother from scorn when, as an infant, he spoke up in her defense and declared himself a prophet, saying "...Peace be upon me, the day I was born, and the day I die, and the day I am raised up alive" (referring to his resurrection on the Day of Judgment). This is a miracle of Jesus not recorded in the Bible.

Chapter 5: The Table

(Verse 3)
Today the unbelievers have despaired of
your religion; therefore fear them not,
but fear you Me.
Today I have perfected your religion
for you, and I have completed My blessing
upon you, and I have approved Islam
for your religion.
(Verse 120)
To God belongs the kingdom of the heavens
And of the earth, and all that is in them,
and He is powerful over everything.

Chapter 93: The Forenoon

(This chapter begins with an oath, which is common in the Qur'an.)
In the Name of God, the Merciful, the Compassionate.
By the white forenoon and the brooding night!
Thy Lord has neither forsaken thee nor hates thee
and the Last [life] shall be better for thee than the First.
Thy Lord shall give thee, and thou shalt be satisfied.
Did He not find thee an orphan, and shelter thee?
Did He not find thee erring, and guide thee?
Did He not find thee needy, and suffice thee?
As for the orphan, do not oppress him,
and as for the beggar, scold him not;
and as for thy Lord's blessing, declare it.

10

Communicating with Arabs

This chapter is about the Arabic language. Though you may never learn Arabic, you will need to know something about the language and how it is used. Arabic is the native language of 300 million people and the official language of some twenty countries. In 1973 it was named the fourth official language of the United Nations, and it is the sixth most widely spoken language in the world.* Arabic originated as one of the northern Semitic languages. The only other Semitic languages still in wide use today are Hebrew (revived as a spoken language only a century ago) and Amharic (Ethiopian), which is from the southern Semitic branch. There are still a few speakers of the other northern Semitic languages (Aramaic, Syriac, and Chaldean) in Lebanon, Syria, and Iraq.

Many English words have been borrowed from Arabic, the most easily recognizable being those that begin with *al* (the Arabic word for "the"), such as *algebra, alchemy, alcove, alcohol,* and *alkali.* Many pertain to mathematics and the sciences; medieval European scholars drew heavily on Arabic source materials in these fields. Other Arabic words include *cipher, algorithm,* and *almanac.* Some foods that originated in the East brought their Arabic names west with them—*coffee, sherbet, sesame, apricot, ginger, saffron,* and *carob.*†

---

*The ranking of the top ten languages is Mandarin Chinese, English, Hindustani, Spanish, Russian, Arabic, Bengali, Portuguese, Malay-Indonesian, French.

†For more examples see Munir Al-Ba'albaki (1982), 101-12.

Varieties of Arabic

Spoken Arabic in all its forms is very different from written Arabic. The written version is Classical Arabic, the language that was in use in the seventh century A.D., in the Hejaz area of Arabia. It is this rich, poetic language of the Qur'an that has persisted as the written language of all Arabic-speaking peoples since that time. Classical Arabic, which has evolved into Modern Standard Arabic to accommodate new words and usages, is sacred to the Arabs, esthetically pleasing, and far more grammatically complex than the spoken or colloquial dialects.

The spoken languages are Formal Spoken Arabic and colloquial Arabic; the latter includes many dialects and subdialects. Although some of them differ from each other as much as Spanish does from Italian or the Scandinavian languages do from each other, they are all recognized as Arabic. When Arabic spread throughout the Middle East and North Africa with the Arab conquests, it mixed with and assimilated local languages, spawning the dialects which are spoken today.

An overview of Arabic language usage reveals the following:

Classical (Modern Standard) Arabic. Classical Arabic is used for all writing and for formal discussions, speeches, and news broadcasts but not for ordinary conversation. It is the same in all Arab countries, except for occasional variations in regional or specialized vocabulary.[‡]

Colloquial Arabic (dialects). Colloquial Arabic is used for everyday spoken communication but not for writing, except sometimes in very informal correspondence, in film or play scripts, or as slang in cartoons and the like.

Formal Spoken Arabic. Formal Spoken Arabic is improvised, consisting principally of Classical Arabic terminology within the structure of the local dialect; it is used by educated people when they converse with Arabs whose dialect is very different from their own.

[‡]Classical and Modern Standard Arabic differ, but differences are technical.

The Superiority of Arabic

It is not an exaggeration to say that *Arabs are passionately in love with their language.* Just speaking and hearing it can be a moving aesthetic experience. Arabs are secure in the knowledge that their language is superior to all others. This attitude about one's own language is held by many people in the world, but in the case of the Arabs, they can point to several factors as proof of their assertion.

Most important, when the Qur'an was revealed directly from God, Arabic was the medium chosen for His message; its use was not an accident. Arabic is also extremely difficult to master, and it is complex grammatically; this is viewed as another sign of superiority. Because its structure lends itself to rhythm and rhyme, Arabic is pleasing to listen to when recited aloud. Finally, it has an unusually large vocabulary and its grammar allows for the easy coining of new words, so that borrowing from other languages is less common in Arabic than in many other languages. In other words, Arabic is richer than other languages, or so it is argued.

While most Westerners feel an affection for their native language, the pride and love Arabs feel for Arabic are much more intense. The Arabic language is their greatest cultural treasure and achievement, an art form that unfortunately cannot be accessed or appreciated by outsiders.

Arabic, if spoken or written in an ornate and semi-poetic style, casts a spell. Hearing the words and phrases used skillfully is a poetic experience, and people respond as much or more to the style as to the content. A talented orator can wield power in this subtle way. Beautiful Arabic conjures up images of once-memorized Qur'an passages or bits of poetry, and it can be just as intricate orally as the most complex Arabic calligraphy designs.

The Prestige of Classical Arabic

The reverence for Arabic pertains only to Classical Arabic, which is what Arabs mean by the phrase "the Arabic language." This was illustrated by the comment of an Egyptian village headman who once explained to me why he considered the village school to be important. "For one thing," he said, "that's where the children go to learn Arabic."

To the contrary, Arabic dialects have no prestige. Some people go so far as to suggest that they have "no grammar" and are not worthy of serious study. Committees of scholars have coined new words and tried to impose conventional usages to partially replace the dialects, but they have had no more success than language regulatory groups in other countries.

A good command of Classical Arabic is highly admired in the Arab culture because it is difficult to attain. Few people other than scholars and specialists in Arabic have enough confidence to speak extemporaneously in Classical Arabic or to defend their written style. In Arabic, the classical language is called "The Most Eloquent Language."

To become truly literate in Arabic requires more years of study than are required for English literacy. The student must learn new words in Classical Arabic (more than 50 percent of the words are different from the local dialect in some countries)[§] and a whole new grammar, including case endings and new verb forms. The literacy problem in the Arab world stems significantly from the difficulty of Classical Arabic. Even people who have had five or six years of schooling are still considered functionally illiterate (unable to use the written language for anything more than rudimentary needs, such as signing one's name or reading signs).

On the other hand, the written language is not truly a foreign language to illiterates or even to preschool children. They hear it passively on a constant basis, in news broadcasts, in speeches and formal discussions, on *Sesame Street,* and in children's books and recordings.

From time to time Arab scholars have suggested that Classical Arabic be replaced by written dialects to facilitate education and literacy. This idea has been repeatedly and emphatically denounced by the large majority of Arabs and has almost no chance of acceptance in the foreseeable future. The most serious objection is that Classical Arabic is the language of the Qur'an. Another argument is that if it were supplanted by the dialects, the entire body of Arabic literature and poetry would become unattainable, and if translated into a dialect, it would lose much of its beauty.

There is a political argument too. Classical Arabic is a cultural force that unites all Arabs. To discard it, many fear, would lead to a linguistic fragmentation which would exacerbate the tendencies toward political and psychological fragmentation already present.

[§]A study was conducted in Tunisia in the early 1970s, comparing the vocabulary of six-year-old Tunisian children with equivalent vocabulary in Modern Standard Arabic, the medium through which they would be taught to read. It was found that over 70 percent of the vocabulary words were different (information from personal communication with professors, University of Tunis).

Eloquence of Speech

Eloquence is emphasized and admired in the Arab World far more than in the West, which accounts for the flowery prose in Arabic, in both written and spoken form. *Instead of viewing rhetoric in a disparaging way, as Westerners often do, Arabs admire it.* The ability to speak eloquently is a sign of education and refinement.

Foreign observers frequently comment on long-winded political speeches and the repetition of phrases and themes in Arabic, failing to understand that the speaker's style of delivery and command of the language appeal to the listeners as much as does the message itself. Exaggerations, threats, promises, and nationalistic slogans are meant more for momentary effect than as statements of policy or belief, yet foreigners too often take them literally, especially when encountered in the cold light of a foreign language translation. *In the Arab world how you say something is as important as what you have to say.*

Eloquence is a clue to the popular appeal of some nationalistic leaders whose words are far more compelling than their deeds. Much of the personal charisma attributed to them is due in large part to their ability to speak in well-phrased, rhetorical Arabic. This was true of the late Gamal Abdel Nasser, for example, and is true of Muammar Qaddhafi today. Repetition of refrains is common, as is exaggeration, which sometimes expresses wish fulfillment and provides a satisfying substitution of words for action.

Arabs devote considerable effort to using their language creatively and effectively. As Leslie J. McLoughlin, an Arabic specialist, says,

> *Westerners are not in everyday speech given, as Arabs are, to quoting poetry, ancient proverbs and extracts from holy books. Nor are they wont to exchange fulsome greetings.... Perhaps the greatest difference between the Levantine approach to language and that of Westerners is that Levantines, like most Arabs, take pleasure in using language for its own sake. The sahra (or evening entertainment) may well take the form of talk alone, but talk of a kind forgotten in the West except in isolated communities such as Irish villages or Swiss mountain communities—talk not merely comical, tragic, historical, pastoral, etc., but talk ranging over poetry, story telling, anecdotes, jokes, word games, singing and acting.*[1]

Speech Mannerisms

Making yourself completely understood by another person is a difficult task under the best of circumstances. It is more difficult still if you each have dramatically different ways of expressing yourself. Such is the problem between Westerners and Arabs, which often results in misunderstanding, leaving both parties feeling bewildered or deceived.

Arabs talk a lot, repeat themselves, shout when excited, and make extensive use of gestures. They punctuate their conversations with oaths (such as "I swear by God") to emphasize what they say, and they exaggerate for effect. Foreigners sometimes wonder if they are involved in a discussion or an argument.

If you speak softly and make your statements only once, Arabs may wonder if you really mean what you are saying. People will ask, "Do you really mean that?" or "Is that true?" It's not that they do not believe you, but they need repetition and a few emphatic "yeses" to be reassured.

Arabs have a great tolerance for noise and interference during discussions; often several people speak at once (each trying to outshout the other), interspersing their statements with threatening (or playful) gestures, all the while being coached by bystanders. Businessmen interrupt meetings to greet callers, answer the telephone, and sign papers brought in by clerks. A foreigner may feel that he or she can be heard only by insisting on the precondition of being allowed to speak without interruption. *Loudness of speech is mainly for dramatic effect and in most cases should not be taken as an indication of how strongly the speaker feels about what he or she is saying.*

In a taxi in Cairo once, my driver was shouting and complaining and gesticulating wildly to other drivers as he worked his way through the crowded streets. In the midst of all this action, he turned around, laughed, and winked. "You know," he said, "sometimes I really enjoy this!"

Some situations absolutely demand emotion and drama. In Baghdad I was in a taxi when it was hit from the rear. Both drivers leaped out of their cars and began shouting at each other. After waiting ten minutes, while a crowd gathered, I decided to pay the fare and leave. I pushed through the crowd and got the driver's attention. He broke off the argument, politely told me that there was nothing to pay, and then resumed the argument at full voice.

Loud and boisterous behavior does have limits, however. It is more frequent, of course, among people of approximately the same age and social status who know each other well. It occurs mostly in social situations, less often in business meetings, and is not acceptable when dealing with elders or social superiors, in which case polite deference is required. Bedouins and the Arabs of Saudi Arabia and the Gulf tend to be more reserved and soft-spoken, at least in more or less formal discussions. In fact, *in almost every respect, protocol is stricter in the Arabian Peninsula* than elsewhere in the Arab world.

The Power of Words

To the Arab way of thinking (consciously or subconsciously), words have power; they can, to some extent, affect subsequent events. Arab conversation is peppered with blessings, which are like little prayers for good fortune, intended to help keep things going well. *Swearing and the use of curses and obscenities is very offensive to Arabs.* If words have power and can affect events, it is feared that curses may bring misfortune just by being uttered.

The liberal use of blessings also demonstrates that the speaker holds no envy toward a person or object; in other words, that he or she does not cast an "evil eye" toward something. Belief in the evil eye (often just called "the eye") is common, and it is feared or acknowledged to some extent by most Arabs, although less so by the better educated. It is widely believed that a person or object can be harmed if viewed (even unconsciously) with envy—with an evil eye. The harm may be prevented, however, by offering blessings or statements of goodwill. We teach students of Arabic a large number of what we call "benedictions." Learning them is not enough; they must also remember to use them.

Foreigners who do not know about the evil eye may be suspected of giving it. When a friend buys a new car, don't express envy, say "May you always drive it safely." When someone moves to a new house, say "May you always live here happily." When meeting someone's children, say "May they always be healthy" or "May God keep them for you." All these are translations of much-used Arabic expressions. Omitting benedictions can be seen as *rude*.

Euphemisms

Arabs are uncomfortable discussing illness, disaster, or death. This trait illustrates how the power of words affects Arab speech and behavior. *A careless reference to bad events can lead to misfortune or make a bad situation worse.* Arabs avoid such references as much as possible and use euphemisms instead.

Euphemisms serve as substitutes, and a foreigner needs to learn the code in order to understand what is really being said. For example, instead of saying that someone is sick, Arabs may describe a person as "a little tired." They avoid a word like *cancer*, saying instead "He has 'it'" or "She has 'the disease,'" and often wait until an illness is over before telling others about it, even relatives. Arabs do not speak easily about death and sometimes avoid telling others about a death for some time; even then they will phrase it euphemistically.

Some years back I was visiting the owner of an Egyptian country estate, when two men came in supporting a third man who had collapsed in the field. The landlord quickly telephoned the local health unit. He got through just as the man slipped from his chair and appeared to be having a heart attack. "Ambulance!" he screamed. "Send me an ambulance! I have a man here who's...a little tired!"

I also had an amusing experience listening to an American life insurance salesman discuss a policy with an Arab. "Now if you should be killed," he began, "or become paralyzed, or blind, or lose a limb...." The conversation ended rather quickly; the Arab decided he did not want to hear about that policy!

These are social manners—in technical situations, of course, where specificity is required (doctor to patient, commander to soldier), explicit language is used.

The Written Word

Arabs have considerable respect for the written as well as the spoken word. Some pious people feel that anything written in Arabic should be burned when no longer needed (such as newspapers) or at least not left on the street to be walked on or used to wrap things, because the name of God probably appears somewhere. Decorations using Arabic calligraphy, Qur'anic quotations, and the name "Allah" are never used on floors (unlike crosses in floors of churches, especially in Europe). They are often seen, however, in framed pictures or painted on walls. If you buy anything decorated with Arabic calligraphy, ask what it means; you could offend Arabs by the careless handling of an item decorated with a religious quotation.

If you own an Arabic Qur'an, you must handle it with respect. It should be placed flat on a table or in its own area on a shelf, not wedged in with many other books. Best of all, keep it in a velvet box or display it on an X-shaped wooden stand (both are made for this purpose). Under no circumstances should anything (an ashtray, another book) be placed on top of the Qur'an.

Written blessings and Qur'anic verses are effective in assuring safety and preventing the evil eye, so they are seen all over the Arab World. Blessings are painted on cars and trucks and engraved on jewelry. You will see religious phrases in combination with the color blue, drawings of eyes, or pictures of open palms, all of which appear on amulets against the evil eye.

Proverbs

Arabs use proverbs far more than Westerners do, and they have hundreds. Many are in the form of rhymes or couplets. A person's knowledge of proverbs and when to use them enhances his or her image by demonstrating wisdom and insight.

Here is a selection of proverbs that help illuminate the Arab outlook on life. Proverbs frequently refer to family and relatives, poverty and social inequality, fate and luck.

- Support your brother, whether he is the tyrant or the tyrannized.
- The knife of the family does not cut.
  (If you are harmed by a relative, don't take offense.)
- You are like a tree, giving your shade to the outside.
  (You should give more attention to your own family.)
- One hand alone does not clap.
  (Cooperation is essential.)
- The hand of God is with the group.
  (There is strength in unity.)
- The young goose is a good swimmer.
  (Like father, like son.)

- Older than you by a day, wiser than you by a year.
  (Respect older people and their advice.)
- The eye cannot rise above the eyebrow.
  (Be satisfied with your station in life.)
- The world is changeable, one day honey and the next day onions. (This rhymes in Arabic.)
- Every sun has to set.
  (Fame and fortune may be fleeting.)
- Seven trades but no luck.
  (Even if a person is qualified in many trades, because of bad luck he may not find work.)
- It's all fate and chance.
- Your tongue is like a horse—if you take care of it, it takes care of you; if you treat it badly, it treats you badly.
- The dogs may bark but the caravan moves on.
  (A person should rise above petty criticism.)
- Patience is beautiful.
- The slave does the thinking and the Lord carries it out.
  (Man proposes and God disposes.)
- Bounties are from God.

And finally, my very favorite:

- The monkey in the eyes of his mother is a gazelle.

Islamic Fundamentalism (Islamism)

Islamic fundamentalism is a political and social issue, not part of the mainstream Islamic religion. For this reason it is considered here rather than in the chapter describing Islam.

Definitions and Numbers

The efforts to understand evolving Islamic social/religious thought have been completely overwhelmed by the (notorious) emergence of fundamentalism. (More accurate terms are *Islamism*, *militant Islam*, or *political Islam*. However, *fundamentalism* has caught on and is the most common word used to designate extremist Islamic thought).*

One problem with using *fundamentalism* in this way is that genuine Muslim fundamentalism refers to the same principles as in other religions: returning to original sacred writings and applying these to moral and social problems in the present. The word *fundamentalist* in Arabic derives from the word for "roots." About 10 percent of the Muslims describe themselves as true fundamentalists (religious conservatives, *not* extremist Islamists). I will use the term *Islamism* to refer to extreme militant Islam.

Extremists exist in every religion. There is no reasoning with people *who know exactly what God wants*. All society can do is try to control them.

---

*Especially recommended is Karen Armstrong's *Islam* (2000), especially the first chapter and the section on militant fundamentalism.

This chapter is intended as a description of militant Islamism in the Middle East and in the West (the United States and Europe). Exploring the various ramifications of the Islamist phenomenon is the goal here.

The militant Muslim groups cannot represent even 1 percent of Muslims in the United States (that would be 50,000) or the world (that would be 15 million). If that were true, we would be overrun with wild-eyed fanatics. Islamists who resort to violence add up to less than one tenth of 1 percent; we only have to consider numbers (surely we do not have 5,000 violent fanatics in the U.S., not even 500, probably not 50).[†] But terrorists do act; they engage in violence, and they are certainly getting most of the publicity.

We need to step back for a moment from the television images — chanting mobs, bombings of innocent people, and violent killings. It is simply common sense to realize that *these groups cannot possibly represent Arab or Muslim societies and people as a whole.* There are 1.5 *billion* Muslims in the world; 450 *million* in North Africa and the Greater Middle East (including non-Arabs); and 215 *million* Arab Muslims.

Some estimates claim that as many as 10 to 15 percent of the Muslims are fundamentalists (meaning militant Islamists). Daniel Pipes claims that the Islamist element includes some 100 to 150 million adherents worldwide, his estimate based on "election data, survey research, anecdotal evidence, and the opinions of informed observers," with no sources cited. He also states (with no sources cited), "Reliable statistics on opinion in the Muslim world do not exist [??], but my sense is that one half of the world's Muslims — or some 500 million persons — sympathize more with Osama bin Laden and the Taliban than with the United States. That such a vast multitude hates the United States is sobering indeed."[1]

One congressman claimed that 85 percent of the mosques in the U.S. have extremist leadership.[2] The author of a 2002 book *American Jihad: The Terrorists Living Among Us*[3] claims that "fundamentalists" control 80 percent of the mosques (his reason being that many mosques are funded at least partially with Saudi money), and stated in 1995 that Islam "sanctions genocide, planned genocide, as part of its religious doctrine."[4]

[†]The U.S. and other countries have been arresting terrorists worldwide since 2001. The largest number ever detained at Guantanamo was around 650. This is assuming that the identification of these terrorists is related to militant Islam. The definition of *terrorist* is in itself unclear; there are many national groups (such as Chechens and Iraqis) who are not counted here.

Statements like these are reckless and alarmist. They are misstated and not backed by empirical data. They fan hysteria, and they libel the entire Muslim community. Anti-American sentiment among Muslims does not imply supporting Bin Ladin or the Taliban (who do hate America). Anti-American Muslims hate America's *political policies* in their region.

When such comments are repeated in the media, most ordinary readers assume that such statements are true of *all* Muslims, or if they don't know the difference, "all those Arabs," unless the Islamist context is *repeatedly* made *very clear* and the difference explained. Arabs frequently talk about the mixing of Islamism and mainstream Islam in the Western media. Islamists have created their own definition of *infidels* and *Jihad*, which are totally unorthodox.

Ordinary Muslims, "the other 99 percent," do *not* go around referring to Christians or Jews as infidels or unbelievers. They would no more do this than we ordinary Westerners would use similar (embarrassing, degrading) Crusade-era terms about them. In 40 years I have never heard this term used by ordinary Muslims to refer to Westerners or their society and institutions, not once. When some Western scholars insist on using terms like *infidel* or *unbeliever* (they are not quoting, they are just being emphatic),† it is insulting to ordinary Muslims because, again, politicians and the media rarely emphasize that such terms are used *only* by Islamists, who also refer to *mainstream Muslims* as unbelievers. Westerners rightly take offense when characterized as infidels, so it is essential that they understand the Islamist source of such labels.

Muslims all over the world just want to get on with their lives, get an education, find a job, raise their children and participate in family and community life. They are not inscrutable. They are not mysterious or exotic. They are ordinary people with *no interest* in harming non-Muslims or interfering with their way of life. That Muslims have normal human priorities is so obvious that it should not need to be stated.

As for Islamists, however, criticism is justified and should not be euphemized if statements are the truth; Islamist militants advocate violence, deny rights to women, and oppose individual freedom. They do

---

†Examples: "The Western world or, as they would put it, the infidel countries;" "They had dealt with one of the infidel superpowers;" "We infidels are the only hope for Islam;" ". . .showing a lack of gratitude or total indifference when we infidels come to their rescue;" ". . .repeated commands for Muslims not to befriend infidels/unbelievers (all non-Muslims)."

not deserve to be protected by a regard for political correctness. *They are doing devastating harm to everyone*, including the vast majority of Arabs and Muslims.

Every society has deviant groups. We as Westerners understand the reasoning and motives of such groups in our own society. Some scholars have compared extremist Islamists to the Ku Klux Klan (KKK) in the U.S., which is Christian but definitely not mainstream. I think a better analogy is the white Aryan groups, because they are more active and they, too, are committed Christians with grievances. They had their own reasons to bomb the federal building in Oklahoma City. But do they represent ordinary Americans? Ordinary Christians? Certainly not. Imagine our outrage if the foreign press depicted Aryan groups as representing mainstream Christianity.

There are *two important factors* in the case of Islamism that explain why it is growing quickly as compared with extremist groups in the U.S. and other societies:

1. Their numbers continue to grow rapidly because they act on perceived grievances *that are constantly being reinforced.*

2. There are many more people in Muslim societies who have no viable personal future or stake in their society, and Islamism provides them with acceptance, a sense of belonging, and a higher purpose (50 to 60 percent of the young men in many countries are unemployed). Such disenchanted individuals acquire a "true believer" mindset, which allows them to confidently believe that whatever they do, they are doing God's work.

It is understandable that Islamists receive a disproportionate amount of attention in the media. To uninformed Westerners such extremists appear to be numerous, but to the thousands of Westerners who visit or live in Muslim countries, they are no more a factor in life than are the fringe groups in our country.

Here is an analogy: All Westerners readily understand the grievances of anti-abortion groups. Some agree and some disagree, some even join rallies, but this does not mean that these supporters are galvanized to condone or participate in violent acts. Understanding motivations and grievances (even sympathizing with them) must not be confused with a willingness to support or join the extremists.

Jihad

Jihad is used here to mean "Holy War," which is how the term is used by Islamic militants and the Western media (only). In this sense, Jihad is the same concept as Crusade, that is, fighting in the name of a religion.

A more accurate interpretation of Jihad refers to the "effort" that a Muslim makes to live and structure his or her personal life, and the wider society, on Islamic principles, a much more benign meaning. Anyone who combats temptations in order to live a righteous life can identify with this.

In January 2002, in the wake of the September 11 tragedy, at a conference of the Muslim World League, Muslim scholars defined *terrorism* and *Jihad*. *Terrorism* is defined as "an unlawful action, acts of aggression against individuals, groups or states [or] against human beings, including attacks on their religion, life, intellect, property or honor."[5] Terrorism, then, is any violence or threat designed to terrorize people or endanger their lives or security. *Jihad* is "self-defense, meant for upholding right, ending injustice, ensuring peace and security and establishing mercy."

Muslims *cannot* initiate an attack and call it a Jihad—a Jihad *must be called in self-defense only*. Extremists have decided that because the West continues to oppress them, they are justified in a "self-defensive" Jihad.

Jihad is not one of the five "pillars" of Islam, and it is not the central prop of the religion, despite the Western perspective. (See Chapter 9 for a discussion of the five tenets.) But it was and remains a duty for Muslims to commit themselves to a struggle on all fronts—moral, spiritual and political—to create a just and decent society.[6] This doctrine is, however, open to distortion.

Islamists and Muslim Society

Islamist mosques are now spreading throughout the Arab world, and *their leaders presume to judge who is or is not a good Muslim*. They do not recognize any interpretations of the Qur'an made by Islamic jurists over the centuries.§ Some people agree with the current, unfounded, interpretations; most people are dismayed. Many people attend these mosques, but they are not necessarily fundamentalist Islamists or terrorists. Very few are attracted to extremist action, which is built on a *deviant* interpretation of religious doctrines. Those who commit to extremist groups belong to a *cult*, which condones violence in the name of a radical vision of Islam.|| Islamists "give a religious covering to a *political* struggle."[8]

In Yemen, a well-known judge, Hamond Al-Hitar, has initiated dialogue with some militants in Yemen, with excellent results. His system is simple: he invites imprisoned militants to use the Qur'an to justify their terrorists acts, and when they cannot, he shows them numerous passages commanding Muslims not to attack civilians, to respect other religions, and to fight only in self-defense. If, after weeks of debate, the prisoners renounce violence (364 had, as of 2004), they are released and offered vocational training and helped to find jobs. Since December 2002, when the first round of dialogues ended, there have been no terrorist attacks in Yemen, and many people believe that this is a significant part of the reason. Judge Hamond said, "Before the dialogues began, there was only one way to fight terrorism, and that was through force. Now there is another way: dialogue."[9] He hopes to speak with Al-Qaeda leaders too.

Many Muslims have found themselves torn between two quite different worldviews. Some seek a synthesis. Others, who may be alienated from their governments and societies, choose the route of total commitment to violent Islamist groups that are hostile to the West. The majority of Islamist followers are poorly educated and believe whatever they are told. Others, the leaders who are better educated, have a political-power agenda.

---

§A good example of a verse often quoted in the Western press and by extremists is "Kill them [infidels] wherever you find them." (2:191) The context of this revelation was the twelve-year persecution of the nascent Muslim community by enemies intent on eradicating it, and it was directed toward the Arabian pagans. This verse in no way refers to noncombatant non-Muslims today.[7]

The Prophet Muhammad himself sent a letter to the monks in St. Catherine's Monastery in Sinai, which is still preserved, assuring them that they would be protected by the Muslims. Muhammad also intentionally shielded Christian Ethiopia from conquest. When Caliph Omar conquered Jerusalem, he issued an edict that all Christian lives and property would be safe, and he allowed the Jews to return (they had been expelled by the Byzantines). One wonders how Islamist zealots accommodate such precedents. They also have to account for this verse in the Qur'an: "Those who believe, and those who follow the Jewish scriptures, and the Christians... Any who believes in God and the Last Day and work righteousness shall have their reward with their Lord." (2:62)

||The beliefs of Islamists are thoroughly discussed in an article, "Middle East Islamism in the European Arena" in the section titled "The Culture of Global Jihad," by Reuven Paz, in the *Middle East Review of International Affairs 6*, no. 3, September 2002.

Some of these groups' interpretations of specific Islamic doctrines are bizarre indeed. For example, because suicide has *never* been a condoned practice in Islam, it would have to be classified as "Jihad martyrdom" to gain any acceptance at all. In fact, the incidence of suicide in Muslim societies is lower than that of any other regional or religious group.[10]

It is also time to put the "72 virgins" to rest; this is a quaint, lurid, provocative interpretation of an obscure passage in the Qur'an, avidly seized upon by Westerners who find it amusing and use it repeatedly to ridicule Islamic belief. Typical is an article in *The Washington Post* that opened, "He was promised a straight shot to heaven and 72 maidens to wait on him once he got there, but Hoshir Sabir Hasan was not ready to die."[11] A brochure from the Institute of Islamic Education states, "The promise of '70 or 72 virgins' is fiction written by some anti-Islam bigots."[12] This belief is to mainstream Muslims as the belief that we will one day be issued wings and a harp, and walk on clouds, is to mainstream Christians.|| I have never seen this refuted in the media.

Mainstream Muslims

Mainstream Muslims living in the United States and the West have spoken out, issued press releases, held conferences and publicized their repudiation of Islamist violence (the most recent is a denunciation from the Islamic Commission of Spain, in March 2005) but usually they get little or no press coverage.[14]

Moderate Muslims and Islamic scholars may be sending the messages, but the general public in America and elsewhere has not heard them. As a group, Muslims in the West are alarmed, embarrassed, and often incredulous at what is happening. They know that Islamism is causing a crisis in the image of their religion that needs to be addressed, and

---

|| "[The] first proponents [of this imagery] had nothing to do with the anti-Islamic myth that martyrs are motivated by the hope of being greeted by dozens of virgins waiting in heaven. It began with Hindu Tamils in Sri Lanka... when it spread to Palestine over the past decade, it was an act of last-resort desperation by frustrated people... Al-Qaeda has merely taken [up] an old technique.[13]

They interpreted these verses from the Qur'an: "Facing each other on thrones, round which will be passed to them a cup from a clear-flowing fountain...and beside them will be chaste women, their glances, with big eyes..." (37:44–48) This is very brief and vague, and it has given rise to many commentaries over the centuries. The Islamist interpretation is based on commentaries.

soon. The vice president of the Islamic Society of North America (the largest in the U.S., with 40,000 members) has stated that Muslims have a "special obligation" to fight extremist Islamism.[15, 16]

Moderates in the West are well aware that *mainstream Islam is also a target of the extremists.*

Many Muslims in America and Europe are immigrants and do not understand methods of attracting publicity, such as signed declarations, protest marches, walks-for-a-cause, and letters to the editor. Sixty percent of the Muslims in America are first or second generation, and 30 percent are black Americans. Younger Muslims who were born in Western countries do understand, and have begun a more active role, from campus events to public rallies. It will be up to them to change the image of Islam. The non-profit organization Free Muslims Against Terrorism was created "to eliminate broad-based support for Islamic extremism and terrorism and to strengthen secular democratic institutions in the Middle East." People are invited to send anonymous reports of any Muslim individuals or groups that (1) "advocate Muslim extremist ideology, (2) engage in apologetic support for terrorist organizations, or (3) advocate Jihad."[17] A website promotes similar goals: "Islam Denounces Terrorism" (www.islamdenouncesterrorism.com).

In the Middle East many people have a conflicted attitude toward Islamist groups because, regardless of their advocacy of violence, most of them provide much-needed social services. This is an important factor and helps explain their success in recruiting. In many countries where the government does not or cannot help the poor (which is considered to be an Islamic obligation on the part of the ruling power), Islamist groups provide services through schools, medical clinics, social welfare agencies, and financial support to families, notably in Egypt, Lebanon, Morocco, Tunisia, Algeria, and Yemen. These groups earn much of their credibility through such activities and programs. Many are well organized and well financed, and have created an institutional structure which is parallel to the state.[18] Because of the social services, Islamists gain support even if people do not agree with their beliefs.

One such organization is the Shia group Hizbollah. The U.S. government is confronting the reality that Hizbollah, classified as a terrorist organization, has become a legitimate political party in Lebanon and holds thirteen seats in the parliament (with the possibility of gaining more in future elections). Hizbollah provides schools, hospitals, pharmacies, dental clinics, jobs, scholarships, and welfare to thousands of Lebanese families.[19]

Islamists (and many fundamentalists) are idealistic (some would say utopian) in that they believe that their vision of Islam can offer the prescription for an ideal state, as in a popular slogan: "Islam is the Solution." Islamists and fundamentalists often function as pressure groups to upgrade the standards of public morality, and many people approve of this.

Anti-Americanism

A guidebook about Arabs cannot ignore the growing sentiment of anti-Americanism among Middle Eastern Arabs and Muslims today. It is an important trend, it is increasing, and we urgently need to try to understand it. Here are some statistics that lend a sense of reality to the worsening anti-American sentiment among Middle Eastern nations.

In a poll in May 2004 surveying six Arab nations, commissioned by the Arab American Institute, the overall approval ratings of the United States ranged between an unprecedented low of 2 percent in Egypt and a high of 20 percent in Lebanon. Those holding a favorable view of the U.S. in Saudi Arabia were 4 percent; in Morocco, 11 percent; in the United Arab Emirates, 14 percent; and in Jordan, 15 percent. These statistics indicate a sharp decline compared with a similar poll held two years previously. Why? The main reason behind the lower percentages was U.S. political policies. Even factoring age and gender into the attitudes toward American foreign policy in the six countries did not seem to have any significant impact.[1]

Before we go further, it must be made clear that *Middle Eastern Muslims and Arabs do not "hate" America.** Nor do they hate the American people. But they are *very angry* at America's government. It is only the extremist fringe that hates America.

I have never heard an ordinary Arab state that he hates America, nor have I heard such reports from others.

If the Arabs are *angry*, then there is hope. And if we understand the reasons for their anger, we can address them, and not misdirect our efforts to bring about change. If they truly *hated* America and America's values, we would have a permanent breach, a real clash of civilizations, and that would be a hopeless situation, one side trying to eradicate the other. *It's not that bad.*

On both sides, anti-American and anti-Arab/Muslim sentiments are as much about *perceptions* as they are about *reality*—who and what people listen to and the conclusions they reach. Both sides generalize and by now, each has a mostly negative, stereotypical image of the other. If people don't know a region or its inhabitants, they have to depend on the media to form their beliefs.[†]

Certainly most Americans truly, sincerely do not understand how this all came about. I think the most objective approach is to let Americans and Arabs speak for themselves. We can look at statements on both sides. One thing we can all agree on is that there are many misunderstandings. Some statements in this chapter use *they* without explaining who "they" is. At times *they* may refer to terrorists; other references are broader, and, given the large volume of commentary and rhetoric, it is often hard to tell how many are intended to refer to Arabs and Muslims in general.

Much that we read or hear is confusing, especially to people who don't know much about the Middle East. If, for example, any of the opinions you read below are difficult for you to understand, you can do several things: (1) ask an Arab or a Muslim in your community (virtually everyone has Arabs or Muslims in their communities); (2) talk with someone knowledgeable who has been to the region; and (3) look it up and read about it. Most important is that you consider statements from all sources and then *make up your own mind* as to the nature of anti-Americanism.

---

*America refers to the United States in this book because *America* is used in the U.S. media and also in the Middle East.

†Unlike the rest of the world, Americans do not see daily images of suffering Palestinians and Iraqis. It's not that other countries have news different from America's—it's *America* that is different.

Because we have already mentioned that most Arabs don't actually hate America but are very angry, let's begin right here.

Reasons for Arab Anger

Arab/Muslim and Some Western Views[‡]

Arabs display favorable attitudes toward many manifestations of America in their midst, including American-made products, science and technology, movies and television, etc. — it is clear that what drives down Arab attitudes toward America is, quite simply, U.S. policy in the region.[2]

In a poll by the Coalition Authorities in May 2004, they found that 92 percent of the Iraqis saw American forces as occupiers, and only 2 percent saw them as liberators.[3]

Anti-Americanism is a recent phenomenon fueled by American foreign policy, not an epochal confrontation of civilizations... Among the vast majority of Arabs today, the expression of anti-American feelings stems less from a blind hatred of the United States or American values than from a profound ambivalence about America: at once an object of admiration for its affluence, its films, its technology (and for some its secularism, its law, its order) and a source of deep disappointment given the ongoing role of the United States in shaping a repressive Middle Eastern status quo.[4]

Politicians, researchers, and observers often talk about this wave of anti-Americanism, but it seems that no one in Washington pays attention, for Washington continues with policies that provoke enmity and hatred. This enmity and hatred is not directed against the American: It is not a racist condition that focuses hatred on the Americans simply because they are American or because the United States is the strongest country in the world, the richest society, or

---

[‡]*Arab/Muslim* here can include some non-Arab Middle Eastern people and exclude some non-Muslim Arabs.

anything like that. It is because of American policies and the posi-
tion of the American administration on other people's rights.[5]

It is important to put the views Arabs and Muslims hold of the
United States in a broader global context. What becomes quickly
evident is that many of the negative views that people in the
Middle East and the Muslim world express about America are
widely shared in other parts of the world.[6]

Americans do not like to hear it, but their government has behaved like
an imperial power in the Middle East [for] more than fifty years.[7]

[There is a] history that is behind perceptions in the Middle East of
the American role there, perceptions that may not match what
Americans think of themselves and their country's role in the world.
Some would cavalierly dismiss these views or address them solely
via glossy public-relations campaigns. This is to underestimate dan-
gerously what is at work here: these perceptions and the history
behind them are extremely important, for it is how those in the
region perceive the United States....[8]

Between 1980 and 2001, the United States engaged in fifteen direct
military operations in the Middle East, all of them directed against
Muslims. There were an equal number of non-military actions such as
the imposition of punitive embargoes, threats through military build-up,
policies in support of some regional states against others, support of
selected opposition groups, and provision of weapons (sometimes
secretly). What matters here is not the diplomatic issue of who America
supported or why, the result has been that *these actions are seen by local*
people as American interference in their region, and resentment has con-
tinued to build. We are talking about perceptions. We are talking about
America's image.[§]

[§]This can be viewed at the *Information Clearing House* website, "U.S. Intervention in the Middle East,"
www.informationclearinghouse.info.

We shouldn't delude ourselves about why there is so much hatred for the United States. It does not come out of the clear blue. It is not because we represent freedom and virtue and light, while the Arabs stand for darkness and repression. American culture may represent something corrosive and immoral to certain Islamic sensibilities – that can't be helped. But that isn't what provokes suicide bombers. American policies often kill, directly and indirectly – and this is why people are willing to sacrifice themselves to kill us in return.[9]

One of the greatest dangers for Americans in deciding how to confront the Islamist threat lies in continuing to believe – at the urging of senior U.S. leaders—that Muslims hate us and attack us for what we are and what we think, rather than for what we do.... America is hated and attacked because Muslims believe they know precisely what the United States is doing in the Islamic world.[10]

Nobody hates America. America used to be a great example, it was not a colonial power in the region. Our sons and brothers work with American businesses. I am very sorry that American policy is threatening the human relations between the nations.[11]

A Shia leader in Lebanon: "We should be clear that we distinguish between the U.S. administration and the American people. We would like to be friends with the American people. Our problem is with the American administration.[12]

Some American Views

1. **They hate our freedom, values, way of life.**

   George W. Bush: *"They hate our freedoms, our freedom of religion, our freedom of speech, our freedom to vote and assemble and disagree with each other."*[13] *"America was targeted for attack because we're the brightest beacon for freedom and opportunity in the world."*[14] *"They hate our values. They hate what America stands for."*[15]

Donald Rumsfeld: *"These were not attacks [9/11] on America alone but...on people everywhere...who believe in freedom, who practice tolerance and who defend the inalienable rights of man."*[16]

George W. Bush: *"I am amazed that there's such misunderstanding of what our country is about that people would hate us. I am like most Americans, I just can't believe it because I know how good we are."*[17]

Bill Maher: *"They hate us because we don't even know why they hate us."*[18]

John McCain: *"They fight to express an irrational hatred for all that is good in humanity....They abhor liberty and justice. We fight for love of freedom and justice."*[19]||

2. They hate our success.

Charles Krauthammer: *"The fact is that the world hates the U.S. for its wealth, its success, its power."*[20]

Dan Rather: *"[People from the Middle East] see themselves as the world's losers. They would never admit that. They see us, we have everything. We win everything. They see themselves and think, "We should be a great people but we're not." It drives them batty. They hate us for who and what we are."*[21]

Ralph Peters: *"Jealous of our success and our power, terrified and threatened by the free, unstructured nature of our societies, and incapable of performing competitively in the twenty-first century, they have convinced themselves that our way of life is satanic...."*[22] *"We are dealing with a delusional civilization."*[23]

Daniel Pipes, interviewed by Chris Matthews: D.P.: *"The Islamic people are in a funk. Things have been going badly for a long time, two centuries. Things are going well for us."* C.M.: *"Lousy government, lousy economies, lousy opportunities in life. Blame it on Israel, blame it on the U.S., is that it?"* D.P.: *"Simply put, yeah."*[24]

||The reference is not clear. He refers to our enemies, they, them, Arab populations, other Arabs, and Saddam. In the last paragraph he mentions our struggle with terrorism.

3. They don't know enough about us.

The American government has recently (post-9/11) undertaken a new initiative—strengthening programs that present information about the country and its values (this is called "public diplomacy"). This is predicated on the assumption that anti-Americanism can be lessened by presenting more accurate or detailed information. The White House has a stated policy that "spreading the universal principle of human liberty" is the key to changing the conditions that spawn terrorism.[25]

> *The administration has made global outreach a priority... increased broadcasting in the Middle East and programs to encourage literacy, democratic reform and education.*[26]

> *Patricia Harrison, former Assistant Secretary of State for Education and Cultural Affairs: "The foundation of our public diplomacy strategy is to engage, inform and influence foreign publics in order to increase understanding for American values, policies, and initiatives."*[27]

> *The State Department spent $15 million for a warm and fuzzy TV advertising campaign called 'Shared Values' intended for broadcast in Muslim countries... The ads...were ultimately dropped after test audiences said they didn't touch on any of the main issues that divide America and the Muslim world.*[28]

> *The results [of a 2002 poll of Arab views] do not reflect an anti-Western sentiment at work...The results appeared contrary to the basic thrust of stepped-up "public diplomacy" outreach.... The programs rest on the premise that anti-American views in the region stem largely from lack of knowledge about U.S. values.*[29]

> *The Pentagon awarded three contracts this week [June 2005], potentially worth up to $300 million over five years, to companies it hopes will inject more creativity into its psychological operations*

efforts to improve foreign public opinion about the United States, particularly the military.[30]

In the "Report of the Advisory Group on Public Diplomacy for the Arab and Muslim World," submitted to the government in 2003 by a group tasked with evaluating public policy initiatives and making recommendations, the report opened with, "While the conduct of [political] policy is the primary determinant of success or failure in this struggle...."[31]

Everyone in the Middle East knows someone who lives in America—a friend, friend-of-a-friend, or a relative. Information from these people is far more credible than any American government-sponsored information campaign.

4. Anti-Americanism is an excuse.

Barry Rubin: *"The basic reason for the prevalence of Arab anti-Americanism, then, is that it has been such a useful tool for radical rulers, revolutionary movements, and even moderate regimes to build domestic support and pursue regional goals with no significant costs."*[32]

Anti-Americanism is how Arab leaders play the Arab people and the United States against each other to preserve their own hides. There is no incentive to be anything but anti-American, and it is very dangerous not to follow the pack.[33]

||Many authors, as well as most reports in the media, wrongly depict the thinking of people in the modern Middle East. I select the writings of Bernard Lewis as an example, because he is widely read and quoted. In all his writings, Dr. Lewis tends to speak in generalities, not distinguishing historical or extremist views from those of ordinary Arabs and Muslims of the 21st century. Repeating and emphasizing insulting remarks about Westerners will resonate with readers and become associated in their minds with Arabs and Muslims, even if they are not relevant today. Dr. Lewis continually uses phrases such as "the enemies of God," "the infidels of the West," and the House of Islam and the House of Unbelief, which are centuries out of date. He writes that "America has become the archenemy, the incarnation of evil, the diabolic opponent of all that is good," which is a belief strictly limited to extremists. I cannot see the relevance today of reading that "studying under infidel teachers was inconceivable." He cannot be describing modern, educated Arabs, but the damage is done. Arabs and Muslims do *not* think in these terms. They admire Western freedoms, science, and technology. Language like this does not reflect what I have been hearing, or overhearing, in the Arab world for 40 years.

Most Western readers simply want to understand 9/11, the Iraqi insurgency, and the current political climate in the Middle East. They don't know what is historical or what is extremist. Such careless writing does not clarify current issues for Western readers; on the contrary, it does incalculable damage.

5. **We share a long history of hatred.**

> Bernard Lewis: *"This is no less than a clash of civilizations—the perhaps irrational but surely historic reaction of an ancient rival against our Judeo-Christian heritage.... The struggle between these rival systems has now lasted for some fourteen centuries."* *"What is truly evil and unacceptable is the domination of infidels over true believers."*[34]II

> Bernard Lewis: *"The motive, clearly, is hatred. . . the hatred has been growing steadily for many years.... It is difficult if not impossible to be strong and successful and to be loved by those who are neither the one or the other....This feeling, with far deeper roots and greater intensity, affects attitudes in the Muslim world toward the Western world or, as they would put it, the infidel countries."*[35]

Unfortunately, the author does not make it clear just who he is talking about. Perhaps only the Islamists, but it reads as if referring to everyone in the "Muslim world." The large majority in the Muslim world would never characterize the Western world as "the infidel countries."

> Samuel Huntington: *"Conflict along the fault line between Western and Islamic civilizations has been going on for 1,300 years.... On both sides, the interaction between Islam and the West is seen as a clash of civilizations."*[36]

> Samuel Huntington: *"A complex mix of factors has increased the conflict between Islam and the West in the late twentieth century... Muslim population growth...the Islamic Resurgence...the West's simultaneous efforts to universalize its values and institutions, to maintain its military and economic superiority...and to intervene in conflicts in the Muslim world...the collapse of communism...increasing contact between...Muslims and Westerners."*[37]

The statements in this section, "Some American Views," cannot be based on interviews with ordinary Middle Eastern Arabs all across the region. Arabs are amazed when they read statements such as these, and they wonder where the authors found the information to justify what they write. No Arabs believe such assertions. Regrettably, Arabs are accustomed to being maligned (some Arabs see the title of this book and are afraid to open it). They also suspect malicious intent.

Arab/Muslim Views on American Culture

In a 2002 poll, 83 to 94 percent of the Arab respondents criticized U.S. policy but stated they love American music, movies, clothes, democracy, and freedom.[38]

In a 2004 poll, 70 percent of respondents in Morocco and 67 percent in Jordan said they would like to know or meet Americans.[39]

The *Arab Human Development Report* 2002 stated that 51 percent of older youths expressed a desire to emigrate, almost all to Europe or America.[40]

Ask anyone in Egypt what country they would like to visit, and they will probably say America," Aly said. "Ask them what movie they would like to see and it will probably be an American film. Ask them what school they would like to attend and they will name an American university. They may disagree violently with American policies, but they don't hate America. This is the paradox.[41]

The American people are very good people. When I go, I'm welcomed. Every young person here wants to go to America. But it's the policy.... There is no hatred toward America, but there is hatred toward a policy which we find unjust.[42]

Views on Western-Style Democracy

Zogby's survey in 2002, reported in What Arabs Think, *said that Arab views do not reflect an anti-Western sentiment and noted that France, Canada and Germany were among countries with highly favorable ratings.... A majority of the respondents in Egypt, Kuwait, Lebanon, and Saudi Arabia, for example, looked favorably on what the survey described as "American freedom and democracy."*[43] *When he asked what most shaped their opinions, those polled said it was U.S. policies, rather than values or culture. When queried, "What is the first thought when you hear America?" the respondents overwhelmingly said "Unfair foreign policy."*[44]

*Curiously, the [Pew Global Attitudes Project*ll*] survey suggested little correlation between support for Bin Laden and hostility to American ideas and cultural products. People who expressed a favorable opinion of Bin Laden were just as likely to appreciate American technology and products as people opposed to Bin Laden. Pro- and anti-Bin Laden respondents also differed little in their views on the workability of Western-style democracy in the Arab world....*[45]

The Pew Report continues: "In most Muslim populations, large majorities continue to believe that Western-style democracy can work in their countries.... Although many Muslims around the world would like to see more religion in politics, this view does not contradict widespread support for democratic ideals among these publics. In fact, in a number of countries, Muslims who support a greater role for Islam in politics place the highest regard on freedom of speech, freedom of the press and the importance of free and contested elections."[46]

In Jordan, over 90 percent of university students believe that there is no contradiction between Islamic teachings and democracy or human rights.[47]

We desperately want change, reform, democracy, prosperity and modernity, but few of us believe that this will come through the barrels of Western guns.[48]

---

ll Part of "Views of a Changing World," the survey was conducted from April 28 to May 15, 2003, among 38,000 interviewees across 44 countries.

Lately, with freedom-and-democracy demonstrations in the news, most Westerners have come to realize that the Arabs love the concept of freedom after all. *They always have. Democracy has an overwhelmingly positive image throughout the world.* This is constantly emphasized in the Arab world, in speech and in writing.

Some American pundits have stated their hope that if the Arabs can gain "freedom" from the Americans, they will leave behind the anti-American political grievances. They will recognize that America is not after their oil—America just wants their freedom.

Charles Krauthammer: *When millions of Iraqis risk their lives and then dance with joy at having been initiated into the rituals of democracy, a fact has been created. And the old clichés that America went to Iraq for oil or hegemony begin to look hollow.*[49]

Demonstrations for freedom in Egypt and Lebanon have taken place because the U.S. military deposed an oppressor.

Charles Krauthammer: *Those who claimed, with great certainty, that Arabs are an exception to the human tendency toward freedom. . .and that the notion the United States could help trigger a democratic revolution by militarily deposing their oppressors was a fantasy—have been proved wrong. The left...is forced to acknowledge that those brutish Americans led by their simpleton cowboy might have been right.... President Bush...declined an invitation to claim vindication for his policy of spreading democracy in the Middle East...partly out of modesty.*[50]

Fouad Ajami: *What we are witnessing in the Arab world is similar to the spring of the European peoples in 1848.*[51] *Now the Arabs, grasping for a new world, and the Americans who have helped usher in this unprecedented moment, together ride this storm wave of freedom.*[52]

But there are fears. It's not simple. Attaining a democracy is not easy everywhere; it can still entail serious risks. We hear some hyperbole and wishful thinking:

We are at the dawn of an Arab Spring—the first bloom of democracy in Iraq, Lebanon, Egypt, Palestine and throughout the greater Middle East.[53]

The idea that the Arab world is not ready for democracy is racist and we should reject it.[54]

But we also hear more sober assessments. An Arab former cabinet minister said,

When you are a Syrian, or an Egyptian or a Saudi and you see what happened to Iraqi society over the past two years, you wonder if democracy deserves such instability and such a sacrifice of people.[55]

The question is, "Do you want freedom and anarchy or do you want dictatorship and security?" If you have a family, it's a big choice to make.[56]

Americans are thinking about democracy, and many Americans are analyzing our own democracy, what it is, what it means. For any democracy to work, it requires *an informed citizenry* (a reasonable level of literacy), *a trust of the opposition* (they will give up power if voted out), and a *national identity* that transcends allegiance based on kin, tribe, religion, or ethnic origin. This is difficult in the Middle East because many national borders were drawn arbitrarily and incorrectly by England and France, after they seized control of the region after World War I, making nations out of people who would not have willingly have been united. Middle Eastern people found themselves defined for the first time by *geography*. Even now, we cannot consider the borders in the Middle East as fixed.

Nobody is saying that Arabs don't want democracy as an ideal—but rather that these conditions have not been met in their countries. The probability is that democracy will *not* be soon realized. Reforms such as pluralism, rule of law, and accountability will come at the expense of the entrenched elites in every country. Arab citizens want more freedom, but we cannot know yet if it has arrived. The situation is too complicated to predict with assurance. Nevertheless, democracy is in the news, and we will see more and more definitions, explanations, and analyses of its meaning in Middle East.

> *Our [America's] wars of liberation will liberate illiberal aspirations, and rather than standing back with incredulity when this happens, we had better give plenty of thought beforehand to the fact that the tyrants we depose will be preferable to the chaos a liberated people will initially endure; that honor is still the currency of value in the Middle East, more so than goods and services; and that the affiliations of blood are immensely more meaningful there than the sovereignty of the individual citizen.*[57]

Rami Khouri, a Lebanese newspaper editor, stated,

> *Personal freedom of the individual is not a central demand or value in most of the developing world, in most of the world. It's not to say that people don't want it. It is not now a central value. In fact, people in most countries of the Middle East, in Asia and Africa give up personal freedom for the benefits they get from belonging to a group, the family, the tribe, the religious group, the clan, the ethnic group.... For most people in the Arab world, the big-sticker items are (1) national liberation from foreign occupation, (2) a sense of dignity, (3) being treated fairly by their own governments, (4) not being subjected to corruption and abuse of power, or being lied to when they turn on their TV news in the evening, (5) being treated decently. Freedom and democracy are six or seven on the list.*[58]

> *[The call for democracy] has already been happening for many years through the work of indigenous reformers and democrats and activists. It is not the American policy of promoting freedom that is starting to show dividends.... What has happened is that the Americans are finally supporting the democrats rather than supporting the tyrants, as they did for the last fifty years.*[59]

Islam

Islam in particular elicits vitriolic attacks and impassioned defenses. These are a very few of the comments; for a bigger picture, you can easily find more on the subject. This list is, of course, selective.

Anti-Islam Comments

Samuel Huntington: *"Some Westerners have argued that the West does not have problems with Islam but only with violent Islamic extremists.... Fourteen hundred years of history demonstrate otherwise.... The underlying problem for the West is not Islamic fundamentalism. It is Islam."*[60]

Franklin Graham: *"I believe it's [Islam] a very evil and wicked religion."*[61] *"In most Islamic countries, it is a crime to build a Christian church.... Christians are not free to worship Jesus in most Muslim countries....*[#] *The Koran provides ample evidence that Islam encourages violence in order to win converts and to reach the ultimate goal of an Islamic world.... The brutal, dehumanizing treatment of women by the Taliban has been well documented...the abusive treatment of women in most Islamic countries is nearly as draconian."*[62]

Bill O'Reilly: *"Teaching our enemy's religion is like teaching Mein Kampf...."*[63]

The world of Islam must now decide whether to wallow in a comforting, medieval form of religion that warms the heart with hatred of others....[64]

[#] Christianity is openly practiced in all Muslim countries except for Saudi Arabia. There are thousands of churches in Muslim countries.

The Koran is the doctrinal guideline for the Muslim, therefore what it says explains their beliefs. What it says to me is that a peaceful Muslim hasn't read it! It is one of, if not the most violence-provoking religion on this earth."[65] **

Defense-of-Islam Comments

We consider the Sept 11… criminal act as foreign to our honored culture, our peaceful and tolerant faith and our hospitable way of life. Terrorism cannot be eradicated until the underlying causes are justly addressed.[67]

George W. Bush: *"Our war is not against Islam, or against faith practiced by the Muslim people."*[68] *"Islam is a faith that brings comfort to a billion people around the world. It's a faith that has made brothers and sisters of every race. It's a faith based upon love, not hate."*[69]

Islam has brought comfort and peace of mind to countless millions of men and women. It has given dignity and meaning to drab and impoverished lives. It has taught people of different races to live in brotherhood and people of different creeds to live side by side in reasonable tolerance.[70]

If Islam were really just the caricature that it is often reduced to, then how would it be so appealing as to become the world's fastest-growing religion?...because it also has admirable qualities that anyone who has lived in the Muslim world observes: a profound

---

**This kind of argument is essentially pointless. Islam is being judged in the context of our time, not the seventh century. The massacres of Joshua in 1230 B.C. must be understood in the context of their time. The people in ancient times lived in a different world, a world of lawlessness and violence. In truth, Muhammad fought fewer than 10 battles in his lifetime, resulting in barely 1,000 casualties on both sides.[66] As in the Bible, every accusation and (selected) quotation can be refuted with an opposite (selected) quotation somewhere, if one keeps looking.

egalitarianism and a lack of hierarchy that confer dignity and self-respect among believers; greater hospitality than in other societies; an institutionalized system of charity, zakat, to provide for the poor. Many West Africans, for example, see Christianity as corrupt and hierarchical and flock to Islam, which they view as democratic and inclusive.[71]

Since the genocide, Rwandans have converted to Islam in huge numbers. Muslims now make up 14 percent of the 8.2 million people here in Africa's most Catholic nation. "We have our own Jihad, and that is our war against ignorance.... It is our struggle to heal," said...the head mufti of Rwanda.[72] *Fundamentalists [from outside] tried to organize and were rejected. During the genocide, Muslims were among the few Rwandans who protected both neighbors and strangers; the churches were not safe.*[73]

We should remember that these are political reactions—disagreements with specific policies. All too often, they are mistaken for an Islamic reaction against Western values, sparking an anti-Islamic backlash.[74]

The subject of anti-Americanism clearly elicits wide-ranging and conflicting opinions, both in explaining its causes and in advocating its possible remedies. This issue is growing increasingly politicized. Because much of the mass media blends entertainment with news, in many instances there is little incentive to present thoughtful analyses of events backed by thorough fact checking.[††] The stakes are high; they couldn't be higher. Every American needs to be knowledgeable on this subject and develop his or her own convictions.

[††]See also Steele and Jamail, "This Is Our Guernica," *The Guardian*, 27 April 2005; William Fisher, "Secrecy, Propaganda Seen Sweeping U.S.," *Inter Press Service*, 3 May 2005; and Bob Herbert, "Lifting the Censor's Veil on the Shame of Iraq," *The New York Times*, 5 May 2005.

13

Arabs and
Muslims in the West

There has been a sharp rise in both Arab and Muslim immigration to the West, which has affected the host countries and also the societies back home. The trend toward increased emigration (except from Saudi Arabia and the Gulf states) continues. Muslims and Arabs, however, are made up of entirely different populations. Statistics for both of these groups are variable, and estimates for both the United States and Europe vary widely.

Arabs in the United States

There are more than three million people of Arab origin in the United States. Of these, more than half (possibly as many as 70 percent) are Christian, and the rest are Muslim.[1] Christians, especially Lebanese and Syrians, got a head start; they began emigrating in the late nineteenth and early twentieth centuries. Half of today's Arab-Americans were born in the U.S. The Arabs who arrived during or after the 1960s are mostly Muslims.

The following is the breakdown of Arabs' countries of origin by percentage:

Countries of Origin, Arab Americans[2]	
Lebanon	47%
Syria	15%
Egypt	9%
Palestine	6%
Iraq	3%
Jordan	2%
Other	8%

Forty-one percent of the Arab Americans have college degrees (compared with 24 percent in the U.S. population as a whole).[3,4]* Seventy-two percent work in professional, managerial, technical and administrative jobs, and 82 percent are citizens. Forty-six percent of Arab American women work (compared with 56 percent in the nation as a whole).[5]

Very few Americans are aware of the contributions Arab Americans have made to the U.S., probably because they are so few in number. The Arab-American Anti-Discrimination Committee's sole purpose is working against the stereotyping of Arabs in the U.S.[6]

In a poll in 2001, 69 percent of the Arab Americans supported an all-out war against countries that support and/or harbor terrorists.[7] After 9/11, they very quickly raised money to donate to the Red Cross and the victims of the attacks. Some notable donations were the following: The National Arab American Medical Association, $100,000; the Arab Bankers' Association, $100,000; Arab Americans in Dearborn, Michigan, $125,000; the Syrian-Lebanese Federation, $20,000; and groups in Texas and Philadelphia, $20,000 and $15,000 respectively.[8] The Arab American communities also sponsored blood drives, rallies, and vigils all over the nation.

Muslims in the United States and Canada

The Muslim population in the United States has increased by 50 percent in the last ten years, and Islam is now the second most commonly practiced religion in America.[9] More than half of the American Muslims live in California, New York, Michigan, Illinois, and New Jersey.[10] By 2001,

---

*Sixty-four percent of those with Egyptian ancestry have a college degree.

there were about 3,000 large and small Islamic centers, mosques, and prayer locations (compared, for example, to 11,000 places of worship for Jehovah's Witnesses).[11] Participation in mosques increased 400 percent between 1994 and 2000.[12]

Of the five million Muslims in the United States,[†] approximately 25 percent are Arabs (Arabs constitute 20 percent of the total Muslim population worldwide). Thirty-three percent of the Muslims in the U.S. are of South Asian origin (India, Pakistan, Bangladesh), 30 percent are black Americans, about 3 percent are of Western or Eastern European origin, and the others are mostly of African or Southeast Asian origin (Indonesia, Malaysia).[14] About 12,000 Muslims have served in the U.S. military.[15]

American immigrants of Middle Eastern Muslim ancestry are more affluent, better educated, and more likely to be married and have children than the average citizen. In the U.S., 77 percent of the Muslims are active in organizations that help the poor, sick, elderly, and homeless. Sixty-nine percent are active in school and youth organizations, and 46 percent belong to a professional organization.[16] Eighty-four percent favor tougher laws to prevent terrorism.[17]

A Zogby poll found that 79 percent of American Muslims were registered to vote and 96 percent favored participation in civic life.[18]

The vast majority of American Muslims were appalled by terrorist attacks; all of these people have a huge stake in the future welfare of America. Many Muslims believe that the mainstream majority has remained silent about extremism and terrorism for too long. The theme of the December 2001 conference of the Muslim Public Affairs Council (MPAC) was "The Rising Voice of Moderate Muslims."[19]

Terrorism has been defined and condemned by Muslim legal scholars, who explain the distinction between terrorism and self-defense. One constantly reads comments by Muslims after terrorist incidents, along the lines of "This is not Islam," and "the people who did this are not Muslims."

A conference titled "Bridging the Divide" was held in December 2004, sponsored by the U.S.-Islamic World Project. A new group was formed, the American Muslim Group on Policy, to focus on ways that the American Muslim community can provide assistance to the U.S. in the war on terrorism and to help build bridges of confidence, trust, and

---

[†]There are 750,000 Muslims in Canada.[13]

communication in the nation. Muslim immigrants also want to play an active role in helping to improve the U.S. image in the Muslim World.[20]

Muslims in Europe

Statistics for the number of Muslims in Europe are indefinite. Muslims come from numerous countries of origin, and Europe's secular governments tend to collect fewer religious statistics than the United States does; furthermore, many Muslims are in Europe illegally and are therefore not counted in any polls or official estimates. Islam is the second most commonly practiced religion in Europe. The Muslim community has doubled in the last ten years, and is now about 15 to 20 million.[21, 22] The approximate breakdown for Muslims in Western Europe is shown in the following chart, which I've pieced together from several different sources.

Number of Muslims in Western Europe 2004[23-30]	
Austria	300,000 –340,000
Belgium	450,000 –500,000
Denmark	160,000 –170,000
Finland	20,000
France	5,000,000 –6,000,000
Germany	3,500,000 –4,000,000
Greece	250,000 –300,000
Ireland	19,000
Italy	600,000 –1,000,000
Luxembourg	6,000
Netherlands	880,000 –950,000
Norway	75,000
Portugal	35,000
Spain	500,000 –1,000,000
Sweden	350,000 –400,000
Switzerland	310,000
United Kingdom	1,600,000
(Australia)	(300,000 –450,000)

Unlike the Muslims in the United States and Western Europe, Eastern European Muslims are mostly indigenous; their ancestors converted to Islam while the region was part of the Ottoman Empire. Shown below are the statistics for Muslims in Eastern Europe.

Number of Muslims in Eastern Europe 2005[31]	
Albania	35,000
Baltic Countries	35,000
Belarus	80,000
Bosnia	2,200,000
Bulgaria	2,600,000
Croatia	400,000
Hungary	80,000
Kosovo	2,000,000
Macedonia	500,000
Moldavia	25,000
Poland	20,000
Romania	120,000
Russia	21,000,000
Serbia	800,000
Slovenia	250,000
Ukraine	2,000,000

Number of Mosques and Islamic Centers in Western Europe 2002[32-34] ‡	
Belgium	300
Denmark	60
France	1500
Germany	141 mosques, 2,400 Islamic centers
Italy	180
Netherlands	450
United Kingdom	1,000 mosques and Islamic centers
(Australia	100)

‡These numbers can refer to large mosques, large Islamic centers, or small nondescript mosques.

Athens is the only European Union capital without an official mosque. The government promised to permit one, but the issue has remained unresolved for almost 10 years; the main opposition is from the Christian Orthodox Church.[35]

Muslims in Western Europe originate from both Arab and non-Arab countries. Muslims in France are primarily from North and West Africa; in Germany, mostly of Turkish origin (3 million out of 3.5 million); in the United Kingdom, South Asian. The mix is slightly different in every country. Europe also receives waves of Muslim refugees periodically; it is affected far more than the United States by destabilization in the Muslim world.

There are crucial differences between the Muslim population in Europe and that in the United States:

- U.S. Muslims are well educated and most are professional and fairly affluent. Muslims in Europe are often not well educated and constitute an underclass, working at menial jobs, and they are often marginalized.

- U.S. Muslims are viewed as potential citizens. In Europe, they are often seen as immigrants or "guest workers," even after two or more generations.

- U.S. Muslims are mostly married, with children. Muslims in Europe are more often unmarried and not as committed to their host country. Many Muslims in Europe initially planned to stay only temporarily, then later decided to remain.

- U.S. Muslims are more geographically spread out than in any single country in Europe.

- U.S. Muslims do not have a particularly high birthrate. In Europe, the Muslim birthrate is three times that of the host countries, which makes them an ever-larger percentage of the total population; their numbers will probably double by 2015.[36]

The result of these differences is that Europeans are more likely to view Muslims as a threat than is generally the case in the United States.[37] Many of the Muslims in Europe came in the 1950s and 1960s, when there was a severe shortage of workers; most were from Turkey, Algeria,

Morocco, Tunisia, and Pakistan. Most stayed and later settled in with their families.

In November 2004, European leaders met at a summit conference to discuss the level of legal migrants needed to compensate for continuing domestic labor shortages and Europe's aging population. An EU report said that the working population in the 25-nation bloc would fall from 303 million to 297 million by 2020, and to 280 million by 2030.[38]

There are two trends that are potentially empowering Muslims in Europe: high birth rates and the opportunities for full citizenship. One scholar has stated, "On the positive side, demographic growth and enfranchisement are already integrating European Muslims into the political mainstream and have the potential to produce a moderate type of Euro-Islam."[39]

The Image of Arabs and Muslims

Both Arabs and Muslims have often been portrayed in Western media and print as excessively wealthy, irrational, sensuous, and violent, and there is little counterbalancing information about ordinary people who live family- and work-oriented lives on a modest scale. The media concentrate on reporting the sensational, not the truly typical. This misleading image has persisted for decades in America and in Europe. No real distinction is made between Arabs and Muslims. *Every time a terrorist incident occurs, those most vulnerable to unfounded suspicion are the Arabs and Muslims living in the West.*

According to Dr. Yvonne Haddad, a specialist on Islam in the West, Muslims have an image problem:

> *For Muslims…discrimination has been aggravated as a consequence of growing hostility towards Islam in the West, sometimes called "Islamophobia." Recently, the religion factor has been especially significant. The stereotyping that has come from media responses to international events usually has repercussions on Muslims living in minority communities in the West. They become the focus of attention and of scapegoating.*[40]

In America

Twenty-five years ago one observer remarked, "The Arabs remain one of the few ethnic groups who can still be slandered with impunity in America."[41] Unfortunately, there has been little improvement. We can read an almost identical statement from 2000, "Arabs are the only really vicious racial stereotypes acceptable in Hollywood."[42] Over the past decade or so, Hollywood has consistently portrayed Arabs as terrorists; examples are *True Lies* and *Executive Decision*. Such stereotypical images are both numerous and well documented.

Ever since the attacks of 11 September 2001, especially in the first year, Muslims have faced increased discrimination, threats, violence, and vandalism. From September 11 to December 6, 2001, the U.S. Equal Employment Opportunity Commission received more than double the number of complaints of discrimination toward Muslims in the workplace compared with the previous year (166 vs. 64).[43] In 2000 the FBI reported 33 anti-Islamic hate crimes across the country; in the four months following September 11, authorities investigated more than 250 incidents.[44]

In late 2004, a poll sponsored by the Council on American-Islamic Relations (CAIR) found that one in four Americans holds negative stereotypes of Muslims.[45]

People in the Muslim community still deal with threats, vandalism, and especially employment discrimination, but they firmly believe that such prejudice is based on a lack of unbiased information about them. Some mosques have open-house receptions, and there are community outreach activities all over the country. The Islamic Society of North America (ISNA) has an informative website. The Islamic Networks Group (ING) maintains a nationwide speakers' bureau. Another lecturing service is Connecting Cultures, Inc.

In Europe and Australia

Despite efforts by governments and civic leaders, hostility toward Muslims is still problematic across much of the European Union; followers of Islam are subject to verbal and physical attacks as well as discrimination in employment and housing.[46] European governments have dealt with the Muslim minorities in various ways—considering them as temporary residents, trying to assimilate them, and giving them citizenship while encouraging them to maintain their cultural identity.

Now, after several terrorist incidents (9/11 in America, the March 11 train bombing in Spain, the murder of Theo Van Gogh in the Netherlands, and the London bombings in July 2005), there is growing concern about the increasing numbers of Muslims immigrating to Europe. With this concern comes negative images of both Arabs and Muslims, which are extensively documented, as in these reports:

> *There is growing intolerance towards Muslim communities in Europe... there is evidence of stereotyping and hostility against Muslim communities.*[47]

> *The International Helsinki Federation for Human Rights reported that there is negative distortion in the media regarding all eleven European countries described in their 2005 report.*[48]

> *An international conference that included representatives of UNESCO, the Arab League, and the Council of Europe met in December 2004 and concluded that European culture contained "an erroneous image, if not images," not just of Arabs and Muslims, but also of Arab culture, Muslim civilization, and above all, of Islam as a faith.*[49]

> *Proposals to build new mosques have met with opposition petition drives and street protests throughout the continent.*[50]

> *A German company, Gfk, and* The Wall Street Journal *polled of 21,000 people in 19 European countries in September and October 2004. The results were discouraging: 52 percent of the respondents in Western Europe saw Muslims in a bad light. The highest percentages were 75 percent in Sweden and 72 percent in the Netherlands. In Austria, Belgium, Denmark, Germany and Switzerland, about two thirds of the responses were negative. The least negative in Western Europe was the United Kingdom, at 39 percent. In sharp contrast, in Eastern Europe 70 percent of the respondents viewed Muslims in a positive light.*[51]

A Pew Research Center poll released in March 2004 reported these favorability ratings for Muslims in these countries:

Favorability Ratings (Percentages) of Muslims[52]			
	Very Favorable	Somewhat Favorable	Unfavorable
U.K.	18	49	18
France	16	48	29
Germany	5	36	46
Russia	15	38	38
U.S.	13	35	32

Unlike the United States, which is a nation of immigrants with no dominant ethnic group, European countries have populations of the same ethnicity, as well as deep historical, cultural, religious, and language traditions. Many Europeans, who are becoming increasingly secular, find the Muslim's emphasis on Islam in their lives difficult to comprehend. (In a Pew Forum poll, 32 percent of the Europeans said that their religion is very important to them, compared with 59 percent in the U.S. A Gallup poll found that Europeans for whom religion was important was an average of 15 percent of the population; in the U.S. it was 44 percent).[53]

Tariq Ramadan, a well-known scholar based in Switzerland, has identified six main topics that he thinks the young generation of European Muslims must attend to: Islam and laicism; European Islamic identity; religious practice in Europe; Islam and the law; citizenship and participation; and promotion of a European Islamic culture.[54] It is significant that he also asserts that the ninth-century division of the world into the House of Islam and the House of War is invalid, out of date, and does not take into account the realities of modern life.[55]

What follows are examples of mostly anti-Muslim remarks in eight Western European countries and Australia. Although many of the European governments are making great efforts to be accommodating to their Muslim populations, repeated terrorist events lead to more fear and calls for restrictions. It is also the case that some of the Muslims in Europe have made little or no effort to assimilate. Probably in another generation something like "European Islam" will evolve; by then most Muslims will have been born and raised in Europe.

United Kingdom. In Britain, negative views of Muslims are quite widespread, although not as much as in the rest of Europe. *BBC News* reported in December 2004 that researchers found a sharp rise in discrimination against Muslims in the United Kingdom, more than in earlier surveys.[56] The latest British statistical report "Focus on Religion" states that Muslims are the most underprivileged group in the country. They have the highest rates of unemployment and the worst health of any religious group.[57]

The Secretary-General of the Muslim Council of Britain stated, "We have been witnessing a relentless increase in hostility toward Islam and British Muslims, and it is clear that existing race relations bodies have been either unable or unwilling to combat this phenomenon effectively. Islamophobia is becoming institutionalized."[58]

A particularly unfortunate event occurred following the Oklahoma City bombing in 1995. Much of the world's press made immediate assumptions and blamed Islam. One of the worst blunders was committed by the British daily *Today*. Its front page on 20 April 1995 showed a picture of a fireman carrying a bloodstained baby under the banner headline, "In the Name of Islam."[59]

Germany. In Germany, some say with bitterness, the government and society have always considered resident foreigners as "guest workers," even after many years. Many Muslims have tended to withdraw into ghetto neighborhoods. The German government now requires that new immigrants take compulsory language and civics lessons. Chancellor Gerhard Schroeder stated, "A democracy cannot tolerate lawless zones or parallel societies. Immigrants must respect our laws and acknowledge our democratic ways of doing things."[60]

In 2004, more than 80 percent of the Germans in a survey associated the word *Islam* with "terrorism" and "oppression of women."[61]

Another poll in September 2004 found that Germans hold negative views about Islam, and a large majority believe there is a "clash of civilizations"; the number increased notably following the Chechen attack on a school on southern Russia. "Germans find Islam foreign and threatening," said the head of Germany's Allensbach polling agency."[62]

While two-thirds of those questioned in a survey commissioned by the Adaneuer Foundation stated that they think Muslims in Germany should be allowed to practice their religion without any restrictions, 46 percent said they did not believe that Islam and Christianity represented the same values.[63]

France. The French Council of the Muslim Faith was established in 2003 to act as a liaison between the Muslim community and the government. With 25 affiliates, it is headed by a moderate imam (cleric) from the Grand Mosque of Paris.

France is developing social problems because of the presence of so many Muslims, who now make up 10 percent of the population. Half of the unemployed workers in France are Muslims.[64] Many live in poverty-stricken areas that have high crime rates.

French society steadfastly holds to "laïcité," which is traditional, strictly enforced secularism. France's law that disallows girls' headscarves in schools, enacted in 1989 and reaffirmed in March 2004, has become a cause célèbre. Unexpectedly, this ban has also meant that some women were unable to marry, vote, or take exams because of [not being allowed to wear] the headscarf.[65]

The French government has decided to deport foreign Islamic preachers who advocate values not in keeping with those of Europe. They hope to encourage domestically trained Islamic clerics to lead congregations of European-born Muslims, believing that the latter will know how to reinterpret Islamic law in a modern environment.

The political attitude toward Islam in France is gradually moving away from hostility toward Islam for two main reasons: the major mosques have not been a threat to public order as feared, and home-grown Islamic extremism has not materialized to the extent expected.[66]

Denmark. The Islamic Information Center in Denmark has been formed to represent the Muslim community, study its needs and problems, and coordinate relations with the government.

A meeting was held in 2003 between the Lutheran World Federation and Muslim representatives regarding the situation of Danish Muslims. They focused on group experiences as a result of "strong political debate in Danish media on the Muslims' right to live and practice their faith in Denmark."[67]

The government announced changes to immigration laws in February 2004, restricting admission of Muslim clerics who often do not understand the situation of Europe's Muslims, who are a minority and face laws different from those in their home countries. A spokesman from the European Islamic Council stated that such clerics "tarnish the image of Islam."[68]

In January 2005, Denmark's Supreme Court ruled that a supermarket chain had the right to fire a young Muslim woman for wearing an Islamic headscarf to work.[69]

Netherlands. The government of the Netherlands has always made an effort to be tolerant, even subsidizing mosques and supporting Islamic schools. But the murder of Theo Van Gogh (who had made a film criticizing Islam's treatment of women) on November 2, 2004, had serious repercussions; after that, 47 percent of people in the Netherlands said that they felt less tolerant toward Muslims. Mosques were set on fire and bombs exploded in Islamic schools.[70]

A far-right party leader called for Muslim imams to be taught separation of church and state and further suggested that Netherlands-born imams be preferred for religious posts, on the assumption that they will be less doctrinaire than those from Islamic countries.[71]

By 2020, it is projected that Amsterdam and Rotterdam will have 50 percent non-Western populations, most of them Muslims. Some right-wing politicians in the parliament are calling for a five-year moratorium on all non-Western immigration. One far-right politician referred to mosques as "houses of terror and recruitment" for Jihad.[72]

Many Dutch do not agree and see this as racist. One elementary-school principal, in a school with 40 percent foreign students of twenty nationalities, was quoted as saying "I understand the emotional problem people have with immigration but... I think we are taking steps backward."[73]

Belgium. Belgian King Albert II issued a royal decree in 2003, recognizing the executive body of Belgium's Muslim Council, ending four years of controversy. The council will primarily focus on combating discrimination against Muslims in schools and workplaces. Asked whether or not the Belgian government might also pass a law banning the Hijab (head cover) in schools, a spokesman for Belgian Muslims said that it would be unlikely, given the fact that secularism in France is more extreme than in Belgium, despite close similarities between the cultures of the two countries.[74] Belgium's top court dealt a blow to one of Europe's most successful anti-immigrant parties by declaring it racist. A new party will be established, to campaign to keep non-European immigrants out of Belgium if they do not adopt the country's "rules and Western values."[75]

Spain. For the Spanish, March 11 is as meaningful as September 11 is to Americans. On March 11, 2004, terrorists bombed a train station in Madrid, killing 191 and wounding more than 1,000 people. Since the Madrid attack, the Spanish have maintained a more negative perspective toward Muslims in their country.[76]

One Muslim leader, the president of the Moroccan Workers' Association, said, "Look, there are two Spains, one before 11 March and another after 11 March."[77] On the first anniversary of the incident, a group of prominent Muslims clerics in the Islamic Commission of Spain issued a *fatwa* (an Islamic edict) against Bin Laden, calling him an apostate and urging Muslims to denounce him.

Spain's president-elect, Jose L. R. Zapatero, has promised to develop a renewed policy against terrorism and show greater commitment to integrating the country's immigrants.[78] The need for Muslims to be more willing to integrate and join the democratic and societal institutions in Spain was echoed in the *fatwa*.

Italy. As Italy's Muslim population has grown, so have Muslim voices expressing a desire to fit in with the host society. Some Muslims stick rigidly to the ways of the old country, while others are creating a hybrid culture of tolerance and experimentation. Stefano Allievi, an Islamic scholar at Padova University, said that contact with Italian society has prompted young Muslims to investigate and question their traditional habits. An individual approach to religion is emerging, he suggested. "In the Middle East, Islamic practices are dictated by tradition," he said. "Here, the context is more individual."[79]

A prominent cleric, Cardinal Biffi, has proposed a law that would allow only Christians to immigrate to Italy. The president of the Senate plans to support it.[80]

The Archbishop of Bologna has called for the closure of the country's mosques and an end to immigration by Muslims, who are, he believes, "outside our humanity."[81]

The Rage and the Arrogance [is] an extended polemical tract in which Italian journalist Oriana Fallaci indicts all the world's Muslims as accomplices to terrorism and followers of a savage, corrupt religion. "They breed like rats," Fallaci says. A disapproving French reviewer notes, "This book has sold 1 million copies in Berlusconi's Italy without arousing any indignation."[82]

Australia. Australia's Muslim population has increased 40 percent since 1996. The government recently announced a partnership program with the Australian Federation of Islamic Councils (AFIC).[83]

It was reported [by a Muslim reporter after a conference in July 2003] that the Australian government and the media continued to maintain an aura of "fear and disdain" for Muslims, thus setting the stage for further reactions by Muslims toward a siege mentality, that will only serve to worsen conditions for Muslims in Australia.[84]

The report of the Human Rights and Equal Opportunity Commission was released in mid-2004. Developed through 69 consultations around Australia over a period of 14 months, the report describes the extent of prejudice against Arab and Muslim Australians: "All round there was a general increase in the level of anti-Muslim, anti-Arab, anti-different type feeling," the acting commissioner said. "This was offset by many positive stories of simple kindness, neighbors assuring support and issuing invitations.... At the grassroots level, there are many organizations making a positive difference."[85]

In December 2004, two Christian pastors were found guilty of "religious vilification of Muslims."[86]

Conclusion

The scholar Tariq Ramadan[§] has proposed a "Third Way," which appeals to many young Muslims. The issue is "how to be at the same time fully Muslim and fully Western." He has stated, "Loyalty to one's faith and conscience requires firm and honest loyalty to one's country: *Sharia* [Islamic law] requires honest citizenship."[87] In his book *Western Muslims and the Future of Islam*, Ramadan stated:

> *We are currently living through a veritable silent revolution in Muslim communities in the West: more and more young people and intellectuals are actively looking for a way to live in harmony with their faith while participating in the societies that are their societies, whether they like it or not. French, English, German, Canadian, and American Muslims, women as well as men, are constructing a "Muslim personality" that will soon surprise many*

§Tariq Ramadan was denied entry into the United States in July 2004.

of their fellow citizens. Far from media attention, going through the risks of a process of maturation that is necessarily slow, they are drawing the shape of European and American Islam: faithful to the principles of Islam, dressed in European and American cultures, and definitively rooted in Western societies. This grassroots movement will soon exert considerable influence over worldwide Islam.[88]

Some neoconservative Americans have called for modernizing Islam, to result in "an American Islam committed to American values." This expresses a hope to mold Islam to suit American interests—everything from promoting the modernization of Islam by directing a message to "substantial numbers of alienated Muslims"[89] to grooming a "Moslem Billy Graham." This was tried in the past, several times, from the outside (mostly through the CIA); it failed decisively. "Were one to formulate a general rule of thumb about how U.S. meddling affects Islam, it would have to be: badly."[90]

I think that if European Islam evolves, and Muslims make these reforms *from within*, it might be considered as a model for America. In New York, a group of Muslims are working to promote gender equality, closer to the Western ideal. They contend that inequality is not a tenet of Islam but a mark of misguided tradition. A woman has led prayers for the group, a practiced approved by an influential scholar of Islamic law.[91]

The number of Arabs and Muslims in the West continues to grow. There is no doubt that Muslims have to work at becoming more integrated into the societies of countries where they live. They will have to integrate smoothly or else remain on the margins indefinitely.

In the United States, there is a heightened interest that is still growing, dating from 9/11. Enrollments in Arabic language, Islamic studies, and Middle Eastern studies have more than tripled. All Westerners have come to realize that the Middle East is an issue that will be important for their own lives and for Western societies in the future.

The Arab Countries:
Similarities and Differences

Generalizing about Arabs is a little like generalizing about Europeans—they have many traits in common, but regional differences are striking. Arabs are more alike than Europeans, however, because they share the same language and, most importantly, they believe strongly that they are a cultural unit, one Arab nation. Arab nationalism has a broad appeal, despite shifting political alliances.

The national, social, and cultural characteristics briefly described below reveal some notable differences among various Arab national groups. The most important single difference that affects foreigners is the distinction between the conservatism of Saudi Arabia (and to some extent, the rest of the Arabian Peninsula) and the more liberal, or tolerant, ways of life elsewhere.

There are dramatic differences among the Arab countries: some are very rich, others are desperately poor. We hear that the Arabs are awash with oil, but in reality, most Arab countries have far less income than developed economies. Relative prosperity can be seen from per capita income in 2003:

Per Capita Income[1-5]

	2003 ($US)
Algeria	1,890
Bahrain	11,260
Egypt	1,390
Iraq	800 ($422 in 2005, $3600 in 1980)
Jordan	1,850
Kuwait	16,340
Lebanon	4,040
Libya	6,400
Morocco	1,320
Oman	7,830
Qatar	30,000+
Saudi Arabia	8,530
Sudan	460
Syria	1,160
Tunisia	2,240
U.A. Emirates	19,755
Yemen	520

The Arab countries discussed below are listed from west to east, north to south.

The Maghrib

The Maghrib is a term used for the entire region of North Africa (the adjective form is *Maghribi*); *Maghrib* comes from Arabic and means "The Arab West." Four countries are of concern to us here: Morocco, Algeria, Tunisia, and Libya.

This region has been inhabited by Berbers for millennia (since at least 3000 B.C.), and today the Berber languages are the mother tongue of 12 million people in the Maghrib, many of whom are bilingual in Arabic. Berber nationalism is growing and will be a significant social and political factor in the future. The number of speakers per country is as follows:

Number of Speakers of Berber[6,7]

Morocco	7.5 million
Algeria	4 million
Tunisia	26,000
Libya	162,000

There are also large numbers of Berber speakers in Mali and Niger.

Regional Maghribi Arabic dialects are distinctive and almost unintelligible to Arabs in the east; they constitute a separate subdialect group called "Western Arabic". The Maghrib has its own special foods, religious practices, style of art and architecture, music, and style of traditional clothing.

Morocco

Morocco, a monarchy, has been strongly influenced by its proximity to Europe and its colonization by France until independence in 1956. Educated Moroccans are bilingual in Arabic and French, and although a campaign of Moroccanization has been underway, French is still needed for most professional and social advancement. Spanish is widely spoken in northern Morocco, and a growing number of Moroccans, particularly younger people with commercial interests, now speak English.

Although a few Moroccans are of Arabian origin, most are descended from native Berber stock. About one fourth of the population are Berber, who are distinct from the Arab-Berber majority in that they speak Berber as their native language and identify themselves as Berbers first. Due to increasing pressure from Berbers, the language is now heard on Moroccan radio, an alphabet has been devised, and newspapers and magazines are appearing. In 2001 the king created the Royal Institute of Berber Culture. Berber was taught in a number of primary schools for the first time in August, 2004,[1] and the teaching and learning of Berber will be mandatory for all Moroccans in all schools, at all levels, within ten years.[2] The Berbers mainly live in the interior highlands of the Atlas Mountains. There are also many Moroccans of sub-Saharan African descent, especially in the southern part of the country.

The royal family traces its descent from the Prophet Muhammad. King Hassan II ruled for 38 years before his death in July 1999; his son King Muhammad VI now rules, and he is making efforts toward political liberalization. This trend is jeopardized, however, because although

Morocco has maintained a tradition of political moderation, large numbers of the younger generations, especially, are now turning toward Islamic radicalism and are playing a bigger role in Islamist militant groups. Several sites in Casablanca were bombed in May 2003, invariably in places that catered to Westerners.[3]

By October 2004, the Moroccan government had arrested 2,100 Islamists and is cooperating closely in tracking Islamic militants; however, Islamist political parties and organizations are becoming increasingly influential.[4]

Morocco sees itself as moderate and pro-Western. It was the first African country to have a free-trade agreement with the U.S., and it was judged eligible for aid from the Millennium Challenge Account. The king has launched dramatic reforms in politics and human rights.[5]

There are three distinct social classes: the royal family and a small educated elite, a growing middle class composed of merchants and professionals, and a lower class that includes more than half of the people. The population was estimated at 32 million in 2005, with a growth rate that is among the highest in the world. Thirty-four percent of Moroccans are under the age of fifteen.

Tribalism is important in Morocco, particularly in the rural areas. Traditional farming remains the occupation of about half of the population. Since the trend toward urbanization, which began early in the twentieth century, cities have grown rapidly (the largest is Casablanca with a population estimated between 3.5 and 5 million), resulting in serious housing shortages and expanding slums with many poor and underemployed urban residents. By 2002, 56 percent of the population lived in urban areas (compared with 38 percent in 1975), and about 40,000 Moroccans migrate abroad each year because of an unemployment rate estimated at 20 to 30 percent.[6] Because of this, about 1.7 million Moroccan men work outside the country, mainly in France and Spain.

Education has increased greatly since Morocco's independence—literacy rose from 15 percent in 1978 to 51 percent in 2002. Both French and Arabic are taught in schools, although only Arabic is the official language. Seventy-nine percent of age-eligible children attend primary school, and 38 percent are in secondary school.

Educated women in Morocco have been entering the professions for a generation, especially in the urban areas. Half of the students in universities are women; 20 percent of the judges in Morocco are women.[7] Although older and more conservative Moroccan women continue to veil in public, most women do not, nor do they always wear the traditional long cloak. Child custody laws were first improved for women in 1994.

In January, 2004, the government revised its family law code to give wives joint responsibility in family matters, and to allow them to initiate divorce, obtain custody of children, and claim an equal share of goods acquired during marriage. The laws also raised the minimum age of marriage for girls from 15 to 18 and restricted polygamy.[8] Although virtually all political parties endorsed the revised law stating "equality of rights and duties" between men and women, controversy still plagues the revisions of women's legal rights.[9] In March of 2000, for example, 400,000 people took to the streets in response to a proposal on the subject—half were for it, half were against it.[10]

Although about 99 percent of the Moroccans are Muslims, other religions have always been practiced freely. Half of the Jews in the Arab world reside in Morocco, estimated at 4,000 to 7,000 (from a high of 350,000 in the 1950s).[11] Morocco's 70,000 Christians are of European origin. The practice of Islam is often mixed with local folk practices, such as the veneration of saints' tombs and their artifacts. Religious brotherhoods, mainly Sufis, are also common.

The Moroccan economy is largely dependent on agriculture, tourism, and phosphate mining (Morocco is the world's largest exporter of phosphates). About 40 percent of the workforce is employed in agriculture and fishing. The textile industry has become increasingly important, the number of textile workers tripling since the 1980s.[12] The textile sector accounts for about 42 percent of Morocco's industrial employment (above 60 percent in some areas).[13]

Moroccans are friendly and hospitable and usually very interested in becoming acquainted with foreigners. The elite are at ease with Westerners because of their exposure to French and European cultures. There are at least three study-abroad programs for young Americans to learn Arabic in Morocco.

Algeria

Algeria is a revolutionary socialist state where Arabization is strongly emphasized, partly as a reaction to the Algerians' experience with French colonization and their long, traumatic war. Independence was achieved in 1962, at a terrible cost – one million Algerians and 28,000 French dead.[1] Despite the fact that Arabic is the official language of the country, French is still widely used, particularly for professional purposes. Both languages are taught in the schools, but only younger Algerians are truly comfortable with Standard (written) Arabic.

Arab nationalism is strong, promoted through government political campaigns, the news media, and the school curriculum. Algeria is in the midst of a desperate political and humanitarian crisis. Open warfare has existed for years between the government and a large number of Islamist activists, the largest of which is the Islamic Salvation Front (FIS), which was formally recognized by the government in 1989. In 1990 FIS candidates gained control in municipal and gubernatorial elections (54 percent of the popular vote), and in January 1992, fearing their total victory, the military government called off national elections and banned the organization (it is still banned). Subsequently, throughout the 1990s, Algeria experienced a rising cycle of violent attacks, many of them random, many in villages; at times 300 to 400 people were being killed per week. Ultimately the figure reached 150,000.[2] These killings were and are met with severe government retaliation. Because 120 foreigners were killed in the 1990s, almost all of them have left the country. The population is still polarized between secular and Islamic groups, radicals and moderates.

Almost all Algerians are of Berber ethnic origin, but about 69 percent identify themselves as Arabs and 30 percent as Berbers. Arabic is the native language of 80 percent of the people; the others speak Berber or are bilingual. Algeria's social classes consist of a small professional and technocratic elite, a growing middle class, and a large number of poor people. The long war for independence resulted in the massive displacement of people from their ancestral lands and social groups, the psychological consequences of which will be felt for a very long time.

Algeria is immense, about four times the state of Texas, but 85 percent of it is in the Sahara Desert region, and only 3 percent is suitable for agriculture, along the temperate northern coast. Algeria's population is 32 million, and its growth rate is one of the highest in the world; 70 percent are under age 30.[3] Schools operate in shifts, health-care facilities and providers cannot keep up, and the housing situation is so desperate that some poorer families even sleep in shifts. The population is expected to reach 52 million by 2025, a fivefold increase since 1950.[4]

In 2004, some two million Algerians were working outside the country, 700,000 of them in France.[5] Although unemployment in the cities is 30 percent, people continue to move from the sparsely populated south to the crowded northern cities seeking work.

Algeria is the world's largest producer of liquefied natural gas and has additional income from oil, mining, and agriculture, but because of the rapid population growth, it remains poor. Despite the government's efforts to diversify (95 percent of foreign earnings are from oil and gas) and industrialize the economy, Algeria, which produced 73 percent of its own food in 1969, was importing 75 percent of its food in 2004.[6]

When Algeria gained its independence in 1962, there were few well-trained Algerians, and it has taken two generations to recover from the loss of the French managerial class. Now, however, a fast-growing number of educated Algerians are entering professional and technical fields. Although almost half of Algeria's university graduates are women, they make up only 12 percent of the workforce, possibly because the high unemployment rate works to their disadvantage.

Family and social traditions are conservative, and more women veil in Algeria than in any other North African country. Algerian women had participated actively during the struggle for independence, so many felt betrayed when, in 1984, the government instituted the Family Code, which restricted women's rights. This is soon to be amended (some are calling for a referendum). The amendments will restrict men's grounds for divorce, grant financial support to divorced wives, and make polygamy difficult. President Bouteflika made this a priority in the last election in April, 2004.[7]

Algerians are accommodating but reserved. Although militant Islam has turned some people against the West, many younger people are ready to befriend Westerners when they visit the country.

Tunisia

Tunisia is a small but diverse country that gained its independence from France in 1956. Since then it has been governed by one secular political party. President Habib Bourguiba, who led the country to independence, was quietly removed in 1987; his successor is President Zayn Al-Abdin Ben Ali. Because Tunisians have always had considerable contact with foreigners, their society is cosmopolitan, at least in the cities, and many Tunisians are well traveled. They are friendly and hospitable to foreign visitors.

The Tunisians are descended from Berber and Arabian stock, but all speak Arabic, the official language. Educated people are bilingual in Arabic and French, and many semi-educated people speak some French. French is taught in the schools alongside Arabic, but there is currently a campaign for the Arabization of education.

Because the Tunisian government encourages private enterprise, about 60 percent of the people are upper and middle class. Tunisia is the most advanced country in the Arab world in terms of equal rights, family planning, education, and medical care, and it is considered a model of success in economic reform. At the same time, however, the Tunisian government has been under severe criticism as a violator of human rights, as it deals harshly with critics and does not tolerate political dissent.[1] It has even been called one of the world's most efficient police states.[2] The government is worried about the threat from growing Islamist activism and is a prominent participant with other nations in the campaign against extremism.

The Tunisian economy depends mainly on a large tourism industry, which brings in 35 percent of its annual income. Of a relatively small population of ten million, about a third work in agriculture, which produces 12 percent of the country's earnings. The government is encouraging diversification and light industry, the latter of which is quickly becoming an important source of employment; in 2001 light industry generated about 30 percent of the national income. Over three-fourths of Tunisia's exports go to Europe, and about the same percentage of its imports are from Europe.[3] Although the government has established agricultural cooperatives and production has been rising, people are still moving to the cities, where they join the urban poor, living in crowded conditions. About 610,000 Tunisians work outside the country, mainly in France and Libya.

The Tunisian government allocates more than 20 percent of its operating budget to primary and secondary education, a figure that is among the highest in the world. In 2001, 92-99 percent of eligible children were in primary schools.⁴ Unfortunately, a good education doesn't guarantee a job after graduation. A large number of the educated young people are unemployed; the unemployment rate was 16 percent in 2004. At the same time, there is a shortage of skilled workers.

Tunisia has been at the forefront of the Arab nations in its effort to liberalize its society. Tunisian women are certainly among the most liberated in the Arab world; they are well educated and active in the workplace in such fields as education, social services, health care, office administration, and the judicial system. Laws benefiting women were enacted in the 1950s. Women have the same divorce rights as men. Polygamy is outlawed, and the minimum age for a woman's marriage is 17. Women's rights were further strengthened in 1992 and 1993, mostly relating to child custody and financial support. The laws were further clarified in 1995, 1996 and 1998.⁵

While most women wear Western clothing, older or traditional women wear loose outer cloaks, which they pull over to partially cover their faces when they are in public. The government has banned the wearing of headscarves in government offices and in schools.⁶

Ninety-eight percent of Tunisians are Muslim. Only about 1800 native Jews remain, half in the capital city of Tunis and half on the southern island of Jerba. The government permits freedom of worship and pays the salary of the Grand Rabbi, in addition to partially subsidizing restoration and maintenance costs of synagogues.⁷

Islam in Tunisia is mixed with a number of folk practices, such as veneration of saints' tombs. Its central city of Kairouan is a pilgrimage site, because of its antiquity and importance to Islam.

Libya

Libya is the only North African nation that was colonized by Italy. Full rule was restored to the Libyan monarchy in 1949. Since the monarchy was overthrown in 1969, Libya has been governed by a leftist military regime under Colonel Muammar Qaddhafi, who has introduced radical socialist and economic development programs, instituted a strong campaign to educate and politicize the people, and set up programs to spur rapid social change. Because of his support for radical revolutionary movements, Libya became something of a pariah state.

Until recently, most Libyans outside the cities were farmers or tribal seminomads, who were largely uneducated and lived simply. In 1951 Libya was considered one of the poorest countries in the world. When oil was discovered in 1959, its effect on the economy was immediate. By 1969 the country's revenues were twenty times greater than they had been in 1962.[1] Lately, the economy has been strained due to U.S. sanctions, which went into effect in 1986 (most were lifted in April 2003), and U.N. sanctions from 1992 to September of 2003. Sanctions by the European Union were lifted in October 2004. Although the economy is now improving, unemployment is about 30 percent.

Libya is a welfare state, and the people (particularly the middle and lower classes) have experienced a dramatic rise in their standard of living, although there are still shortages of some basic goods. There are steady improvements in health and nutrition programs, transportation, and communications. Before oil was marketed, 25 percent of the population was urbanized; the figure increased to 88 percent in 2001, and, like elsewhere, migration continues from the rural areas to the cities.

Libyans are a homogeneous ethnic group of mixed Berber and Arabian descent, and all speak Arabic. Tribalism is an important source of identity, particularly among rural people. Although there are theoretically no social classes because of the government's policy of strict egalitarianism and rule "by the people," in reality rule is authoritarian, and only a few people are part of the elite upper class.

Libya's economic viability is almost entirely dependent on oil; its soil is poor, its natural resources and water sparse. Less than 10 percent of the land is suitable for agriculture (90 percent is desert), and 75 percent of the country's food is imported. Because Libya badly needs trained and skilled workers (its population is only about 6 million), large numbers of foreigners have lived and worked there, approximately 1 to 1.5 million in 1995, before Qaddhafi expelled large numbers of them, mainly Egyptians, Sudanese, and Palestinians. The official estimate of foreign workers in 2004 was one million, although the unofficial number may reach as high as two million.[2]

Universal education has been available since the 1970s, and now 82 percent of the people are literate. Libya has a history of sending university students abroad, especially to the United States and Europe. In 1978, more than 3,000 students were studying in the U. S. alone. By 2002 that figure had dropped to just 33 as a result of sanctions and travel restrictions imposed in 1986.[3] Libyan women now constitute 21 percent of the workforce, and they are encouraged to work in education, nursing, clerical services, and factory jobs.

Late in 2003, the Libyan government pledged to end its support of international terrorism and end its nuclear weapons effort. The country plans to liberalize its socialist-oriented economy and to apply for World Trade Organization membership. The United States is slowly re-establishing formal contacts with Libya, and recently, meetings have been held to discuss increasing the number of Libyan graduate students in the U.S. to possibly 500 and facilitating student exchanges.[4] The British Council signed a cultural agreement with Libya at the end of 2003. There are currently more than 3,000 Libyan students enrolled at British institutions of higher education, 90 percent of whom are on Libyan government scholarships.[5]

Libyans are conservative and 99 percent Muslim, and Islamic law is generally followed, although with some modifications. The government promotes Islam mixed with a strong revolutionary message in order to guide social change and control dissent. Arab nationalism and pan-Arab unity are extolled. Libyans are not encouraged to interact with foreigners and are hesitant to display customary Arab hospitality to them. As a result, the people have had relatively little contact with foreigners.

Northeastern Africa

Egypt

Egypt's long history and ancient traditions have resulted in a homogeneous and distinctive society with a unique culture. Egyptians all speak Arabic, except for some Nubians in the far south, and English is the most common second language. French is also spoken by many.

Egypt has by far the largest population of any Arab nation, approximately 76 million in 2005. As in many Arab countries, the proportion of young people is high—32 percent under age 15 in 2005 (down from 40 percent in 1990). The population doubled between 1947 and the early 1980s; its rate of increase was as high as 4.1 percent per year in the late 1980s. But as a result of vigorous government campaigning, the rate decreased to 1.7 percent in 2001. Because only 3 to 4 percent of Egypt's land is habitable (the rest is desert), its population density is among the highest in the world. Ninety-five percent of the people live on 5 percent of the land.

About 10 percent of the Egyptians are in the elite upper class, which dominates the country politically and economically. The middle class is expanding; nevertheless, about 55 percent of the people are still peasant farmers or villagers, and there are many urban poor.

Because of its long tradition of education for the upper and middle classes, Egypt has an abundance of professionally trained citizens. At any given time there are about 2.5 million Egyptians working abroad as teachers, doctors, accountants, and laborers.[1] Until the mid-1980s the largest percentage of expatriate Egyptians were working in the Arabian Peninsula and Libya. Since then many have been forced to return because of the decline in the oil industry in the host nations. Unemployment is 15 to 20 percent overall, and in the age group of 15 to 25, it runs to 70 percent, a serious and growing problem.

Intensive agriculture has always been central to the Egyptian economy. The government promotes industry and manufacturing; the main sources of income are oil, cotton, and other agricultural products. Tourism is the most important of all. Egypt's relative poverty makes it heavily dependent on aid from the United States. Once an exporter of food (since ancient times and up to about 1960), Egypt now produces only 22 percent of the food needed for local consumption. Agriculture yields only 32 percent of the national income.

Poverty is increasing. The cost of living rose by 20 percent in 2004, and in May 2004, the government reintroduced vouchers to subsidize 25 staple foods, reversing its intention to abolish the subsidies due to vehement opposition. The government estimates that 88 percent of the population will be entitled to the vouchers.[2].

The Egyptian government has been socialist since 1952, when the current regime seized power from the monarchy. Although the government is stable, it faces a serious challenge from several militant Islamist movements, the most prominent of which are the Muslim Brotherhood, the Islamic Group, and Islamic Jihad. These groups are illegal, as are all political organizations based on religion or ethnicity, and members are subject to arrest.[3] Islamist organizations have gained support because they provide social services not available from the government; this has been especially noticeable in times of disasters. There have been several terrorist attacks, mainly against the government but also against tourists. The government has reacted harshly and continues to make widespread arrests, bring Islamists to trial, and hold thousands in custody. The estimate is that in 1999, Egypt had 16,700 political prisoners, most of them Islamists, of whom 7,891 were being held without trial. The government released 1,000 of them as a conciliatory gesture, shortly after the Islamic Group renounced violence and called for a peaceful rapprochement with the entire society.[4] Discussion of this issue is a constant feature in the Egyptian press. The Grand Mufti of Egypt has strongly denounced Islamist philosophy; this is a courageous stance to take.[5] Almost all of the 53,000 mosques are now regulated by the state.[6]

The Egyptian government is authoritarian and recently cracked down on opposition groups that were making efforts to stop President Mubarak from extending his rule to a fifth six-year term in office (there is also suspicion that he may be planning to hand over power to his son).[7] Criticism of the president has been widespread. Under pressure, Mubarak announced in February 2005 that he would direct the parliament to change the constitution and permit multiparty popular elections.[8] The plans for change are convoluted and the election will not be entirely free.

Health has improved dramatically due to government programs instituted in the 1960s; unfortunately, education has not fared as well. Despite the fact that free education has been available to all children since the 1960s, the rate of literacy is still only about 56 percent.

Egyptian women have enjoyed considerable personal freedom in pursuing their interests and have been integrated into the workforce at all levels for many years. Half the university students are women. Egypt was in fact the first Arab country to admit women to its national university, in 1928, and education is entirely coed. In 1957 two Egyptian women were the first to serve in an Arab parliament, and in 2004 Egypt had two women ministers, one judge (appointed in 2003 with much publicity), and 14 female ambassadors. There are more than 300 women's organizations in Cairo. In a recent study, it was found that 28 percent of university professors are women, compared to 24 percent in the United States.[9]

The government has amended women's rights laws constantly, as shown, for example, in divorce laws. In 1979 the divorce law was amended but was declared unconstitutional in 1985. In 2000, the divorce law was again amended, granting women much broader grounds for divorce. However, in 2004 a study showed little public awareness of changes.[10] And in 2005, the right to divorce was still gender-biased.[11] Although virtually no women covered their hair in the 1960s, a growing number (perhaps 80 percent) have now made the decision to do so. Many also wear very conservative dress.

About 94 percent of the Egyptians are Muslims, and, officially, about 6 percent are Christians, mostly Copts (the Coptic church estimates 15 percent). Islam is Egypt's official religion, but religious tolerance has long been practiced. There have been serious clashes with Islamic extremists, however, especially in the early 1990s, which is an issue of growing concern to the Christians and the government. Egyptian society, which was among the most liberal in the Arab world in the 1960s and 1970s, has become more conservative due to social trends and pressure from the Islamists.

Egypt is vibrant with cultural energy—it is the leader of the Arab nations in such fields as filmmaking and journalism. It has long been a dominant political and cultural influence in the Arab world, partly because of its large population, which makes up about 40 percent of all the Arabs. At any given time there are about 400 young Americans studying in Egypt and improving their Arabic, most of them at the American University in Cairo. Most of them want to return to Egypt as soon as they can, and many want to live there. Cairo, home to 14 million people, is a big, hot, crowded, polluted, poor city—still, *to know it is to love it.*

The Egyptian people are known to be especially friendly and good-humored, and they are very outgoing toward foreigners.

Sudan

Sudan is the largest country in Africa, with an area of one million square miles. It is tribal and diverse, with considerable sub-Saharan African influence on its social structure and ethnic composition. Sudan has one of the most ethnically diverse populations in the world, with over 400 languages, 19 major ethnic groups, and 597 subgroups, most of them in the non-Arab south.[1] It is one of the 25 poorest countries in the world, with 90 percent living below the poverty line.[2]

The country is divided into two distinct regions: the Arab north and the non-Arab south. Northern Sudanese are Arabs (in language, only partially in ethnicity). Tribalism is dominant in the north as well as in the south, where many men are marked with identifying facial scars, as is common in sub-Saharan Africa. Arabic is the only official language, but it is spoken by only about 60 percent of the population, despite an Arabization program that has been in place for decades. About 70 percent of the Sudanese are Sunni Muslim, another 5 percent are Christian, mainly in the south, and the rest adhere to local or indigenous religions. Some tribes in the south, who are related culturally and historically to the peoples of east Africa, still live autonomously, barely influenced by the government, and some areas still do not have a cash economy. The Sudanese government decreed Islamic law in 1983, and since 1989 Sudan has had the only avowed Islamist (fundamentalist) government in place in the Arab world (Saudi Arabia is conservative but not Islamist). The government is attempting to modernize within the Islamic system.

There has been an on-going civil war between the Arab Islamic north and the African south virtually since Sudan's independence from the United Kingdom in 1956. The conflict, the first phase of which was 1955–1972, escalated again in 1983, and despite a formal pact signed in January 2005, rebel groups in the south continue their resistance. The war has been devastating—this is one of the world's worst sustained conflicts since World War II. Large-scale famine and unchecked disease continue to ravage the south; about two million are dead and four to five million have been displaced from their homes, mostly civilians in the south (the largest number of displaced persons in the world).[3,4] The government (or groups it tolerates) has been repeatedly accused of genocide,* human rights abuses, and the toleration of slavery; the world views the situation as a major humanitarian crisis. Thousands of people, including orphaned or abandoned children, are living in refugee camps. Many international relief organizations are present, both in the south and among the people in camps around Khartoum.

Since 1989, after a military coup led by President Omar Al-Bashir, the Sudanese government has been authoritarian. In 1993 Sudan was placed on the U.S. list of countries that sponsor international terrorism. The U.S. imposed comprehensive economic sanctions in 1997, and

---

*The International Criminal Court called it abuse, not genocide.[5]

these were extended in November 2001.[6] New sanctions by the U.N. have been threatened since mid-2004.

The American embassy was closed in 1996, and in 1998 the United States carried out a cruise missile attack, which (notoriously) destroyed a pharmaceutical plant. Osama Bin Laden came to Sudan after he was expelled from Saudi Arabia, and it was there that he set up the Al Qaeda organization.

Unlike most urbanized Arab populations, in Sudan 80 percent live in rural areas and work in agriculture, although in this huge country, only about 7 percent of its land is arable. The southern region, if developed, has a huge economic potential in its oil and minerals, rare timbers, and abundant water.[7]

Population density is low in Sudan, with a population of about 36 million in the entire country, 75 percent of whom live in the north. The population of Khartoum is six to seven million. Forty-four percent of Sudan's population is 14 years old or younger.

The government has promoted irrigation and land reclamation projects to develop the immense agricultural potential of much of the country (Sudan could feed almost all of Africa if it were developed). About 65 percent of the people are villagers and small farmers or herders. Tourism could be a potential draw, although by now, much of the big game that flourished a generation ago is gone.

Because education has been available for the upper and middle classes for decades, this group is highly literate; the rate is 60 percent in the country as a whole. Although there is a large pool of well-educated Sudanese professionals, because of low salaries at home, many work abroad, mainly in the Arabian Peninsula. This has caused a shortage of trained manpower in the country; at the same time, the overall unemployment rate was 19 percent in 2002.

Although education for women is increasing, only about 28 percent of Sudanese women work outside the home, mainly as teachers and social workers. Sudan is extremely conservative in its view of women's rights (the birth rate is an average of 5 children per woman). Women do not cover their faces, but they all wear a long cloak and voluminous scarves in public.

Sudanese are known throughout the Arab world as friendly, sincere, generous, and scrupulously honest, and they are proud of this reputation.

The Levant

The Levant, a French term, is used to identify the countries of the Eastern Mediterranean: Lebanon, Syria, and Palestine (and perhaps Jordan and Iraq). The adjective form is *Levantine*.

The Levantine people in Lebanon, Syria, and Palestine are mainly from the same Semitic origin, descended from indigenous inhabitants of the region (from Neolithic times). They constitute a linguistic and cultural unit and identify with each other. Jordanians, however, are of Bedouin descent, from the northern Arabian Peninsula (now Saudi Arabia). Many Iraqis are Arabian too, because Iraq was seriously depopulated and then repopulated by Bedouin tribes from Arabia (the dialect of Baghdad is a Bedouin dialect).

Lebanon

Lebanon is a small country, both in size and in population (about four million), with a diverse geography and a long history of commercial and maritime importance. Its people are descended from the same (non-Arabian) Semitic stock, mainly Phoenician and Canaanite. Religious diversity and social class have been divisive and have created barriers to social integration. All Lebanese feel an intense loyalty to their own clan and religious group.

From 1975 to 1991, Lebanon experienced a disastrous civil war, during which 25 percent of the population was displaced and at least 130,000 people were killed. Religious tensions were in part the cause — the Christians (30 percent) have traditionally had more wealth and power than have the more numerous Muslims (70 percent), who in turn are divided among Sunnis and Shia (slightly more Shia than Sunnis). A third influential denomination is the Druze religion, which originated in Lebanon in the eleventh century and is derived from Shia Islam. Altogether, five Muslim and 14 Christian sects are recognized, and there are 19 different types of religious law.[1] The social and political effects of this mix of religions and sects can well be imagined; it has affected government stability.

The Lebanese speak Arabic, and educated people also speak French, English, or both. Some minority groups, notably the Armenians, speak their own languages but are bilingual in Arabic.

Prior to the beginning of the civil war, the Lebanese government was pro-Western and pro-capitalist, and the country was a leader in service industries such as banking and commerce. The Lebanese had the highest standard of living in the Arab world and the most cosmopolitan way of life, at least in Beirut. This is rapidly returning (but the Gulf States are catching up). It is worrisome that violence and assassinations have not completely ended.

Since the end of the war, Lebanon has rebuilt extensively and recovered its infrastructure. It has reclaimed many of the services for which it was known, and many of the people who fled to Europe or the United States during the war have returned. Prosperity is evident everywhere, but with it has come a higher cost of living, now the highest in the Arab world.

Social classes are clearly defined in Lebanon, with a small upper class, a growing middle class, and a large lower class made up of about half of the people. The lower classes are quite poor, and the majority live in urban areas. Agricultural production is limited by inadequate natural resources, and imports far exceed exports. Unemployment is 15 to 20 percent.[2] The population is about 3.5 million, including about 400,000 Palestinian refugees.[3]

The Lebanese have migrated abroad in great numbers since the late nineteenth century (more live outside the country than inside), and the sustained contacts with these emigrants all over the world has influenced the society and economy. Many Lebanese work in other Arab countries, mainly as managers and professionals.

The Lebanese are highly educated. Free public education has long been available, and the literacy rate is 86 percent, one of the highest in the Arab world. In the mid-nineteenth century, French and American missionaries established schools and universities in Lebanon. The missionaries had a strong influence on society, and they trained many future leaders and intellectuals of the Arab world. Standards of health care and social services are once again high, as they were before the war.

Urban Lebanese women, especially Christians, are active in the professions, commerce, and social organizations. Women constitute 29 percent of the workforce, one-fourth of them in the professional sector. They generally dress in the Western manner and mix freely in society. In contrast, women in rural areas are restricted by the prevailing traditional values.

Women received the right to vote and to run in elections in 1952. The government instituted a National Action Plan to improve the status of women from 1997 to 2000 and has instituted a National Authority on Women's Issues as well.[4] In 2004 two women were finally appointed to the national cabinet, one as minister of industry and one as minister of state. There are active organizations seeking to place more women in leadership positions and seeking to replace some Islamic laws with civil ones.

The Lebanese people are well traveled and sophisticated, and they are politically oriented and very patriotic. Some, mainly Christians, believe that Lebanon should be more Western than Arab and should identify with Europe; others, mainly Muslims, identify with pan-Arab sentiments and want to de-emphasize Western influences.

The society in Lebanon remains divided. Lebanon has not conducted an official census since 1932 because it could upset the delicate religious balance. The three highest-level positions in the government are designated for a Christian, a Sunni Muslim, and a Shia Muslim; this was set up based on the 1932 census, when Christians made up 56 percent of the population. The Parliament has an equal number of Christians and Muslims, but the Christians control the country. (Lebanon was created from the region of Greater Syria as a haven for Christians, who had suffered massacres by the Druze and the Turks in the 1860s. This was done through an agreement between Europe's Great Powers—France even sent troops—and Ottoman authorities.) The Christians in Lebanon do not want this to change. If Lebanon became a democracy, the Shia majority might well rule, with an enhanced role for Hizbollah.

There is internal disagreement on important issues—in March 2005, a poll was taken in which half of the Maronite Christians said they wanted the Syrian army to leave Lebanon, while only one third of the people in other groups (Orthodox, Sunni, Shia, Druze) agreed. On the issue of disarming the Lebanese militia, 60 percent of the Druze said yes, while only 5 percent of the Shia agreed, 13 percent of the Sunnis, 17 percent of the Maronites, and 16 percent of the Orthodox.[5] There are two large pro-Syrian parties supported by a majority of Lebanese.[6] In a poll in November 2004, 58 percent of the Lebanese were opposed to the U.N. resolution engineered by the U.S. and France, demanding a Syrian pullback (They had approved Syrian intervention during the civil war because their army provided stability.).[7] It was sectarian disagreements of this kind that caused the long civil war.

Beirut is exceptionally built up and modernized, and it is beautiful; there is a long road along the Mediterranean seacoast, and mountains are not far away. Beirut is known as "the Paris of the Middle East." Life in the city is liberal (by far the most liberal in the Arab world), luxurious, and highly social, and there is an active nightlife. Many students from Europe and the U.S. have studied at the American University in Beirut, as well as several other universities. Westerners feel comfortable there.

Syria

Syria's civilization has reached high levels in its long history, but it has also been subjected to frequent invasions and conquests, mainly because of its strategic location. The nation's population is diverse. Of its 18 million people, about 90 percent are Muslims (74 percent of those are Sunni; the rest belong to other Islamic sects). Minority groups in Syria include Christians, 5 to 10 percent, and Druze, about 3 percent. Of the Sunni Muslims, one-tenth are Kurds. The most notable Muslim sect is that of the Alawites (a variation of Shiism), who comprise only 14 percent of the population but have controlled the government since 1970 when the current regime took power. Jews are no longer a significant part of the population; only 85 Jews remained in 2004, most of them in Damascus.[1] There are still 300,000 Palestinian refugees in the country.

Syria's socialist government is authoritarian, secular, nationalistic, and cautious in its relations with the West. With the death of President Hafez Al-Assad in 2000, his son Bashar assumed the presidency, and he appears to be making efforts to liberalize the country and to reform the economy; nevertheless, the future remains hard to predict. The government finds itself on the defensive, accused of supporting international terrorism, which affects both its tourism and its trade. The United States imposed sanctions on Syria in May 2004 and was considering adding more, but announced a delay in February 2005. The threat of additional new sanctions looms, although its effect would be more political than economic. Rumors continue to exist that the American government wishes to see a regime change in Damascus.*

---

*In 1990, Syria was the first Arab country to condemn Iraq's invasion of Kuwait, and contributed 20,000 soldiers during the first Gulf War in 1991.[2]

The Syrian government has long attempted to control Islamists. In 1982 an Islamist threat was harshly put down, during which at least 20,000 civilians died. Islamism is again on the rise, partly in response to the war in Iraq. Many Syrians fear political Islam and the religious revival, but the government may well decide to give religious leaders positions in the government so that it will appear more Islamic. While clerics insist that secular government has not worked, many of the intelligentsia and middle class have spoken out against the religious trend.[3] A Syrian Baath Party spokesman recently stated, "The basic attitude of the Baath Party is totally secular and against religious interference."[4] If Syria's secular government falls, it will very likely be replaced by one that is based on religion. A Sunni cleric runs the country's largest Islamic education and charitable foundation.[5] One reporter has given this assessment: "There would be little public regret if the regime did just fall apart. Yet few in the opposition really want it that way. They fear that with ethnic and sectarian tensions, civil war—even another Iraq—could occur."[6]

Syria is one of the most densely populated of all the Arab countries. About half of its land is habitable. The population growth rate is such that 40 percent of the people are under the age of 14. The upper and middle classes make up about 35 percent of the population. Education and health care are widely available, and literacy has reached 83 percent.

Agricultural production is an important factor in the economy, as are oil, phosphates, and textiles. Land reform and the establishment of agricultural cooperatives have led to improvements in the lives of small farmers, who make up about one third of the population. The standard of living in urban areas continues to improve. New government policies are designed to attract foreign investment and rejuvenate the economy. Twenty-five percent of the workforce was unemployed in late 2004.

Most Syrians identify strongly with Arab nationalism and their Arab/Muslim heritage, and they are generally quite conservative. Few Western tourists have visited Syria in recent decades, so contact is fairly recent and tourism is just getting started. French is spoken more widely than English.

Syrian women of the upper class have been well educated for two generations and have long been working, primarily in education and medicine; women hold 39 percent of the positions in the national university system. In 1998, women comprised 28 percent of the labor force.

Most of them dress in Western styles. In 2001, 26 women were members of the parliament, out of 250, and in 2003 there were 24. There are also two women in the cabinet.[7]

Syrians are friendly and welcoming to Westerners and to Americans. There are study-abroad programs for young Americans learning Arabic, and more are in the planning stage. Currently, there are a few hundred Western students living and studying in Damascus, and about 50 of them are Americans. Western students have greatly enjoyed their experiences there.

Jordan

Jordan is a relatively new nation. It was created under a British mandate at the end of World War I as a kingdom to be ruled by the Hashemites (Hashemites are originally from the Hejaz region of western Saudi Arabia, where they fought against the Turks in the Arab Revolt during World War I). Jordan became independent of Britain in 1946. Its borders are artificial—Jordan's territory is essentially the leftovers when the borders of adjoining nations were determined by the British (for their own interests). Jordan ceded the West Bank (of the Jordan River, occupied by Israel since 1967) to the Palestinian Authority in 1988.

About 60 percent of Jordan's 4 to 5 million people are Palestinians (figures vary from 20 to70 percent), most of whom arrived after the events of 1948 and 1967. Most are well educated and many are wealthy. Palestinians have been granted Jordanian citizenship and have the same political and economic rights as Jordanians do.

There is a significant distinction between Palestinians (who identify more readily with Lebanese and Syrians) *and Jordanians.* The Palestinian dialect is predominant in the urban centers, but elsewhere the Jordanians speak their own dialect, close to the Bedouin dialects. Jordanian Arabic has been encouraged and promoted in television programs. About 65,000 Jordanians are still Bedouins; with government encouragement, they are becoming more settled every year. Jordanians (not Palestinians) hold most of the administrative posts in the country.

Jordan has 950,000 registered Palestinian refugees, of whom 18 percent live in thirteen refugee camps, ten of which are administered by UNRWA (the U.N. Relief and Works Agency). The U.N.'s temporary relief services have become permanent. Jordan went through a traumatic civil war in 1970, when Palestinians attempted (unsuccessfully) to take over the government.

Most Jordanians are Sunni Muslim, but between 5 and 8 percent of the population is Christian. Religion has not been a divisive factor in this society. Eighty-six to 90 percent of the population is literate, and English is widely spoken. The Jordanian government has been viewed in the past as moderate and pro-Western. After the death of King Hussein in February 1999, his son Abdullah assumed the throne and has been promoting efforts toward economic and political openness. Jordan is probably the most democratic of all Arab countries.

There is opposition, however; the Islamist Muslim Brotherhood won a majority of the seats in the parliamentary elections of 1989, a large number in 1993, and about one-fourth of the seats in 2003 (they boycotted the elections of 1997). And despite the government's relatively pro-Western policies, it still has to contend with the results of a Pew Global Attitudes Project poll in 2003, in which 99 percent of the people viewed the U.S. unfavorably.[1]

Jordan is poor in natural resources, and despite numerous economic initiatives, the nation is heavily dependent on foreign aid. There are serious water shortages, which are worsening. Only 6 percent of the land is arable, and 20 percent of the people are farmers. A notably successful innovation has been a microfund program that lends small amounts of money to low-income women. Established in 1996, it had made over 61,000 loans by 2001.[2]

Jordan's location between Israel and Iraq is a disadvantage; it has suffered because of both neighbors. Before the Gulf War of 1991, 75 percent of its trade was with Iraq ($1 billion per year); this was reduced to one quarter of that amount.[3] Some 380,000 people returned from jobs abroad, mainly in the Arabian Gulf, and unemployment rose to 30 percent; it was still 25-30 percent in 2001.[4] The second Gulf War caused an even greater crisis in the energy supply situation, as oil had been imported (below market cost) from Iraq. Recently, economic growth has resumed, in part due to the Jordan-U.S. Free Trade Agreement of 2001. Jordan joined the World Trade Organization in April 2000.

Jordan's economy is based on tourism, mining, industry, trade, and agriculture. Tourism has been especially hard-hit by both Gulf Wars. Most people have experienced a decrease in income in the last decade. Approximately 40 percent of the population now lives in poverty.[5]

Jordan's education system is excellent, and 21 percent of the government's total expenditure is spent on education. The literacy rate had climbed to 87 percent by 1998; it is now 91 percent. There is also an excellent nationwide health program. Jordanians all speak Arabic, and many speak English as their second language.

Jordanian women are well educated and working in a wide array of fields; about 20 percent of them are in the workforce. Women have been voting since 1974. Queen Rania is publicly championing the cause of women's rights. In the parliamentary elections of June 2003, women gained 5.5 percent of the seats in the lower house and 12.7 percent in the upper house.[6]

Jordanians are very personable, warm, and welcoming. They enjoy friendships with foreigners. Many American students choose to study in Jordan, and even more travel there. They are unanimous in their praise of the Jordanians.

Iraq

What can be said about Iraq? Like Syria, it has a proud history and was the home of five magnificent ancient civilizations. But time after time, Iraq was beset by invasions and conquests. Unlike heavily populated Egypt, Iraq (Mesopotamia) is underpopulated (about 25 million), although its land is as fertile and its history as old as Egypt's, the consequence of repeated wars and devastation. Iraq's location has always made it a strategic battlefield for the region.

Only 75 percent of the Iraqis are Arabs, and 20 percent are Kurds, who are bilingual in Arabic and Kurdish. (Note: Kurds are not Arabs, they are ethnically Aryan.) The remainder are minority ethnic groups: Turkomans, Assyrians, Armenians, and some other peoples of Iranian origin. Arabic is the official language, and English is widely spoken by the educated. Ninety-seven percent of the Iraqis are Muslim, of whom 60 percent are Shia; 3 percent are Christians. Iraq has been strongly influenced by its Islamic heritage because several sites sacred to Shia Muslims are located here and have long been the object of religious pilgrimages.

Iraq's revolutionary socialist government was established after the Hashemite monarchy was overthrown in 1958, and there have been four coups since then. Saddam Hussein's regime took power in 1968.

Iraq has been hard-hit by two wars, ten years apart (not to mention an eight-year war with Iran prior to these two). The first phase was Gulf War I, followed by an international embargo imposed in 1991 (referred to by Iraqis and other Arabs as "the American sanctions"). In ten years the sale of oil went from generating 95 percent of the foreign exchange to 10 percent. Social services declined drastically, and money that was intended for food and medicine in the oil-for-food program was mostly diverted to government loyalists. By 2001 an estimated 800,000 to 1.2 million people had died because of the embargo, half a million of them children under the age of five.[1] Because of scarcities, the people became more dependent on the government for necessities, including drinking water.

Then came Gulf War II, the American invasion of March 2003. The chaotic results are well known, and they continue. Even as 8 million Iraqis voted and exuberantly demonstrated their love of freedom and democracy in the elections of January 2005, at the same time 92 percent of them wanted the Americans out.

Almost half of Iraq's population consists of children. In 2003 about 25 percent of Iraq's children were malnourished, which is up 73 percent from 1991. Infant mortality more than doubled between the late 1980s and early 2000s. By 2001 it was about 133 per 1,000 births (as compared with 4 to 5 in Western Europe and 6.7 in the United States).[2] A United Nations report stated, "The country's fall on the UNDP Human Development Index from 96 to 127 reflects one of the most rapid declines in human welfare in recent history."[3] A UNICEF report stated that in mid-2005, 4,000 children under the age of five died every day.[4]

Enrollments in primary schools dropped from 100 percent in 1980 to 85 percent in 1996, and then to 76 percent in 2003. Ninety-two percent of the population was once literate, dropping to 40 percent in 2003.[5]

Only 12 percent of Iraq's land is cultivated, and efforts have long been underway to reclaim more (it was irrigated and fertile in ancient times). About 30 percent of the Iraqis work in agriculture.

Iraqi women have always been among the most liberated in the Middle East, and are thoroughly integrated into the workforce as professionals. Within a span of 20 years, thousands of women became lawyers, physicians, professors, engineers, writers and artists. In 1959, Iraq became the first country in the Middle East to have a female minister and four female judges, as well as women scientists and politicians. The 1959 Code of Personal Status gave women equal political and economic rights, and extensive legal protections.[6] The ruling Baath Party was secular, and promulgated laws specifically aimed at improving women's status. It set up the General Federation of Iraqi Women, which coordinated more than 250 rural and urban centers for job training, education, and social programs. Women were granted equal opportunities in the civil service sector, maternity leave, and freedom from harassment in the workplace. In 1976, women constituted 38 percent of those working in education and 15 percent of the civil servants.

The status of women has worsened dramatically because of the two Gulf wars. After the first Gulf War, Saddam decided to embrace Islamic and tribal traditions as a political tool in order to consolidate power.[7] Many steps toward women's advancement were reversed. There were changes to the personal status laws and the labor code. As the economy grew worse, women were pushed out of the labor force to ensure employment for men. All state ministries were required to enforce restrictions on women working. Freedom to travel abroad was restricted, and coeducational high schools were changed to single-sex only.

Most Westerners would prefer a system that separates church and state, and many see an opportunity to promote such a system. Unfortunately, it has become more difficult when the current trend in the U.S. is to mix faith and government.[8]

Until recently, most Iraqis were determinedly secular. There was no sectarian tension; in fact, people frequently married across Sunni-Shia lines. Now it is doubtful that Iraq will ever again have a secular government.

Baghdad is still a beautiful city, with its parks and its broad boulevards illuminated against the Tigris river at night. It was designed in the eighth century, had a million inhabitants by the tenth century, and was the very heart of Islamic civilization during its Golden Age from the eighth to the eleventh centuries. There are still traces of the inner city's circular, geometric plan.

Iraq once had one of the highest living standards in the Middle East. It had an educated populace, a relatively small population, and plenty of money. Baghdad was filled with universities, museums, libraries, restaurants, and art galleries. Iraq was a cosmopolitan center of culture, art, and intellect. No longer.

The Arabian Peninsula

The Arabian Peninsula is the homeland of the Semitic Arabian people, in the true ethnic sense. This region has had the least contact with foreigners and is the most conservative in its traditions. In the Peninsula (often called Al-Jazeera), by law the men wear the long robe and head cloth ("the national dress") on official occasions and at work. Most women wear long dresses and frequently add a covering cloak when in public. Veiling (full face cover) is common in this region, but this is by no means universal. Veiling is required by law only in Saudi Arabia.

The Peninsula can be divided into three distinct regions: Saudi Arabia, Yemen, and the Arabian Gulf states. Saudi Arabia is rich (although less so than before), Yemen is poor, and the Arabian Gulf states are fabulously rich, their societies changing very quickly. Most foreigners particularly love the Gulf states—the people are friendly and hospitable, the cities are flamboyantly sleek and modern, with every convenience, and yet there is a desert Arab charm and a simplicity of values that permeates everything. Many foreigners who first come to the Gulf states for work are soon trying to extend their stay as long as possible.

Saudi Arabia

Saudi Arabia has always been prominent in the news because of its wealth, its size, and its location. It is a relatively new nation, is mostly desert, and has a population of 25 million (up from 6 million in 1970). The population growth rate is 2.4 percent per year, and 60 percent of the people are under age 18.[1] The young population has nearly tripled since 1980.

Prior to its unification in 1935 by King Abdel-Aziz Ibn Saud, the region that is now Saudi Arabia was loosely governed and inhabited by numerous Bedouin tribes. The Hashemites controlled the west coast region, with its port of Jeddah and its holy cities, Mecca and Medina. Ibn Saud conquered the region in 1924 (and other areas in the 1920s), and his descendants still rule. Saudi Arabia has evolved into a viable nation since its official founding in 1932, and most of the people have a Saudi identity.

Two important elements influence Saudi society: the fact that Arabia was the birthplace of Islam, and the discovery of oil, which led to sudden wealth. Religiosity, conservatism, wealth, and foreign workers—all of these factors are present in Saudi Arabia and result in ever-changing attitudes and social policies.

Muslim pilgrimages to the holy cities of Mecca and Medina, throughout the year and especially at the annual Hajj Pilgrimage season, are a significant source of income and prestige for the nation; one of the king's titles is "Keeper of the Two Holy Mosques." During the Hajj, the entire country is filled with pilgrims, two million from all over world. There are special airports, camping areas, and health facilities. Saudi Arabia is often referred to as the Holy Land; its Islamic history is central to its identity.

Saudi Arabia is the world's leading producer and exporter of oil. Although oil was first produced in 1938, the real effects of wealth were not felt until the 1960s and 1970s. The Saudis' immense wealth has made them influential in the Muslim world, and they are in the forefront of efforts to promote Islam. Saudis own many influential newspapers and broadcasting companies that are concerned with promoting modernization, but within the values of conservative Islam. The proposals of modernizers inside Saudi Arabia are constantly balanced by demands from the religious authorities.

Until the 1960s, most of the population was nomadic or seminomadic; due to rapid economic and urban growth, more than 95 percent of the population is now settled. Some cities and oases have densities of more than 1,000 people per square kilometer.

In 2005 there were at least 5.6 million foreign workers in Saudi Arabia, half of the total workforce, both laborers and professionals. Many of the foreign workers are from other Arab countries, along with many from Asia, particularly India, Pakistan, Bangladesh, Indonesia and the Philippines. There are about 100,000 Westerners, of whom 40,000 are from the United States and 30,000 from Britain.[2] This number will drop as the Saudi government fulfills its aim to reduce the number of foreigners to less than 20 percent of its total population, or two million, by 2013.[3] The plan is to replace them with Saudis, especially in management and professional positions.

Young university graduates, who were once assured of good positions, are finding jobs and upward mobility far less certain; national income has fallen drastically since the heyday of the 1970s. In fact, Saudi Arabia has been struggling through an economic recession, and some public projects were curtailed. Unemployment is 20 to 30 percent.[4] The demography of Saudi Arabia is very skewed, with 70 percent of the people under age 30.[5] Two hundred thousand people enter the Saudi workforce every year.

Oil prices fell by over 80 percent between 1982 and 1999. Personal income fell from $26,000 in 1981 to $6,800 in early 2002.[6] It was $4,511 in 2005. But oil revenues (90 to 95 percent of total export earnings) were up sharply in 2004 and are expected to remain high in 2005 and 2006.[7]

Saudi Arabia is a welfare state. The government subsidizes food, water, electricity and other consumer products, and provides interest-free loans. In April 2000, tariffs on electricity were increased, but this was reversed in October because of widespread public opposition.[8] The government still plans to cut subsidies and increase taxes, but with the recent rise in its oil income, it can move more slowly.

Health programs, first instituted in the 1960s, have achieved far-reaching results. Life expectancy rose from 40 to 68 in two generations (1955-2000). Money has been lavished on public health facilities: there are almost 400 hospitals, 26 opened in 2004 alone, 88 more are planned, and 2,000 more primary care centers are slated to be built by 2010. The government must plan for a projected population of 37 million by 2020.[9] Unfortunately, training has not kept up with demand; 65 percent of the physicians and nurses are foreign.

Education has shown an equally dramatic increase. In 1960, 22 percent of boys and 2 percent of girls were enrolled in primary school. In 1981 enrollments were 81 percent of boys and 43 percent of girls (education is free but not compulsory). Now, half of the students are girls. Literacy now stands at 94 percent, compared with less than 3 percent in the early 1960s!

At the university level, the number of male students increased by 95 percent between 1983 and 1989, and the number of female students increased by 132 percent. In 2003, 56 percent of the university graduates were women (up from a total of 70 women in 1965), and women's enrollment in technical schools rose tenfold between 1994 and 2001.[10,11] There are 7 universities and over 50 women's colleges.[12]

The class system in Saudi Arabia is four-tiered: royalty (8,000 princes and 40,000 other members of the royal family),[13] a growing educated elite, an expanding middle class, and a lower, uneducated class. The latter may be poor but just as often they are simply isolated from social services and live in their traditional manner. Saudi Arabia is now 87 percent urban.[14]

In this austere Sunni Wahhabi country, 5 to 15 percent of the population are Shia (estimated officially at 200,000 to 400,000), who make up one-third of the population of the oil-rich Eastern Province.*

The Shia have limited employment opportunities; they are rarely accepted into national-security positions, such as the military and the Ministry of Interior. There are none in the National Guard. Most of them work in lower-level jobs. The number of Shia admitted to universities is also restricted, as are the construction of Shia mosques and schools (the building of Shia mosques was banned for thirty years.)[17] There are no Shia cabinet ministers and only two in the 120-member Consultative Council.[18]

Many of the skilled and semi-skilled Saudi employees of Aramco (the Arabian-American Oil Company) are Shia, mainly because the Eastern Province is the source of the country's oil wealth. In 1979 the Shia rioted, demanding a more equitable share of the money. In 2003 the government instituted a "national dialogue" to give a hearing to minority religious groups. The Shia are deeply ambivalent about their Saudi identity and feel newly empowered by Shia advances in Iraq.[19]

There is no freedom of religion in Saudi Arabia. The government prohibits public practice of non-Muslim religions, and there are no non-Muslim places of worship (Christians usually meet in private homes). Saudi Arabia is absolutely unique in the Muslim world in this respect. *Unfortunately, thousands of foreigners have worked in Saudi Arabia, and Westerners often see its society and laws as representative of all Arab and Muslim governments.* But Saudi Arabia is unique in its restrictions.

Alcohol, pork products, "pornography" (pictures of nude paintings or statues, photos of women wearing little clothing, non-Muslim religious pictures), and religious artifacts such as Bibles, crosses, or statues of Buddha are all forbidden. Print materials from abroad are subject to censorship. Even Muslims from other countries need time to adjust to the harsh social control.

---

*The State Department's "Religious Freedom Report" for 2004 estimates the number of Shia at two million, or 40–50 percent of the population of the Eastern Province.[15] The "Minorities at Risk" project estimates the number at three million, or 15 percent of the total Saudi population.[16] This is a highly sensitive issue, and a census has never been taken.

There are several dissident Islamist factions in Saudi Arabia that oppose the rule of the royal family and want to impose even stricter Islamic law, ruling through an "Islamic state." Bin Laden's group is one of these. Islamists have been influential for some time: in November of 1979 Islamic zealots briefly seized and occupied the Great Mosque in Mecca and had to be removed by military force. Pressures to reform are also coming from liberal intellectuals, technocrats, and women.[20]

In 2003 a six-month security campaign was launched, the likes of which the country had never seen. In a period of six months authorities arrested more than 600 Islamists, and killed dozens in nightly police raids.[21] The foreign minister recently said, "Our efforts are aimed at ending this scourge from the region."[22]

Liberalization is slowly taking place. For the first time in more than 40 years, local elections were held in February 2005. Half of the seats in newly created municipal councils were elected; the government appointed the other half.[23] Islamic activists won a sweeping victory, and many of them were well-educated professionals.[24] Critics have been calling for an independent judiciary and an elected national assembly; they say that municipal councils will have no power.[25] Women were not allowed to vote or run for office.

The legislature, the Consultative Council (Shura), is appointed, but many liberals hope the Council will some day be democratically elected. Two-thirds of its members are American-educated. Some reformers worry that if America pushes the Saudis to change too quickly, it could create a backlash.[26]

Saudi Arabia has by far the most severe restrictions on women in the Middle East, if not the world. Women are fully veiled in public, in a long black cloak. They may not travel alone, leave the country without permission from male relatives, or drive cars (many Muslims from Arab countries and elsewhere find this outrageous). In December 2001, women were issued separate identification cards, so now they finally have a fully legal identity.[27] Few work outside the home (only about 5.5 percent of eligible women); those who do, work in all-female environments such as schools, universities, and even "women's banks" (this requirement is eased for health workers).[28] The government has eased restrictions on women's obtaining commercial licenses, and many women own their own businesses, often computing companies and retail stores. In Jeddah, one-fourth of the private businesses are owned by women.[29]

This exclusion of women from voting was favored by 60 percent of the men in Riyadh just prior to the recent elections.[30] One Saudi journalist has written, "Saudi society must realize that it cannot do without the talents and abilities of half of its population if it is to develop and prosper."[31]

The image of Saudi Arabia for a visitor or resident is one of modern cities with high-rise buildings, huge freeways, luxury shopping malls thronged with people, fast-food shops, and perfume shops. Saudis like American consumer goods, especially music, and many Saudis express admiration for America's freedoms and way of life.[32]

Saudis are reserved, not quick to welcome foreigners into their private lives. Once a friendship is established, however, Saudis are generous and hospitable in the time-honored Arab way.

Yemen

Yemen, long isolated from outside contact and influences, is one of the most colorful and tradition-oriented countries in the Arab world. It was called "Arabia Felix" by the Romans and was known as the main source of incense.

Social practices have changed relatively slowly since modernization programs were introduced in the late 1960s. Much of the country is rugged, and outside of the cities it is a land of tribes and guns. Many of Yemen's 20 million people live in remote villages; only 25 to 40 percent of the people are urbanized. Yemen's architecture is traditional and distinctive, mainly stone-mud high-rise buildings decorated with white geometric designs. It is one of the poorest countries in Arab world, but it is spectacularly beautiful, with its mountains, valleys, and terraced hillsides. Unlike the rest of the Peninsula, Yemen has a temperate climate and much of it is green.

For three hundred years Yemen was divided into two separate nations: North Yemen and South Yemen (formerly Aden). The king of Yemen was deposed in 1962; in the north, the current regime has been in power since 1976; Aden was ruled by pro-Soviet Marxists beginning in 1971. In 1990 the two countries were united under a broadly socialist government. Since the union, numerous clashes have occurred, including a civil war in mid-1994, when the south tried to break away from the north.

In 1993 Yemen conducted the only fully free elections ever held in the Arabian Peninsula.[1] Ali Abdullah Saleh was elected president in 1999, for a term of seven years. Parliamentary elections were held in April 2003. The government is under pressure to assert control over terrorism, particularly after the bombing of the *U.S.S. Cole* in 2000. Its control is limited, though — there are thousands of miles of unpatrolled coast, and another thousand miles of wide-open frontier.[2]

A major problem in trying to control extremists and terrorists (Yemen has been listed as a haven) is that doing so is widely unpopular. Nevertheless, the government has deported many foreign Muslims, closed down 1,300 religious schools, and started a public campaign against extremism.[3]

Yemenis are Arabian Muslims. In the north, the most distinctive division is between Sunni Muslims and the Zaidi (Shia) sect, which dates to the thirteenth century; each group has well-defined geographic boundaries. In the south almost all the people are Sunni and they have intermarried extensively with African and Indian peoples (it was from Yemen that early travelers went to Indonesia and Malaysia, which are now Muslim countries.)

Yemenis speak Arabic, including some unusual, isolated dialects in remote areas, and educated Yemenis speak English as a second language. Yemeni men wear distinctive dress, a sarong-like skirt and a wide belt in which they place the traditional *jambiyya* (dagger).

The climate of Yemen has made intensive agriculture possible, much of it on terraced land, but only 2.7 percent of the land in the country is cultivated.[4] Coffee and cotton are major sources of revenue (the first coffee in Europe was imported from Yemen, probably through the port of Mocha). Traditional skills include construction and stonemasonry, carpentry, and metalworking. Before the first Gulf War of 1991, many thousands of Yemenis worked abroad, their wages strengthening the nation's economy. After the war, however, Saudi Arabia expelled over one million Yemenis (the Yemeni government supported Iraq), with serious economic consequences. Thirty-seven percent of the workforce is now unemployed, and over 40 percent of the people live in poverty.[5]

Southern Yemen has a semiarid climate, and the people have traditionally been fishermen and merchants (in the coastal area) as well as farmers and herders. The south's geographical location has been advantageous for commerce with countries of the Indian Ocean. A large share of the area's income derives from the procurement and distribution of petroleum products.

Yemen's great hope for the future is oil, first exported in 1993. In 2000, oil exports constituted nearly 97 percent of total exports; in 2004 the percentage dropped to just above 90 percent.[6] Sixteen percent of the country's income is money sent back by people working abroad. Yemen also depends on foreign aid. It faces a looming problem of inadequate water, especially in the capital city, Sanaa. Groundwater will be pumped dry in Sanaa within ten years; it is such a problem elsewhere that the rural economy could disappear within a generation.[7]

Productivity and prosperity are also affected by the social custom (mostly among men) of chewing a leaf called *Qat*, which produces a feeling of mild euphoria. Qat is chewed every day, beginning in early afternoon. Unfortunately, much fertile land is devoted to growing this plant.

Health programs are growing; nonetheless, Yemen's health facilities are among the least developed in the Arab world: infant mortality is still very high (63 per 1,000 births), and life expectancy is only age 61. In general, sanitation is poor and awareness of general health practices very low. Health care is also hampered by a severe shortage of qualified practitioners, particularly in rural areas.

Yemen faces a severe problem in its population growth. It was estimated at 3.4 percent in 2004, when the fertility rate was 6.75 children per woman.[8] Forty-eight percent of its people are under age 14.

Education is improving. The government spent 22.3 percent of its expendable income on education in 2001.[9] Attendance of eligible children is 67 percent in primary school and 37 percent in secondary school. The literacy rate was 46 percent in 2002. The government has launched a crash education program (including adults), emphasizing science, engineering, and technology.

Women in northern Yemen are fully veiled in public and many are uneducated; still, 27 percent work outside the home, owing to financial necessity. Women voted in national elections in 1993, the first women in the Arabian Peninsula to do so. Their participation was enthusiastically supported by tribal leaders and by the Islamist political party. There are women in parliament, a woman is minister of human rights, and Yemen has a woman ambassador.[10] In south Yemen, formerly Aden, women were granted equal status by law under the then-Marxist government (the only communist government in the Middle East) and were recruited into the labor force in fields such as accounting and mechanics, or in factories. Women in south Yemen are more integrated into society than in any other Arabian Peninsular country.

In Yemen's five universities, all men and women students share classes together. In 1995, women represented 28 percent of the professionals in medicine, 13 percent in the judicial field, and 6 percent in politics.[11]

There are good-quality programs in Sanaa for foreign students to study Arabic. Westerners find the country fascinating and charming.

Yemenis are admired for their industriousness and skills. They are friendly and curious about the outside world, and are very accommodating to foreigners.

The Arabian Gulf States*

The five Arabian Gulf states—Kuwait, Bahrain, Qatar, the United Arab Emirates (UAE), and Oman—are situated along the eastern coast of the Arabian Peninsula. Most were under British administration until 1971.

These countries, as well as Saudi Arabia, are joined in the Gulf Cooperative Council (GCC), which promotes economic integration in the region. Income is high and population is low, but rapidly increasing. Citizens pay no income taxes or import taxes, and for citizens, corporate taxes are non-existent or very low. Most countries can afford to generously subsidize many of the people's living costs.

This is a dramatic change from the poverty of the past. The traditional sources of income had been trade, herding, fishing, pearling, and piracy. Everything has been turned upside down in the last fifty years.

Kuwait

Although Kuwait is small, it is an important country, mostly because of its vast oil wealth, the basis of its economic and political influence among the Arab states. It gained its independence from Britain in 1961 and has since been ruled by the Al Sabah royal family. Kuwait has had a national assembly and parliamentary elections off and on since 1962, most recently in 2003. Power lies in the hands of the ruler, the Emir, who

---

*The Arabs do not use the term *Persian Gulf*.

suspended the parliament from 1976 to 1981, and again from May to July, 1999.

The election of 2003 was a major victory for Islamists; they and tribal representatives loyal to the royal family dominate the parliament.[1] There were so many restrictions that only 15 percent of the 800,000–900,000 eligible citizens were actually allowed to vote.[2]

In many ways Kuwaiti society resembles that of Saudi Arabia. Both are tribal, religious, and conservative, and the two countries have long had close ties. Kuwaitis are Arabian Muslims; about 65 percent are Sunni and 35 percent are Shia. Their practice of Islam is not, however, as austere as that of Saudi Arabia, although alcohol is banned.

The population of Kuwait is about 2.4 million—45 percent Kuwaitis and the rest foreign workers. So many foreign workers have come to Kuwait that they once constituted 80 percent of the workforce. Many Palestinians and others were forced to leave after the Gulf War of 1991, and since then the government has prioritized replacing foreign workers with Kuwaitis in professional and managerial jobs. Even so, 70 percent of the workforce was still foreign in 2004.

The dominant fact of life in Kuwait is the government's enormous oil-based wealth; oil sales are 85 percent of the public revenues. Per capita income is one of the highest in the world, although it has dropped slightly. Production of oil began in 1946, and within fifteen years poverty was virtually eradicated.[3] Like Saudi Arabia, Kuwait is a welfare state. It also has the reputation of being the shrewdest and most sophisticated of the major Arab overseas investors.

Another factor that will dominate Kuwaiti affairs for many years is the Iraqi invasion of 1990, followed by the Gulf War. Although the economic effects have largely been overcome, the psychological consequences will last for a long time. Kuwaitis have begun reassessing their role as a nation, especially vis-à-vis the rest of the Arab world.

Kuwait cooperated with the U.S. in the second war with Iraq, the invasion of 2003, and it was the main staging area for military preparations. In early 2005 there were about 30,000 American military personnel in the country. The Kuwaitis are the most pro-American in the Arab world; they still feel gratitude for their liberation in the first Gulf War. Even they have been shaken by recent events, however, and many are beginning to reconsider their unqualified political support.

Class distinctions and class consciousness are strong in Kuwait, even as wealth has become more widespread. Progress in health, education, and economic development has completely changed the Kuwaiti way of life over the last fifty years. The literacy rate is was 83 percent in 2002. Life expectancy is 78, the highest in the Arab world. The people have everything money can buy. Virtually all of Kuwait's water comes from seawater desalinization plants, an expenditure impossible for governments with less money and more people.[4] The government encourages large families, and the average size of a traditional Kuwaiti family is 8.2 members.[5]

Kuwaiti women are generally veiled in public, although this is changing. Many are active in education and commerce, and some own their own businesses. Unlike Saudi Arabia, Kuwaiti women are not prohibited from working in the same environment as men. Women are also making progress in education and currently receive two-thirds of the bachelor's degrees granted each year. The number of women working in 2004 was 34 percent.[6]

Women in Kuwait were given full political rights, including the right to vote and run for office, in a parliamentary amendment to the country's election law, enacted on an "order for urgency" basis, in mid-May 2005. This follows years of struggle and demonstrations by Kuwaiti women. The ruler had proposed full rights in 1999, but it was repeatedly blocked by the parliament. This is seen as a major victory and a sign of changing times.[7]

Kuwaitis are very cordial to foreigners but not quick to establish strong personal friendships. They prefer private and family social circles.

Bahrain

Bahrain, an island in the Arabian Gulf, is the most modernized of the Gulf states. It was the first to produce oil, which brings in about 60 percent of the nation's income, but supplies are declining. The government has diversified into dry-dock ship services, aluminum production, and light engineering. Bahrain's development as a major financial center has been the most widely heralded aspect of its diversification effort; it also has excellent tourist facilities. As long as 5,000 years ago, when it was the ancient civilization of Dilmun, Bahrain was a trading center.

Bahrain's population was 660,000 in July 2003, including 235,000 foreigners. It is one of the most densely populated countries in the Middle East, with 89 percent of the people living in two principal cities.

The population of Manama, the capital, is 144,000 (compared with 62,000 in 1960). Arabic is the official language, and English is widely used as a second language.

Bahrain imports almost all of its food; agriculture is less than 1 percent of its income. The land is almost entirely desert, and the people have always made a living from the sea.

Bahrain was a British protectorate from 1861 until its independence in 1971. Bahrain is ruled by an emir, and it elected its first parliament in 1973. In 1975 the National Assembly attempted to legislate the end of the Al-Khalifa family's rule and also to expel the U.S. Navy. The emir dissolved the National Assembly, and in 1992 he appointed a consultative council (*Shura*), which now has 40 members. There were some incidents of political violence in the 1990s stemming from the disaffection of the Shia majority.[1]

In February 2002 the current ruler, Shaikh Hamad, pronounced Bahrain a constitutional monarchy (rather than heredity emirate) and changed his status from emir to king. The first elections in nearly thirty years were held at that time, with women being allowed to vote and also to run for office.[2]

Bahrain's small size and population have contributed to its rapid modernization. Life expectancy is 74. Health and education programs are universal, and the literacy rate was 89 percent in 2004. Bahrain is working to establish itself as a regional center of higher education and already boasts two universities.

Bahrain is not without problems. Seventy percent of its people are Shia Muslims, and the remaining 30 percent are Sunnis. The ruling family is Sunni. Unemployment is 15 percent, twice as high among the Shia. The government, military, and corporate sectors are all controlled by Sunnis. Human rights groups have called for reforms in the treatment of dissidents.[3]

Bahraini women, many of whom are well educated, constitute about 24 percent of the workforce, up from 17 percent in 1991.

Bahrain is a favorite tourist destination in the Gulf. It is very liberal and has an active nightlife. It is connected to Saudi Arabia by a causeway.

Qatar

Qatar (pronounced KA-tar) is a small peninsula, fabulously rich in both oil and gas. Eighty percent of the population lives in the capital city, Doha. Since the discovery of oil in 1949, Qatar's population has exploded: 100,000 in 1970, 350,000 in 1991, and 840,000 in 2004, of whom only about 170,000 were citizens.[1] Foreigners comprise about 75 percent of the population, and 80 to 90 percent of the workforce.[2]

Until the discovery of oil, the Qatari people were engaged in fishing, pearling, and trading, many living in dire poverty. The ruling family signed a treaty with Britain in 1868, and it was a British protectorate from 1916 until it gained its independence in 1971.

Oil and gas account for 85 percent of Qatar's annual income. Although only a little over 1 percent of the land is arable, Qatar produces half of the vegetables it consumes. Most people maintain large herds of goats, sheep, camels and cattle, and fishing is still a mainstay.[3]

Health programs are numerous and lavishly funded; life expectancy is now 73 years of age. Qatar had a phenomenal population growth rate of over 6 percent between 1990 and 1998, and the government encourages large families. Twenty-four percent of the Qataris are under age 15 and the annual growth rate is now 2.75 percent.

Qataris are Arabian Muslims; they speak Arabic and use English as their second language. Fifteen percent of the people are Shia, who are restricted from working in positions related to national security.[4]

The country is ruled by a hereditary emir (now king), and the society is conservative. The country is so small that the emir runs the government like a family business and rules in conjunction with an advisory council. A Qatari constitution was overwhelmingly approved by referendum in April 2003 and took effect in October of the same year. It guarantees freedom of expression, assembly, and religion.[5] In 1998 the emir abolished the Ministry of Information, thus ending censorship of print and broadcast media.[6] Qatar is home to the phenomenally successful Al-Jazeera satellite television channel, an important, and occasionally controversial source of news and other programming across the Middle East. The government does not regulate Al-Jazeera's content.

Qatar has made the news lately because of agreements with the American military. When Qatar agreed to allow the U.S. to base its main Gulf region command center there in 2002, the decision was controversial but largely favored by the Qataris. Qatar then hosted the Coalition headquarters during the invasion of Iraq in 2003. The government and people are generally pro-Western; nevertheless, in view of changing events, soldiers have been advised to avoid Doha, at least in large groups.[7]

Education has made enormous strides and receives priority funding. The literacy rate is 85 percent. Qatar is making an effort to attract foreign students to study Arabic at the University of Qatar, providing scholarships for that purpose. Through an initiative of the Qatar Foundation, sponsored by the ruler's wife, Sheikha Muza, exchange agreements have been arranged with five American universities to date: Texas A & M University, Cornell Medical College, Carnegie-Mellon University, Georgetown University, and Virginia Commonwealth University. Some smaller exchange programs exist as well. A large area has been allocated for a compound to be called Education City.[8]

The social organization of Qatar is still tribal and strongly family-oriented; many people live in compounds that hold several related families. Educated young men are beginning to assume professional and managerial positions. Qatari women currently comprise only 13 percent of the workforce, but many are becoming educated. Now more than half of the employees of the Ministry of Education are women, as is the minister. Qatari women are free to drive and wear jeans and blouses.[9] Women first voted in 1999 and have participated politically since. Qatar and Bahrain are the only Gulf states that allow women to run for elective office.

Qataris are outgoing and friendly to foreigners, many of whom have lived there for years.

United Arab Emirates

The United Arab Emirates (UAE) is a federation of small territories that was created as an independent nation in 1971–1972 by uniting seven of the Trucial States (so called by the British, to replace the infamous name "Pirate Coast"). The combined population is 2.6 million (some estimates go as high as 4 million).[1] UAE citizens comprise about 20 percent of the population, and 40 percent of them live in Abu Dhabi. The country is 87 percent urban. There are so many foreign workers that 71 percent of the total population is male. The government is working to increase the number of its own citizens in the workforce.

Abu Dhabi is by far the largest of the former territories, comprising 87 percent of the UAE's total area. Abu Dhabi is the capital city; Dubai is the main port and has become a huge, prosperous commercial center for the whole Gulf region. The city created the Dubai International Financial Centre, intended to become a regional financial center on a par with New York and London.[2]

The union of emirates has worked out well on the whole, and rulers of the smaller states realize that they have attained a larger degree of influence and economic benefit through alliance with their larger neighbors than would have been possible otherwise. The people are Arabian Muslims, of whom about 80 percent are Sunni and 20 percent are Shia. All seven states are ruled by Sunnis.

Abu Dhabi began oil production in 1962, Dubai in 1969, and Sharjah in 1973. Life has been transformed—former fishing villages are now modern cities filled with high-rise buildings and superhighways. The other four small emirates (Ajman, Umm al Qaiwain, Ras al-Khaimah, and Fujairah), each with a small population, have no oil and are changing more slowly. The entire country has been transformed.

Per capita income in the UAE is the second highest in the Gulf. Oil accounts for 88 percent of the government's revenues. Previously, people made their living mainly from fishing, pearling, oasis-farming, and animal herding. Abu Dhabi and Dubai are the only emirates that contribute to the UAE's finances.[3] All of the emirates earn income through the sale of exotic postage stamps!

Ambitious programs have been established in education, health, and agricultural production (there had been no arable land, only oases). Literacy is 79 percent, and life expectancy is 75 years. The society is still very traditional and conservative (at least outside the cities). Women are veiled and most participate little in public life. This is changing, however, now that women's education through the university level is strongly encouraged by the government; 70 percent of eligible women attend university. Women are about 12 percent of the workforce, and they constitute 65 percent of the teachers. They do not yet have the right to vote.

There are at least seven universities (depending on how one interprets the term *university*), including the American University of Dubai and the American University of Sharjah.[4] The AUS has a program in Arabic, and a growing number of Western students are studying there.

Citizens of the UAE are affluent, all poverty has been eradicated, and they are known to be the biggest spenders in the Arab world.[5] Many are outgoing and friendly, some are more reserved.

Oman

Oman is situated in the southeast corner of the Arabian Peninsula, in a very strategic location at the entrance to the Arabian Gulf. It is larger than the other Gulf countries but not as rich. Oman is ruled by a sultan, whose family has ruled since 1744 (after gaining independence from Iran).

Oman's population was almost 3 million in 2004, of whom 20 percent were foreigners (over half of them from the Indian subcontinent and other parts of Asia). Eighty-five percent of the Omani citizens are Arabians, and the rest are of Zanzibari, Baluchi, or of South Asian origin. Almost everyone speaks Arabic; some non-Arabic Semitic languages are still spoken in the far south. Tribalism is still the main source of identity for the Omani people.

About 70 percent of the Omanis belong to the Ibadi sect (a branch of Shia Islam), which contributed to an isolationist tendency in the past. Twenty-five percent are Sunnis. Indian Hindus are the principal non-Muslim minority group; they have resided in Oman for centuries.

Oman was forced to become a British protectorate in 1891 because of piracy; in fact, *musketeer* originally referred to someone from Muscat. It became independent in 1971.

The discovery of oil in 1967 exacerbated impatience with the old sultan, who was reactionary and oppressive: he sanctioned slavery, and the Omani people were beset with poverty, disease, illiteracy, and social restrictions (e.g., prohibition against smoking and travel inside the country). All of this had caused 600,000 people to go into exile. Oil income was spent on defense only. In 1970 the sultan was deposed by his British-educated son Qaboos, who still rules and is very popular. He began the extensive modernization of the country.

Under Qaboos' leadership, Oman has seen dramatic changes in health, education, and commercial development. Electricity, telephones, radio, television, public education, roads, hospitals, public health programs—all are new since 1970. Seventy-eight percent of Oman's income comes from oil, but 40 percent of the people still work in oasis agriculture and in fishing. Although Oman has a considerable amount of potentially arable land, it lacks manpower and water. In some remote interior areas the people have little contact with the rest of the country.

With all the development, life is getting better, phenomenally better. Literacy is 76 percent (up from 18 percent in 1970), partly due to adult literacy programs. Sixty-three percent of the eligible children are in school. Because of improved health care, the growth rate of the population has been truly amazing. Between 1965 and 1990 it tripled, and it is now about 3.5 percent per year. Fully 42 percent of the population is under age 14. The average number of children is 6 per woman, and life expectancy is 73 years.[1]

The sultan is known to be one of the most innovative rulers in the Gulf. He has promoted two areas in particular: higher education and women's participation in society. Oman's two universities, as well as colleges of medicine, engineering, business, and others are proof of the sultan's commitment to his first objective. The goal is to gradually phase out foreign workers so that by 2010, the workforce will be 90 percent Omani.[2] Oman joined the World Trade Organization in November 2000.

Qaboos has been equally successful with his second objective: in 2004, 70 percent of university students were women. Eighteen percent are in the workforce, and this is increasing rapidly. Women can vote; the ruler enfranchised all adult citizens age 21 and over, ending restrictions that had allowed only a quarter of citizens to vote.[3]

Oman is the leader in the Gulf in terms of women in government. In late 2004, a woman was named minister of social development; she is the third woman to hold a Cabinet portfolio and the fourth with ministerial rank. There are nine women in the Parliament and two in the Consultative Council. There is also one female ambassador abroad.[4]

Omanis are very friendly, warm people. Many foreigners greatly enjoy living there.

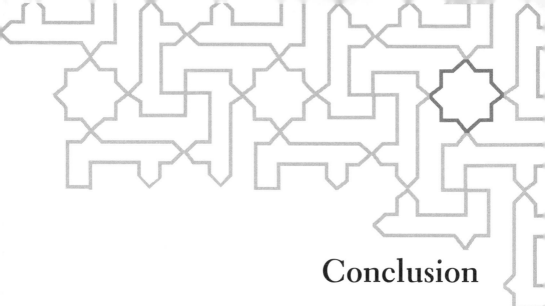

Conclusion

The more you socialize and interact with Arabs, the sooner you will abandon your stereotyped impressions of them. Individuals behave differently, but patterns emerge if you look for them. Soon you will be able to understand and even predict actions and reactions, some of which may be different from what you expected. Your task is to become aware of how and why things happen in order to feel comfortable with new social patterns as soon as possible.

Arab culture is complex but not unfathomable or totally exotic; many people find it similar to life in the Mediterranean area and Latin America.* Arabs are demonstrative, emotional, and full of zest for life, while at the same time bound by stringent rules and social expectations. Westerners need not feel obliged to imitate Arabs in order to be accepted. All that is necessary for harmonious relations is to be nonjudgmental and to avoid any actions that are insulting or shocking. Westerners, especially Americans, are accustomed to being open and upfront with beliefs and feelings. This forthrightness needs to be tempered when operating in the tradition- bound culture of the Middle East.

---

* This is due, in part, to the fact that the Arabs ruled Spain for the seven centuries preceding the discovery of the New World.

Arabs are accustomed to dealing with foreigners and expect them to behave and dress differently and to have different ideas from themselves. Foreigners are forgiven a great deal; even conservative people make allowances, particularly when they trust your motives. The essential thing is to make a sincere, well-meaning effort to adapt and understand. This attitude is readily apparent and will go a long way in helping you form comfortable work relations and friendships. Perhaps you will find yourself on good enough terms with an Arab friend to ask for constructive criticism from time to time. If you do, tactful hints will be offered—listen for them.

Most Arabs are genuinely interested in foreigners and enjoy talking to and developing friendships with them. But their attitude toward Westerners is a mixture of awe, goodwill, and puzzled wariness. They admire Westerners' education and expertise, and most of them have heard favorable reports from others who have visited Western countries. Many Arabs express the hope that they can visit or study in the West, and in some countries, travel and immigration to Western countries are popular.

At the same time Arabs feel that Western societies are too liberal in many ways and that Westerners are not careful enough about their personal and social appearance. Arabs have a great deal of pride and are easily hurt; thus, they are sensitive to any display of arrogance by Westerners and to implied criticisms. They also disapprove of and resent Western political policies in the Arab world.

Moving to an Arab country or interacting with Arabs need not be a source of anxiety. If you use common sense, make an effort to be considerate, and apply your knowledge of Arab customs and traditions, it will be easy to conduct yourself in a way which reflects creditably on your background and home country. At the same time, you will have a rich and rewarding experience.

Appendix:
The Arabic Language

Learning Arabic is indispensable for gaining a real insight into Arab society and culture. If you intend to study Arabic, you should choose the type that suits your own needs best.

Arabs associate foreign learners of Arabic with scholars, who (in the past) have tended to concentrate on Classical Arabic, so if you ask an Arab to give you lessons in Arabic, he or she will usually want to start with the alphabet and emphasize reading. If your interest is mainly in learning spoken Arabic, you will have to make that clear from the outset.

When you speak Arabic, you will find that your use of even the simplest phrases, no matter how poorly pronounced, will produce an immediate smile and comment of appreciation. I have had literally hundreds of occasions on which my willingness to converse in Arabic led to a delightful experience. A typical example occurred once when I was shopping in a small town in Lebanon and spent about half an hour chatting with the owner of one of the shops. When I was about to leave, he insisted on giving me a small brass camel, "because you speak Arabic."

Arabs are flattered by your efforts to learn their language (although they are convinced that no foreigner can ever master it), and they will do everything to encourage you. Even just a little Arabic is a useful tool for forming friendships and demonstrating goodwill.

Colloquial Arabic Dialects

The Arabic dialects fall into five geographical categories:

Category	Dialects	Native or Other Language Influence
1. North African (Western Arabic)	Moroccan Algerian Tunisian Libyan Mauretanian	Berber
2. Egyptian/Sudanese	Egyptian Sudanese	Turkish, Coptic, Nilotic
3. Levantine	Lebanese Syrian Palestinian	Local Semitic languages (Aramaic, Phoenician, Canaanite)
4. Arabian Peninsular	Jordanian Saudi Yemeni Kuwaiti Bahraini Qatari Emirates (Emirati) Omani	Farsi (in the Gulf states), Bedouin dialects, South Arabian languages
5. Iraqi*	Iraqi	Local Semitic languages (Assyrian, Chaldean) Farsi, Turkish

*Iraqi is essentially a non-urban dialect, with three distinct varieties, similar to both Jordanian and Kuwaiti Arabic.

Speakers of dialects in two of the categories — Egyptian/Sudanese and Levantine — have relatively little difficulty understanding each other. The North African, Iraqi, and Arabian Peninsular dialects, however, are relatively difficult for other Arabs to understand.

The most noticeable differences among dialects occur in the vocabulary, although there are grammatical discrepancies too. These variations should be taken into account when you are choosing a dialect to study, since it is almost useless to study a dialect different from the one spoken in the country to which you are going.

Simple words and phrases, such as greetings, vary widely, while technical and erudite words are usually the same. Educated Arabs get around this problem by using classical words, but a foreigner is more likely to experience each dialect as a different language. The following are examples of differences among dialects.

		Slightly Different		
	Egyptian	**Saudi**	**Moroccan**	
paper	*wara'a*	*waraga*	*werqa*	
	Jordanian	**Moroccan**	**Egyptian**	
beautiful	*jameela*	*jmila*	*gameela*	
	Saudi	**Tunisian**	**Lebanese**	
heavy	*tageel*	*thaqeel*	*ti'eel*	

		Completely Different		
	Lebanese	**Egyptian**	**Iraqi**	**Tunisian**
How are you?	*keefak?*	*izzayyak?*	*shlownak?*	*shniyya hwalak?*
	Moroccan	**Egyptian**	**Jordanian**	**Saudi**
now	*daba*	*dilwa'ti*	*halla'*	*daheen*
	Lebanese	**Kuwaiti**	**Moroccan**	**Egyptian**
good	*mneeh*	*zayn*	*mezyan*	*kwayyis*

Attitudes Toward Dialects

Arabs tend to regard their own dialect as the purest and the closest to Classical Arabic; I have heard this claim vigorously defended from Morocco to Iraq. In fact, though, where one dialect is closer to the Classical with respect to one feature, another dialect is closer with respect to another. No dialect can be successfully defended as pure except possibly the Najdi dialect spoken in central Arabia, which has been the most isolated from non-Arabic influences.

Arabs view the Bedouin dialects as semiclassical and therefore admirable, although a bit archaic. Most Arabs find the Egyptian dialect to be the most pleasing to listen to because the pronunciation is "light." Eastern Arabs tend to look down on western Arabic (North African) because of their difficulty in understanding the dialect (which they attribute, wrongly, to Berber usages). Most of the differences between western and eastern Arabic stem from changes in pronunciation and word stress.

Because all Arabs view their local dialect as the best, they are quick to advise a foreigner that theirs is the most useful, but usefulness depends entirely on where you are in the Arab world.

The Structure of Arabic

The structure of Arabic is like that of all Semitic languages. Its most striking feature is the way words are formed, which is called the "root and pattern" system. A root is a set of three consonants that carry the meaning of the word. The vowels in a word form patterns and, depending on how they are intermixed with the consonants, determine the part of speech of a word. The consonants and vowels have different functions in a word, and together, their combinations yield a rich vocabulary. Here are some examples from Classical Arabic, distinguishing roots and patterns (patterns may contain affixes — additional syllables added at the beginning, in the middle, or at the end of words).

		Meaning
Roots:	k-t-b	writing
	r-k-b	riding

Patterns:	-a-(a)-a	(completed action, past tense)
	(i)	
	-aa-i-	agent (one who does an action)
	ma—a-	place (where the action is done)
Words:	kataba	he wrote
	rakiba	he rode
	kaatib	writer, clerk
	raakib	rider
	maktab	(place for writing) office, desk
	markab	(place for riding) boat
	markaba	vehicle

As you learn vocabulary, you will notice that words that have the same core meaning come in varying patterns, but almost all can be reduced to a three-consonant base. For example, other words that share the consonants *k-t-h* are:

kitaab	book
kitaaba	writing
maktaba	library, bookstore
maktuub	letter, something written, fate

Personal names in Arabic usually have a meaning. Below is a group of names from the same three-consonant base, *h-m-d,* which means "to praise":

Muhammad	Hamdy
Mahmoud	Hammady
Hameed	Hamoud
Hamed	Ahmed

You can see why foreigners find Arabic names confusing.

Arabic pronunciation makes use of many sounds that do not occur in English, mostly consonants produced far back in the mouth and throat. Some of these consonants show up in the English spelling of words, such as *gh* (Baghdad), *kh* (Khartoum), *q* (Qatar), and *dh* (Riyadh). In Classical Arabic there are twenty-eight consonants, three long vowels, and three short vowels. In the Arabic dialects, some consonants have been dropped or merged with others, and some consonants and vowels have been added—features which distinguish one dialect from another.

Arabic Writing

The Arabic alphabet has twenty-eight letters and is written from right to left. Numerals, however, are written from left to right. Most letters connect with the preceding and following letters in the same word. Sometimes two or three sounds are written using the same letter; in this case they are differentiated from each other by the arrangement of dots, for example:

b	ب	r	ر	s	س
t	ت	z	ز	sh	ش
th	ث				

Because consonants carry the meaning of words, the Arabic alphabet (like all Semitic alphabets) includes only the consonants and the long vowels (for example, *aa*, which is a different vowel from *a* and is held longer when pronounced). The short vowels do not appear in the alphabet, but the Arab reader knows what they are and can pronounce the words correctly because these vowels come in predictable patterns. Additional signs (diacritical marks) mark short vowels, doubled consonants, and the like, but these are used only in texts for beginners—and are always included in the text of the Qur'an in order to assure correct reading.

The numerals in Arabic are very easy to learn. We refer to our own numbers as "Arabic numerals" because the system of using one symbol for 0 through 9 and adding new place values for tens, hundreds, and so forth, was borrowed from the Arabs to replace the Roman numeral system.

Nevertheless, although their numerals are used the same way as ours, they are not alike (note especially their numbers 5 and 6, which look like our 0 and 7).

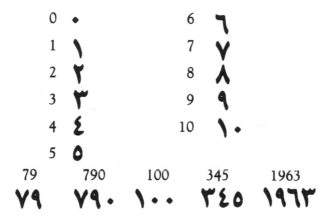

There are several styles of handwriting, and in each the shapes of the individual letters are slightly different. The difference between North African or western script, for instance, and eastern script is especially noticeable.

Calligraphy As an Art Form

Decorative calligraphy, as you might guess, is one of the highest artistic expressions of Arab culture. Most letters of the alphabet are full of flowing curves, so an artist can easily form them into elaborate designs. Calligraphy usually depicts Qur'anic quotations or favorite proverbs, and the patterns are often beautifully balanced and intricate. Calligraphic designs are widely used to decorate mosques, monuments, books, and household items such as brass trays.

Calligraphy and arabesque geometric designs have developed because of the Islamic injunction against paintings and statues in places of worship. This emphasis is very evident in Islamic architecture.

Social Greetings

Arabs use many beautiful, elaborate greetings and blessings—and in every type of situation. Most of these expressions are predictable—each situation calls for its own statements and responses. Situational expressions exist in English, but they are few, such as "How are you?"/"Fine," "Thank you"/"You're welcome," and "Have a nice day." In Arabic there are at least thirty situations that call for predetermined expressions. Although these are burdensome for a student of Arabic to memorize, it is comforting to know that you can feel secure about what to say in almost every social context.

There are formulas for greetings in the morning and evening, for meeting after a long absence, for meeting for the first time, and for welcoming someone who has returned from a trip. There are formulas for acknowledging accomplishments, purchases, marriage, or death and for expressing good wishes when someone is engaged in a task, or has just had a haircut! All of these situations have required responses, and they are beautiful in delivery and usually religious in content. Some examples follow.

English (Statement/Response)	Arabic Translation (Statement/Response)
Good morning./Good morning.	Morning of goodness./Morning of light.
Good-bye./Good-bye.	[Go] with safety./May God make you safe.
Happy to see you back./Thanks.	Thanks be to God for your safety./May God make you safe.
(Said when someone is working)	God give you strength./ God strengthen you.
(Said when discussing future plans)	May our Lord make it easy.
Good night./Good night.	May you reach morning in goodness./And may you be of the same group.
I'm taking a trip. What can I bring you?/What would you like?	Your safety.
I have news. Guess what I heard.	[May it be] good, God willing.

Conversational ritual expressions are much used in Arabic. Sometimes a ritual exchange of formalities can last five or ten minutes, particularly among older and more traditional people.

The Arabs have the charming custom of addressing strangers with kinship terms, which connotes respect and goodwill at the same time. One Western writer was struck by the use of these terms with strangers in Yemeni society (they are as widely used elsewhere).

"Brother, how can I help you?"

"Take this taxi, my sisters, I'll find another."

"My mother, it's the best that I can do."

"You're right, uncle."[1]

Ritualistic statements are required by etiquette in many situations. Meeting someone's small child calls for praise carefully mixed with blessings; for example, "May God keep him" or "[This is] what God wills." Such statements reassure the parents that you are not envious (you certainly would not add, "I wish I had a child like this!"). Blessings should also be used when seeing something of value, such as a new car or a new house. When someone purchases something, even a rather small item, the usual word is *Mabrook*, which is translated "Congratulations" but literally means "Blessed." Some of the most common phrases are given here.

English	Arabic
Hello./Hello.	*Marhaba./Marhabtayn.*
Good morning./Good morning.	*Sabah alkhayr./Sabah annoor.*
Peace be upon you./And upon you peace.	*Assalamu 'alaykum./Wa 'alaykum assalam.*
Good-bye./Good-bye. ([Go] with safety./May God make you safe.)	*Ma'a ssalama./Allah yisallimak.*
Thank you./You're welcome.	*Shukran./'Afwan.*
Congratulations./Thank you. (Blessed./May God bless you.)	*Mabrook./Allah yibarik feek.*

Welcome./Thanks. (Welcome./ Welcome to you.)	*Ahlan wa sahlan./Ahlan beek.*
If God wills.	*Inshallah.* (Said when speaking of a future event)
What God wills.	*Mashallah.* (Said when seeing a child or complimenting someone's health)
Thanks be to God.	*Alhamdu lillah.*
Thanks be to God for your safety.	*Hamdillah 'ala ssalama.* (Said when someone returns from a trip or recovers from an illness)

Some Arabic expressions sound much too elaborate to be used comfortably in English. There is no need to use them exactly in translation if you are speaking English, as long as you express good wishes.

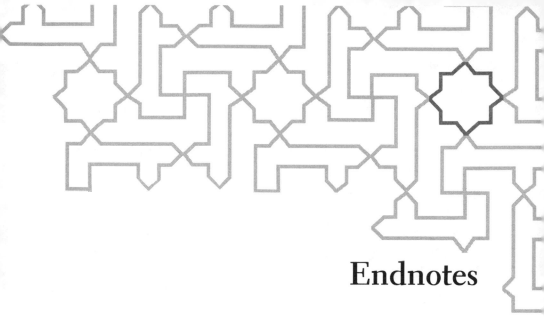

Endnotes

Preface

1. David Fromkin, *A Peace to End All Peace* (New York: Henry Holt, 1989), 306.

2. Raphael Patai, *The Arab Mind* (1973; reprint, Long Island, NY: The Hatherleigh Press, 2002).

3. David Bukay, "Islamic Fundamentalism and the Arabic Political Culture," *NATIV Online*, 3 April 2005, <http://www.acpr.org.il/ english-nativ/index.htm>.

Introduction: Patterns of Change

1. "Primary School-Age Population" and "Total Secondary Enrollment," *Global Education Database*, U.S. Agency for International Development, Center for Development Information and Evaluation, 2001, <http://www.esdb.cdie.org>.

2. "Saudi Arabia: Education," *MapZones*, 2002, <http://www. map-zones.com>.

3. "Saudi Arabia: Population, Health and Well-Being," *EarthTrends*, World Research Institute, 2002, <http://www.earthtrends. wri.org>.

4. "Middle East and North Africa 2001," *Europa*, European Union, 2001, <http://www.europa.edu.int>.

5. "Tertiary Gross Enrollment Ratio," *Global Education Database*, U.S. Agency for International Development, Center for Development Information and Evaluation, 2002, <http://esdb.cdie.org>.

6. Elizabeth Fernea, "Islamic Feminism Finds a Different Voice," *Foreign Service Journal* (May 2000): 30.

7. "The World's Women 2004, Trends and Statistics," U.N. Statistics Division, Demographic, 2004, <http://www.unstats.un.org>.

8. "Countries in Order of People per Doctor," *World Development Indicators*, 2001, <http://www.worldbank.org>.

9. "Physicians per 1000 Population," *Human Development Report 2004, Commitment to Health*, U.N. Development Programme, 2004, <http://hdr.undp.org/reports/global/2004>, 159.

10. "Statistics and Indicators on Men and Women," U.N. Statistics Division, Demographic, 2005, <http://www.unstats.un.org>.

11. "Population Growth," *Human Development Report 2005*, U.N. Development Programme, 2005, <http://hdr.undp.org>.

12. Ibid.

13. "Middle East Population Set to Double," *Popline*, Population Institute, 25 April 2002, <http://www.populationinstitute.org>.

14. "Growing Urbanization," *Human Development Report 1999*, UN Development Programme, 1999, < http://hdr.undp.org>.

15. Mostafa Kharoufi, "Urbanization and Urban Research in the Arab World," UNESCO, 1996, <http://www.unesco.org>.

16. "1999 Revision: Key Findings," *World Urbanization Prospects, World Global Trends*, 1999, <http://www.t21.ca>.

17. Mostafa Kharoufi, "Urbanization and Urban Research."

18. "Internet Users per 1,000 People," *Human Development Report 2004*, UN Development Programme, 2004, <http://www.hdr.undp.org>.

19. Colum Lynch, "Report Urges Arab Governments to Share Power," *The Washington Post*, 6 April 2005.

20. Marina Ottaway, "Listen to Arab Voices," *The Washington Post*, 5 April 2005.

21. David K. Willis, "The Impact of Islam," *Christian Science Monitor*, weekly international edition, 18–24 August 1984.

22. Ahmad S. Mousalli, *Moderate and Radical Islamic Fundamentalism* (Gainesville: University Press of Florida, 1999), 181–86.

23. Benazir Bhutto, "Politics and the Modern Woman," in *Liberal Islam, A Sourcebook*, edited by Charles Kurzman (New York: Oxford University Press, 1998), 107.

24. Muhammad Sayyid Qutb, "The Role of Religion in Education," in *Aims and Objectives of Islamic Education*, ed. S. N. Al-Attas (Jeddah: King Abdulaziz University, 1979), 60.

25. Osman Bakar, *The History and Philosophy of Islamic Science* (Cambridge, England: Islamic Texts Society, 1999), 214.

26. Thabet Asim, "The Muslim Science Wars: Modern Muslim Discussion on Science," *Muslims Under Progress* (UK), 2005, <http://www.underprogress.blogs.com>.

27. "Current Religious Affairs Consultation Meeting, Final Communique," Higher Council of Religious Affairs, 18 May 2002, <http://www.turkishpolicy.com>.

Chapter One: Beliefs and Values

1. "Egypt," *Encarta Online Encyclopedia 2005*, Microsoft, 2005, <http://uk.encarta.msn.com>.

2. Desmond Stewart, *The Arab World* (New York: Time Life Books, 1972), 9–10.

3. Halim Barakat, *The Arab World: Society, Culture, and the State* (Berkeley: University of California Press, 1993), 21.

4. Patricia Donovan, "The 'Illegitimacy Bonus' and State Efforts to Reduce Out-of-Wedlock Births," *Family Planning Perspectives 31, no. 2*, March/April 1999, <http://www.agi-usa.org>.

Chapter Two: Friends and Strangers

1. Recorded December 2004 in Doha, Qatar.

2. David K. Shipler, *Arab and Jew, Wounded Spirits in a Promised Land* (New York: Penguin Books, 1986), 387.

3. Ghada Karmi, *In Search of Fatima, A Palestinian Story* (London: Verso, 2002), 181.

Chapter Three: Emotion and Logic

1. George N. Atiyeh, *Arab and American Cultures* (Washington, DC: American Enterprise Institute for Public Policy Research, 1977), 179.

2. T. E. Lawrence, *The Seven Pillars of Wisdom* (New York: Doubleday, 1926), 24.

Chapter Four: Getting Personal

1. Edward T. Hall, *The Hidden Dimension* (New York: Doubleday, 1966), 15.

2. Anthony Shadid, "Hussein's Baghdad Falls," *The Washington Post*, 10 April 2003.

Chapter Five: Men and Women

1. Dina Ezzat, "Fortifying Women's Rights," *Al-Ahram Weekly*, 17–23 June 2004, <http://www.weekly.ahram.org.eg>.

2. Ibid.

3. Elizabeth Fernea, "Islamic Feminism Finds a Different Voice," *Foreign Service Journal* (May 2000): 27.

4. Julia Choucair, "Dates of Women's Suffrage and Current Ministerial Positions Held by Women in Arab Countries," Carnegie Endowment for International Peace, 2004, <http://www.ceip.org>.

5. Jim Hoagland, "The Unheralded Revolution," *The Washington Post*, 24 February 2005.

6. Julia Choucair, "Women in Parliament in the Arab World," Carnegie Endowment for International Peace, 2004, <http://www.ceip.org>.

7. Joelle Bassoul, "Iraqi Women Poised for Parliament," *The Monday Phenomenon*, 15 February 2005, <http://www.iafrica.com>.

8. "Enhancing Women's Political Participation through Social Measures in the Arab Region," *International IDEA*, National Council for Women (Egypt), U.N. Development Programme, 2005, <http://www.ncwegypt.com>.

9. Karen Armstrong, *Muhammad, A Biography of the Prophet* (San Francisco: HarperSanFrancisco, 1992), 198.

10. Ibid., 199.

11. Megan Stack, "The Many Layers of the Veil," *Los Angeles Times*, 12 January 2005.

12. Thomas Omstad, "The Casbah Connection," *U.S. News and World Report*, 9 May 2005, 28.

13. Theodore Bergstrom, "On the Economics of Polygyny," Centre on Economics Learning and Social Evolution (ELSE), 1994, <http://www.nctec.mcc.ac.uk>.

14. Bernard Lewis, "Targeted by a History of Hatred," *The Washington Post*, 10 September 2002.

15. Donna Lee Bowen and Evelyn A. Early, eds., *Everyday Life in the Muslim Middle East* (Bloomington: Indiana University Press, 1993), 77.

16. "Quotation of the Day," *The New York Times*, 13 April 2005.

Chapter Six: Social Formalities and Etiquette

1. Aida Hasan, "Arab Culture and Identity—Arab Food and Hospitality," *Suite University Online*, 1999, <http://www.suite101.com>.

Chapter Eight: The Role of the Family

1. Thomas Collelo, ed., *Syria: A Country Study*, 3 ed. (Washington DC: Department of the Army, 1988), 81–82.

2. Alean Al-Krenawi, and John R. Graham, "Principles of Social Work Practice in the Muslim Arab World," *Arab Studies Quarterly* 25, no. 4 (Fall 2003): 85.

3. "Fatima Urges Protection of Arab Family," *UAE Interact*, Ministry of Information and Culture, 1999, <http://www.uaeinteract.com>.

4. Hanan Hamamy, "Consanguineous Marriages in the Arab World," National Centre for Diabetes, Endocrinology and Genetics, Amman, Jordan, *The Ambassadors*, July 2003, <http://www.ambassadors.net>.

5. Ibid.

Chapter Nine: Religion and Society

1. Ziauddin Sardar, *Introducing Muhammad* (New York: Totem Books, 1994), 48.

2. Thomas Lippman, *Understanding Islam, An Introduction to the Muslim World* (New York: Penguin Books, 1990), 13.

Chapter Ten: Communicating With Arabs

1. Leslie J. McLoughlin, *Colloquial Arabic (Levantine)* (London: Routledge and Kegan Paul, 1982), 2–3.

Chapter Eleven: Islamic Fundamentalism (Islamism)

1. Daniel Pipes, *Militant Islam Reaches America* (New York: W.W. Norton & Co., 2003), 247, 248.

2. Mark Clayton, "How Are Mosques Fighting Terror?" *Christian Science Monitor*, 12 August 2004.

3. Steven Emerson, *American Jihad, The Terrorists Living Among Us* (New York: Free Press, 2002), 41.

4. Eric Boehlert, "Terrorists under the Bed," *Salon.com*, 5 March 2002, <http://www.salon.com>.

5. Abdul Wahab Bashir, "Scholars Define Terrorism, Call for Joint Action to Defend Islam," *Arab News*, 12 January 2002, <http://www.arab-news. com>.

6. Karen Armstrong, *Muhammad, A Biography of the Prophet*, (San Francisco: HarperSanFrancisco, 1992), 168.

7. Riad Saloojie, "The Nature of Islam," *The Globe and Mail* (Canada), 16 January 2000, <http://www.theglobeandmail.com>.

8. Daniel Williams, "Unveiling Islam: Author Challenges Orthodox Precepts," *The Washington Post*, 7 March 2005.

9. Peter Williams, "Fighting through Listening," *Al-Ahram Weekly*, 8–14 April 2004, <http://www.ahram.org.eg>

10. "Worldwide Suicide Rates," Suicide and Mental Health Association International, February, 2005, <http://www.suicideandmental healthassociationinternational.org>.

11. Jackie Spinner, "An Attack Burns Anguish into Kurdish Region," *The Washington Post*, 6 February 2005.

12. "Islam, Jihad, and Terrorism," Institute of Islamic Information and Education, 14 October 2004, <http://www.iiie.net>.

13. Jonathon Steele, "Terrorism Is Not an Enemy State that Can Be Defeated," *The Guardian* (UK), 23 November 2003, <http://www.guardian.co.uk>.

14. "Spanish Muslims Issue Fatwa against Usama," *U.S. and World*, Fox News.com, 11 March 2005, <http://www.foxnews.com>.

15. Deborah Caldwell, "'Something Major Is Happening: Are We Witnessing the Beginnings of an Islamic Reformation?" Beliefnet, December 2001, <http://www.beliefnet.com>.

16. Mary Beth Sheridan, "Sensitizing Police Toward Muslims," *The Washington Post*, 6 October 2003.

17. "Report Instances of Extremism or Support of Terrorism," Free Muslims Against Terrorism, 2005, <http://www.freemuslims.org>.

18. Erica Simmons, "A Passion for Justice," *New Internationalist*, no. 210, August 1990, 9.

19. Robin Wright, "In Mideast, Shiites May Be Unlikely U.S. Allies," *The Washington Post*, 16 March 2005.

Chapter Twelve: Anti-Americanism

1. Khaled Dawood. "Arab Opinions," *Al-Ahram Weekly*, 30 July 2004, <http://www.ahram.org.eg>

2. James J. Zogby, *What Arabs Think* (Washington, DC: Zogby International, 2002), 64.

3. Jonathon Schell, "Iraq's Unpredictable Politics," *The Nation*, 11 February 2005, <http://www.thenation.com>.

4. Ussama Makdisi, "Anti-Americanism in the Arab World: An Interpretation of a Brief History," *Journal of American History* 89, no. 2 (September 2002): 538–39.

5. Mahmoud Al-Tohami, "The Reasons for the Enmity and Hatred," *Alam-al-Youm* (Egypt), 1 September 2002, <http://www.worldpress.org>

6. Shibley Telhami, *The Stakes* (Boulder, CO: Westview Press, 2002), 39.

7. Sheldon Richman, "Another Frankenstein's Monster," *Commentaries*, The Future of Freedom Foundation, 27 December 2002, <http://www.fff.org/comment>.

8. Rashid Khalidi, *Resurrecting Empire: Western Footprints and America's Perilous Path in the Middle East* (Boston: Beacon Press, 2004), xii.

9. Scott McConnell, "Why Many Arabs Hate America," Media Monitors Network, 12 September 2001, <http://www.mediamonitors.net>.

10. "CIA Insider: The Threat We Refuse to Get," *The Washington Post*, 11 July 2004.

11. Anthony Shadid, "Old Arab Friends Turn Away from U.S.," *The Washington Post*, 26 February 2003.

12. Larry Johnson, "Commentary," *Seattle Post Intelligencer*, 20 June 2004, <http://www.seattlepi.nwssource.com>.

13. M. Shahid Alam, "The Clash Thesis: A Failing Ideology?" Common Dreams News Center, 2004,< http://www.commondreams.org>

14. "Complete Text of President Bush's National Address," *Globe and Mail* (Canada), 12 September 2001, <http://www.theglobeand-mail.com>

15. Gilbert P. Blythe, "We Are All Jews Now," *The Last Ditch*, WTM Enterprises, 19 October 2003, <http://www.thornwalker.com>.

16. Donald Rumsfeld, "Rumsfeld on Message of 9–11," International Broadcasting Bureau, U.S. Government, 11 September 2002, <www.ibb.gov>.

17. Alam, "The Clash Thesis."

18. Ibid.

19. John McCain, "The Road to Baghdad," *Time*, 9 September 2002, 107.

20. Philip Kennicott, "An About-Face on America," *The Washington Post*, 24 August 2004.

21. Rime Allaf, "Dangerous Delusions," *The Daily Star* (Beirut), 3 October 2001, <http://www.worldpress.org>.

22. Ralph Peters, *Beyond Terror* (Mechanicsburg, PA: Stackpole Books, 2002), 35.

23. Ibid., 54.

24. "Why the Islamic World Has Such Hate for the U.S." *Hardball with Chris Matthews*, MSNBC, 19 October 2001, <http://www.msnbc.msn.com>.

25. "Hughes's Role To Be Outreach to Muslims," *The Washington Post*, 15 March 2005.

26. Robin Wright, "U.S. Struggles to Win Hearts, Minds in the Muslim World," *The Washington Post*, 20 August 2004.

27. Ibid.

28. Michael Holtzman, "Washington's Sour Sales Pitch," *The New York Times*, 4 October 2003.

29. Karin DeYoung. "Poll finds Arabs Dislike U.S. Based on Policies It Pursues," *The Washington Post*, 7 October 2002.

30. Ranae Merle, "Pentagon Funds Diplomacy Effort," *The Washington Post*, 11 June 2005.

31. Edward Djerejian (Chairman), "Changing Minds, Winning Peace," (submitted to the Committee on Appropriations, U.S. House of Representatives), 1 October, 2003, 5.

32. Barry Rubin, "The Real Roots of Arab Anti-Americanism," *Foreign Affairs*, (November/December 2002): 80.

33. Lee Smith, "Democracy Inaction: Understanding Arab Anti-Americanism," *Slate*, 23 April 2004, <http://www.slate.msn.com>.

34. Bernard Lewis, "The Roots of Muslim Rage," *The Atlantic Monthly* 266, no.3 (September 1990): 56.

35. _____, "Targeted by a History of Hatred," *The Washington Post*, 10 September 2002.

36. Samuel P. Huntington, "The Clash of Civilizations," *Foreign Affairs* 72, no. 3 (Summer 1993): 31–32.

37. _____, *The Clash of Civilizations and the Remaking of World Order* (New York: Simon and Schuster, 1996), 211.

38. Mary McGrory. "Nuancing the Mideast Dilemma," *The Washington Post*, 14 April 2002.

39. Dawood, "Arab Opinions."

40. "UN Report: Most Arab Youth Want to Emigrate to Europe, U.S.," *World Tribune.com*, 21 July 2002, <http://www.worldtribune.com>.

41. "Anti-Americanism: What's New, What's Next?", *World Economic Forum*, 2002, <http://www.weforum.org>.

42. Sharon Waxman. "I Love You, Now Go Away," (quoting Farouk Hosny, Egyptian Minister of Culture), *The Washington Post*, 17 December 2001.

43. DeYoung, "Poll Finds Arabs Dislike U.S."

44. Dafna Linzer, "Poll Shows Growing Arab Rancor at U.S.," *The Washington Post*, 23 July 2004.

45. Michael Dobbs, "Arab Hostility toward U.S. Growing, Poll Finds," *The Washington Post*, 4 June 2003.

46. "Views of Changing World," *Pew Global Attitudes Project*, June 2003, <http://www.people-press.org>.

47. Abdel Mahdi Abdallah, "Causes of Anti-Americanism in the Arab World: A Socio-Political Perspective," *Middle East Review of International Affairs* 7, no. 4 (December 2003): 68.

48. Rami Khouri, "For Arabs, A Cruel Echo of History," *The Daily Star* (Beirut), 21 March 2003, <http://www.dailystar.com.lb>.

49. Charles Krauthammer, "Why It Deserves the Hype," *Time*, 14 February 2005, 80.

50. _____, "What's Left? Shame," *The Washington Post*, 18 March 2005.

51. Fouad Ajami, "Bush Country," *The Daily Star* (Beirut), 23 May 2005, <http://www.dailystar.com.lb>.

52. _____. "The Meaning of Lebanon," The Foundation for the Defense of Democracy, 1 May 2005, <http://www.defenddemocracy.org>.

53. Charles Krautthammer, "Syria and the New Axis of Evil," *The Washington Post*, 1 April 2005.

54. Elizabeth Cheney, "U.S. Supports Democracy in Every Nation, Culture," U.S. Department of State, 14 June 2005, <http://usinfo.state.gov>.

55. Neil MacFarquhar, "Syria Reaches Turning Point, But Which Way Will It Turn?" *The New York Times*, 12 March 2001.

56. David Barsamian, interview: Robert Fisk, *The Progressive*, June 2005, 42.

57. Joshua Mitchell, "Not All Yearn to Be Free," *The Washington Post*, 10 August 2003.

58. "Unprecedented Opportunity," The Center for Public Integrity, interview with Rami Khoury, 16 March 2005, <http://www.publicintegrity.org>.

59. Ibid.

60. Huntington, "The Clash of Civilizations," 209, 217.

61. Nicholas Kristof, "Bigotry in Islam and Here," *The New York Times*, 9 July 2002.

62. Franklin Graham, "My View of Islam," *Covenant News*, 9 December 2001, <http://www.covenantnews.com>.

63. "A Conservative Christian Group Sues the U.N.C. for Assigning a Book on Islam," *Democracy Now*, 8 August 2002, <http://www.democracynow.org>.

64. Ralph Peters, *Beyond Terror* (Mechanicsburg, PA: Stackpole Books, 2002), 6.

65. "Islam Is Violent," *Jesus-Is-Lord*, <http://www.jesus-is-lord.com>.

66. Alexander Kronemer, "Understanding Muhammad," *Christian Science Monitor*, 9 December 2002.

67. Nassir M. Al-Ajmi, "Heart to Heart Talk—A Friend to Friend Discussion," The Ladah Foundation, 23 October 2003, <http://www.ladah.org>.

68. "Not at War against Islam," *Bush on Muslims*, 5 January 2002, <http://www.muslimsforbush.com>.

69. "Islam Is Love," *Bush on Muslims*, 10 September 2002, <http://www.muslimsforbush.com>.

70. Ian Buruma, "Lost in Translation," *The New Yorker*, June 2004, 186.

71. Kristof, "Bigotry in Islam."

72. Emily Wax, "Jihad Is Taught as Struggle to Heal," *The Washington Post*, 23 September 2002.

73. Rodrique Ngawi, "Rwanda Turns to Islam after Genocide," *Times Daily*, 7 November 2002, <http://www.timesdaily.com>.

74. Kofi Annan, "Confronting Islamophobia: Education for Tolerance and Understanding," Address to the DPI Seminar, Document SG/SM/9637, 7 December 2004, <http://www.un.org>.

Chapter 13: Arabs and Muslims in the West

1. Ray Hanania, "Failure to Understand Arab-Muslim Issues Exposes Nation to Attacks," 11 March 2005, <http://www.hananiacreators.blogspot.com>.

2. "Census 2000: Portrait of the Nation," *The Washington Post*, 5 June 2002.

3. Ibid.

4. Genaro Armas, "Census Bureau Says People of Arab Descent Doing Well in the United States," *Detroit Free Press*, 9 March 2005.

5. Helen Samhan, "Arab Americans," Arab American Institute, 2001, <http://www.aaiusa.org>.

6. Mazin Qumsiyeh, "100 Years of Anti-Arab and Anti-Muslim Stereotyping," *The Prism*, Arab-American Anti-Discrimination Committee, January 1998, <http://www.ibiblio.org/prism>.

7. Hanania, "Failure to Understand."

8. "Healing the Nation: Arab American Response to September 11 Attacks," Arab American Institute, 2001, <http://www.aaiusa.org>.

9. Jonah Blank, "The Muslim Mainstream," *U.S. News and World Report*, 20 July 1998, 22.

10. D'Vera Cohn, "Statistics Portray Settled, Affluent Mideast Community," *The Washington Post*, 20 November 2001.

11. Abdul Malik Mujahid, "Muslims in America: Profile 2001," SoundVision.com, 2001, <http://www.soundvision.com>.

12. Ihsan Bagby, Paul Perl, and Bryan Froehle, "The Mosque in America: A National Portrait," Washington D.C.: Council on American Islamic Relations, 26 April 2001, <http://www.cair-net.org>.

13. Abdul Malik Mujahid, "Profile of Muslims in Canada," *Toronto Muslims.com*, 20 April 2004, <http://www.torontomuslims.com>.

14. "How Many Muslims Are in the U.S. and the Rest of the World?" Ontario Consultants on Religious Tolerance, 2002, <http://www.religioustolerance.org>.

15. Mike Barber, "Muslims in the U.S. Military Are as Loyal as Any, Chaplain Says," *Seattle Post-Intelligencer*, 20 October 2001.

16. John Zogby, "American Muslim Poll, November-December 2001," Washington DC: Zogby International, 2001, <http://www.amperspective. com>.

17. Virginia Culver, "Many American Muslims Well-Off, College Educated, Poll Shows," *The Denver Post*, 18 January 2002.

18. Jane Lampman, "Muslim in America," *Christian Science Monitor*, 10 January 2002.

19. Ibid.

20. M. A. Muqtedar Khan, "American Muslims Push for Role in Policy Planning," The Brookings Institution, *Daily Times*, 25 December 2004, <http://www.brookings.edu>.

21. Ross Douthat, "A Muslim Europe?" *The Atlantic Monthly*, January/February 2005, 58.

22. "Intolerance and Discrimination against Muslims in the EU: Developments since September 11," International Helsinki Federation for Human Rights, March 2005, <http://www.ihf-hr.org>, 11.

23. Tamer Abul Einein and Ahmed Al-Matboli, "Austrian Muslims Score Big in 2004," *American Muslim Perspective*, Islam Online, 4 January 2004, <http://www.islamonline.net>.

24. Douthat, "A Muslim Europe?"

25. Charles Bremmer, "Stoned to Death: Why Europe Is Starting to Lose Its Faith in Islam," *Times Online* (UK), 4 April 2004, <http://www.timesonline.co.uk>.

26. Robin Shepherd, "In Europe, Is It a Matter of Fear or Loathing?" *The Washington Post*, 25 January 2004.

27. Keith Richberg, "French President Urges Ban on Headscarves," *The Washington Post*, 18 December 2003.

28. Alaa Bayoumi, "Integrating European Muslims: Europe's Fearful Bid," Islam Online, 17 March 2004, <http://www.islamonline.net>.

29. Tracy Wilkinson, "Promise of Mosque Unfulfilled in Athens," *The Washington Post*, 17 March 2004.

30. "Intolerance and Discrimination," 11–12.

31. "Muslim Communities in Eastern Europe and Baltic Countries," Islam Online, February 2005, <http://www.islamonline.net>.

32. Jeffrey Fleischman, "Minarets Rise in Germany," *Los Angeles Times*, 17 March 2004.

33. "France Pledges Protection for Mosques." Islam Online, 9 March 2004, <http://www.islamonline.net>.

34. Ridwaan Jawdat, "Islam Fastest Growing Faith in Australia," *Arab News*, 25 October 2004, <http://www.arabnews.com>.

35. Wilkinson, "Promise of Mosque."

36. Omer Taspinar, "Europe's Muslim Street," *Foreign Policy* 135, (March/April 2003): 77.

37. Jim Hoagland, "In Europe, The Enemy Within," *The Washington Post*, 26 February 2004.

38. Taspinar, "Europe's Muslim Street."

39. "EU Opens Debate on Economic Migration." EurActiv, 14 January 2005, <http://www.euractiv.com>.

40. Yvonne Haddad and Jane Smith, eds., *Muslim Minorities in the West: Visible and Invisible* (New York: Altamira Press, 2002), xii.

41. Shelley Slade, "The Image of the Arab in America: Analysis of a Poll of American Attitudes," *Middle East Journal* 35, no. 2 (Spring 1981): 143.

42. Brian Whitaker, "Why the Rules of Racism Are Different for Arabs," *The Guardian* (UK), 18 August 2000.

43. Kerstin Grimsley, "More Arabs, Muslims Allege Bias on the Job," *The Washington Post*, 12 February 2001.

44. Alan Cooperman, "September 11 Backlash Murders and the State of Hate," *The Washington Post*, 20 January 2002.

45. Caryle Murphy, "Distrust of Muslims Common in U.S., Poll Finds," *The Washington Post*, 5 October 2004.

46. William J. Kole, "Hostility and Discrimination toward Muslims Widespread in EU," *Al-Jazeerah*, 14 September 2004, <http://www.aljazeerah.info>.

47. "EU Laments Growing Hostility to Muslims since 9/11," *EU Business*, 22 May 2003, <http://www.eubusiness.com>.

48. "Intolerance and Discrimination," 11–12.

49. Dina Ezzat, "Rewriting the Textbooks," *Al-Ahram Weekly*, 16–22 December 2004, <http://www.weeklyahram.org.eg>.

50. Fleischman, "Minarets Rise in Germany."

51. "Majority of Europeans Unhappy with Muslims," *Euro-Islam.Info*, World Affairs Board, December 2004, <http://www.worldaffairsboard.com>.

52. "A Year after Iraq War," The Pew Research Center, 16 March 2004, <http://www.people-press.org>.

53. Peter Ford, "What Place for God in Europe?" *Christian Science Monitor*, 22 February 2005, <http://www.people-press.org>.

54. Tariq Ramadan, *Western Muslims and the Future of Islam* (Oxford: Oxford University Press, 2004), 143.

55. _____, "Muslims in Italy," in *Muslims in the West: From Sojourners to Citizens*, edited by Yvonne Haddad (New York: Oxford University Press, 2002), 161.

56. Dominic Casciani, "Rise in Muslim Discrimination," *Community Affairs*, BBC News, 16 December 2004, <http://www.bbc.co.uk>.

57. Jan Jun, "U.K.: Report Says Britain's Muslims Most Underpriviledged Religious Group," Muslim Public Affairs Committee U.K., 25 October 2004, <http://www.forum.mpacuk.org>.

58. Dominic Casciani, "Islamophobia Pervades UK—Report," *Community Affairs, BBC News*, 2 June 2004, <http://www.news.bbc.co.uk>.

59. Vertovec, Steven, and Ceri Peach, eds. "Introduction," in *Islam in Europe, The Politics of Religion and Community* (London: Macmillan, 1997), 3–47.

60. Ray Furlong, "Germans Argue over Integration," *BBC News*, 30 November 2004, <http://www.bbc.co.uk>.

61. "Anti-Muslim Bias Spreads in EU," *BBC News*, 7 March 2005, <http://www.bbc.co.uk>.

62. "Germans Have Negative View of Islam," *Expatica*, BUPA International, 16 September 2004, <http://www.expatica.com>.

63. "Study Shows What Germans Think about Islam," *Deutsche Welle* (Broadcaster), 27 July 2003, <http://www.dw-world.de>.

64. Christopher Caldwell, "Allah Mode: France's Islam Problem," *The Weekly Standard* 7, no. 42, (15 July 2002), <http://www.weeklystandard.com>.

65. "Anti-Muslim Bias."

66. Jocelyne Cesari, "Islam in France: The Shaping of a Religious Minority," in *Muslims in the West: From Sojourners to Citizens*, edited by Yvonne Haddad (New York: Oxford University Press, 2002), 39.

67. "Situation of Muslims in Denmark: A Major Part of LWF Inter-religious Study on Conflict," Lutheran World Federation, 11 December 2003, <http://www.lutheranworld.org>.

68. Mustafa Abdel-Halim, "Denmark Imposes Restrictions on Imams," Islam Online, 18 February 2004, <http://www.islamonline.net>.

69. "Denmark Rejects Headscarf Plea," *BBC News Europe*, 21 January 2005, <http://www.news.bbc.co.uk>.

70. Shada Islam, "The Plot Thickens: Testing European Tolerance," *Yale Global Online*, 17 November 2004, <http://www.yaleglobal.yale.edu>.

71. Dan Bilefsky, "In Netherlands, Some Muslims Work to Convince Voters Islam Is Tolerant," *The Wall Street Journal*, 23 May 2002.

72. Tom Carter, "Tolerance Tested in Holland," *Washington Times*, 20 December 2004.

73. Ibid.

74. Hadi Yahmid, "Belgium Recognizes Muslim Executive Body," Islam Online, 2003, <http://www.islamonline.net>.

75. "Belgium Bans Popular Racist Party," *Dhimmi Watch*, November 2004, <http://www.jihadwatch.org/dhimmiwatch>.

76. Al-Amin Andalusi, "Spanish Muslims Renew Anti-Terror Stand," Islam Online, 9 March 2005, http://www.islamonline.net.

77. "When the Voiceless Speak," *Al-Ahram Weekly*, 1–7 April 2005, <http://www.ahram.org.eg>.

78. Ibid.

79. Daniel Williams, "Immigrants Keep Islam–Italian Style," *The Washington Post*, 24 July 2004.

80. "News from Italy: Immigrazione Pera," *Euro-Islam.info.*, 29 December 2004, <http://64.207.171.242/pages/news_italy.html>.

81. Abdal-Hakim Murad, "Muslims and the European Right," *The American Muslim*, September/October 2000, <http://www.theamerican muslim.org>.

82. Jim Hoagland, "The Word in Paris," *The Washington Post*, 21 July 2002.

83. Jawdat, "Islam Fastest Growing Faith."

84. Hanan Dover, "Siege Mentality: Current Australian Muslim Response," Forum on Australia's Islamic Relations (FAIR), 2 November 2003, <http://www.fair.org.au>.

85. Jayne-Maree Sedgman, "Discrimination Isolates Muslim Australians," *ABC News Online*, 17 June 2004, <http://www.abc.net.au>.

86. Robert Spencer, "Death Knell of the West," *FrontPageMagazine.com*, 22 December 2004, <http://www.frontpagemag.com>.

87. Sarah Wildman, "Third Way Speaks to Europe's Young Muslims," *International Reporting Project*, Johns Hopkins University School of Advanced International Studies, Spring 2003, <http://www.journalismfellowships.org>.

88. Ramadan, "Western Muslims," 6.

89. Martin A. Lee, "Not a Prayer," *Harper's Magazine*, June 2004, 77.

90. Ibid., 79.

91. Jeff Chu and Nadia Mustafa, "Her Turn to Pray," *Time*, 28 March 2005, 49.

Chapter 14: The Arab Countries—Similarites and Differences

1. Suleiman Al-Khaledi, "Iraqi Economic Recovery Seen in 2005—World Bank," Global Policy, 2004, <http://www.globalpolicy.org>.

2. "Tasks and Challenges of the Reconstruction of Iraq," *Baghdad Economic Research Center*, Center for International Private Enterprise, 2001, <http://www.cipe.org>.

3. "Libya: Economy," *ExxUN*, 2003 <http://www.exxun.com>.

4. "Qatar is the Richest Arab Nation; Among Top 20 in the World," Qatar National Bank, 2004, <http://www.qnb.com.qa>.

5. Ibid.

The Maghrib

6. "Berber Languages," *Columbia Encyclopedia*, 6th ed. 2005, <www.bartleby.com>.

7. "Berber Languages," *Wikipedia*, 2004, <http://www.en. wikipedia. org>.

Morocco

1. Nabil Oumimoun, "Teaching Berber in the Moroccan Primary Schools," Amazigh World, 2004, <http://www.amazighworld.net>.

2. Sebastian Usher, "The Berber Language Is Being Taught in Moroccan Schools for the First Time on Monday," *BBC News World Edition*, 15 September 2003, <http://www.bbc.co.uk>.

3. Craig Whitlock, "Moroccans Gain Prominence in Terror Groups," *The Washington Post*, 14 October 2004.

4. Ibid.

5. Thomas Omestad, "The Casbah Connection," *U.S. News and World Report*, 9 May 2005, 24.

6. "Working Conditions in Morocco," CCC, Spanish Clean Clothes Campaign, 2003, <http://www.cleanclothes.org>.

7. Elizabeth Fernea, "Islamic Feminism Finds a Different Voice," *Foreign Service Journal* (30 May 2000): 30.

8. "Morocco: Country Reports on Human Rights Practices 2004," U.S. Department of State, 28 February 2005, <http://www.state.gov>.

9. "Morocco: Husbands and Wives Now Equal," *Cairo Times*, 26 January-11 February 2004, <http://www.cairotimes.com>.

10. Susan Sachs, "Where Muslim Traditions Meet Modernity," *The New York Times*, 17 December 2001.

11. David Lamb, "In a Region of Hate, Morocco is the Land of Harmony," *Los Angeles Times*, 25 October 1995.

12. "Historical Ties Leave Trying Legacy," *Christian Science Monitor*, 27 January 1993.

13. "Working Conditions in Morocco."

Algeria

1. Historical Ties Leave Trying Legacy," *Christian Science Monitor*, 27 January 1993.

2. Craig Smith, "Voices of the Dead Echo across Algeria," *The New York Times*, 18 April 2004.

3. "Algeria: Agri-Food Country Profile," *Agri-Food Trade Service* (Canada), July 2004, <http://atnriae.agr.ca>.

4. "Where the North Meets the South, the Pollution Charges Fly," *Christian Science Monitor*, 27 January 1993.

5. "Algeria Election: Reluctant Youth," *Arab-American Journal* (23 December 2004), <www.arabamerican.com>.

6. "Algeria: Agri-Food Country Profile."

7. Paul DeBendern, "Algeria to Press Ahead with Women's Rights Bill," *Jordan Times*, 16 September 2004, <http://www.jordantimes.com>.

Tunisia

1. "Tunisia," *World Report*, Human Rights Watch, 2004, <http://www.hrw.org>.

2. Kamel Labidi, "The Wrong Man to Promote Democracy," *Los Angeles Times*, 21 January 2004.

3. "Tunisia: Economy," Travel Document Systems, 2005, <http://www. traveldocs.com>.

4. "Tunisia: Education," Tunisia Online, 2001, <http://www.tunisiaonline.com>.

5. "Tunisia: Women and Civil Rights," Tunisia Online, 2002, <http://www.tunisiaonline.com>.

6. "Tunisia: International Religious Freedom Report 2003," Bureau of Democracy, Human Rights and Labor, U.S. Department of State, 18 December, 2003, <http://www.state.gov>.

7. Ibid.

Libya

1. J. A. Allen, *Libya: The Experience of Oil* (Boulder, CO: Westview Press, 1981), 22.

2. "Human Trafficking in Libya," *The Villager* 74, no. 34 (December/January 2004), <http://www.thevillager.com>.

3. Nick Clark, "Education in Libya," *World Education News and Reviews*, July/August 2004, <http://www.wes.org>.

4. "Libya: Economy," *CIA World Factbook 2004*, 2004, <http://www.cia.gov>.

5. Ibid.

Egypt

1. "Egypt," *Encarta Online Encyclopedia*, Microsoft Corp., 2005, <http://www.encarta.msn.com>.

2. Paul Mitchell, "Egypt Reintroduces Food Vouchers as Poverty Worsens," World Socialist Web Site, 5 May 2004, <http://www.wsws.org>.

3. Sharon Waxman, "I Love You, Now Go Away," *The Washington Post*, 17 December 2001.

4. Lee Smith, "Egypt's Islamist Dilemma," *The Nation* 227, no. 18 (1 December 2003): 23.

5. Willow Wilson, "The Show-Me Sheikh," *The Atlantic Monthly*, July/August 2005, 40.

6. "Distribution of the Islamic Ruling on Smoking in 53,000 Mosques across Egypt," *Tobacco Free Initiative*, World Health Organization, 2005, <http://www.enro.who.int>.

7. Daniel Williams, "Egypt Reins in Opponents of Longtime Leader," *The Washington Post*, 2 January 2005.

8. _____, "Egyptian President Says He Will Push Multiparty Elections," *The Washington Post*, 26 February 2005.

9. Louise Sheldon, "Reflections on the Status of Women in Islam," *Baltimore Chronicle and Sentinel*, 2 June 2004, <http://www.baltimorechronicle.com>.

10. Brian Katulis, "Women's Rights in Focus: Egypt," Freedom House, The Communication Initiative, 19 October 2004, <http://www.comminit.com>.

11. Charles Levinson, "Egyptian Women See Divorce as Religious Right," Women's e-News, 9 January 2005, <http://www.womensenews.org>.

Sudan

1. "Sudan: Population," *Encyclopedia Britannica Online*, 13 February 2005, <http://www.britannica.com>.

2. Tessa Morrod, "Too Little: The Vicious Circle of Drought in North Darfur," Intermediate Technology Development Group (UK), October 2003, <http://www.itdg.org>.

3. Irving Greenburg and Jerome Shestack, "Carnage in Sudan," *The Washington Post*, 31 October 2000.

4. William Finnegan, "The Invisible War," *The New Yorker*, 25 January 1999, 71.

5. Colum Lynch, "U.N. Panel Finds No Genocide in Darfur but Urges Tribunals," *The Washington Post*, 1 February 2005.

6. Karl Vick, "Sudan, Newly Helpful, Remains Wary of U.S.," *The Washington Post*, 10 December 2001.

7. John Daniszewski, "A Ray of Hope in a War-Torn Sudan," *The New York Times*, 18 October 1997.

Lebanon

1. "Gender: Lebanon," *POGAR, Programme on Governance in the Arab Region*, U.N. Development Programme, 2004, <http://www.pogar.org>.

2. Will Rasmussem, "LIA Chief Eager to Dabble in the Bigger Picture," *The Daily Star* (Beirut), 6 February 2005, <http://www.dailystar.com.lb>.

3. "The Forgotten: Palestinian Refugees In Lebanon," Ockenden International (UK), 6 February 2005, <http://www.ockenden.org.uk>.

4. "Gender: Lebanon."

5. "New Polling Shows Deep Fractures among Lebanese," Zogby International, 7 March 2005, <http://www.zogby.com>.

6. Scott Wilson, "Rallies Highlight Rifts in Lebanon," *The Washington Post*, 15 March 2005.

7. Scott Wilson, "Religious Surge Alarms Secular Syrians," *The Washington Post*, 23 January 2005.

Syria

1. "Syria, International Religious Freedom Report 2004," Bureau of Democracy, Human Rights, and Labor, U.S. Department of State, 15 September 2004, <http://www.state.gov>.

2. "Syria," *Columbia Encyclopedia*, The Free Dictionary.com, 2005. <http://columbia.thefreedictionary.com>.

3. Scott Wilson, "Religious Surge Alarms Secular Syrians," *The Washington Post*, 23 January 2005.

4. Ibid.

5. Ibid.

6. David Hirst, "Syria's Unpredictable Storm," *Los Angeles Times*, 7 June 2005.

7. "Great Hopes Pinned on Syria's Women and Education Forum," *Aman Daily News* (Jordan), 2 February 2003, <http://www.amanjordan.org>.

Jordan

1. "Arab Democracy," *Outpost*, Americans for a Safe Israel, July/August 2003, <http://www.afsi.org>.

2. Kimberley Harrington, "Microfund for Women: Building a Better Future for Women in Jordan," *Jordan Times*, 7 December 2001.

3. Neil MacFarquhar, "Syria Reaches Turning Point, but Which Way Will it Turn?" *The New York Times*, 12 March 2001.

4. "Economy: Jordan," *CIA World Factbook 2004*, 2004, <http://www.cia.gov>.

5. Yusuf Mansur, "Combating Poverty in Jordan," *Aman Daily News*, 14 February 2004, <http://www.amanjordan.org>.

6. "Women in Parliament in the Arab World," Carnegie Endowment for International Peace, 2003, <http://www.ceip.org>.

Iraq

1. "Half Million Child Deaths 1991–1998, Global Policy Forum, United Nations, 2000, <http://www.globalpolicy.org>.

2. "Health Situation in Iraq," World Health Organization, United Nations, 2003, <http://www.who.int>.

3. "Iraq: Briefing Paper on Health," Office for Coordination of Humanitarian Affairs, United Nations, 18 May 2002, <http://www.ochaonline.un.org>.

4. John Pilger, "Squeezed to Death," *The Guardian* (UK), 4 March 2005, <http://www.guardian.co.uk>.

5. "Literacy," *CIA World Factbook 2004*, 2004, <http://www.cia.gov>.

6. "Iraqi Women and Children's Liberation Act of 2004," S 2519, *The Orator*, U.S. Congress, 15 June 2004, <http://www.theorator.com>.

7. "Background on Women's Status in Iraq Prior to the Fall of the Saddam Hussein Government," *Human Rights Watch Briefing Paper*, Human Rights Watch, November 2003, <http://hrw.org>.

8. Susan Jacoby, "*Sharia*: Iraq's Dark Cloud," *Los Angeles Times*, 21 March 2005.

Saudi Arabia

1. Scott Wilson, "Saudis Fight Militancy With Jobs," *The Washington Post*, 31 August 2004.

2. Divya Pakkiasamy, "Saudi Arabia's Plan for Changing Its Workforce," *Migration Policy Institute*, 1 November 2004, <http://www.migrationinformation.org>.

3. "Saudi Arabia's Foreign Workforce," *BBC News World Edition*, 13 May 2003, <http://news.bbc.co.uk>.

4. Muhammad Ibrahim Al-Helwa, "Creating Civil Society: An Insider's View," *Al-Sharq Al-Awsat* (London), 9 December 2003, <http://www.asharqalawsat.com>.

5. Catherine Taylor, "Fundamentals of Democracy," *The Australian*, 1 December 2003, <http://www.theaustralian.news.com>.

6. Al-Helwa, "Creating Civil Society."

7. "Saudi Arabia," *Country Analysis Briefs*, U.S. Department of Energy, January 2005, <http://www.eia.doe.gov>.

8. Ibid.

9. "Healthcare in Saudi Arabia," Mediwales, 25 May 2004, <http://www.mediwales.com>.

10. Hugh Pope, "For Saudi Women, Running a Business is a Veiled Initiative," *The Wall Street Journal*, 2 January 2002.

11. Farzaneh Roudi-Fahimi and Valentine M. Moghadam, "Empowering Women, Developing Society: Female Education in the Middle East and North Africa," Population Reference Bureau, November 2003, <http://www.prb.org>.

12. Ali A. Mosa, "Pressures in Saudi Arabia," Center for International Higher Education, Boston College, 2000, <http://www.bc.edu>.

13. Robert Kaiser, "Enormous Wealth Spilled into American Coffers," *The Washington Post*, 11 February 2002.

14. Helen Chapin Metz, ed., *Saudi Arabia: A Country Study*, 5th ed. (Washington, DC: Library of Congress Federal Research Division, 1993), 62.

15. "Saudi Arabia, International Religious Freedom Report 2004," Bureau of Democracy, Human Rights, and Labor, U.S. Department of State, 15 November 2004, <http://www.state.gov>.

16. "Shi'i [Shia] in Saudi Arabia," *Minorities at Risk Project*, Center for International Development and Conflict Management, University of Maryland, 15 July 2004, <http://www.cidcm.umd.edu>.

17. Scott Wilson, "Shiites See an Opening in Saudi Arabia," *The Washington Post*, 28 February 2005.

18. Saudi Arabia, "International Religious Freedom Report."

19. Marian Douglas, "U.S. Support of Saudi Arabia? Mideast, Oil, Terror," *The Guardian* (UK), 5 June 2004, <http://www.guardian.co.uk>.

20. Neil MacFarquhar, "Under Pressure to Change, Saudis Debate Their Future," *The New York Times*, 23 November 2003.

21. Subhi Hadidi, "Can Saudi Arabia Save Itself?" *Al-Quds Al-Arabi* (London), 28 November 2003, reprinted in *World Press Review*, February 2004, <http://www.worldpress.org>.

22. Craig Whitlock, "Saudis Confront Extremist Ideologies," *The Washington Post*, 6 February 2005.

23. Scott Wilson, "Saudi Men Cast Ballots in First Election Since '63," *The Washington Post*, 11 February 2005.

24. Mohamed Bazzi, "After a Period During Which Change Seemed Impossible, Saudi Family Tightens Grip," *Newsday*, 26 October 2004 <http://www.newsday.com>.

25. David Kaplan, "Of Bedouins and Bombings," *U.S. News and World Report*, 24 November 2004, 28.

26. Pope, "For Saudi Women."

27. "Saudi Arabia Ends Ban Limiting Female Employment," *U.N. Wire*, U.N. Foundation, 11 June 2004, <http://www.unwire.org>.

28. Pope, "For Saudi Women."

29. Wilson, "Saudi Men Cast Ballots."

30. Raid Qusti, "Our Female Problem," *The Washington Post*, 9 July 2002.

31. Kaplan, "Of Bedouins."

Yemen

1. Deborah Pugh, "Yemen's Remarkable Elections Are a First for Arabian Peninsula," *Christian Science Monitor*, 29 April 1993.

2. Karl Vick, "Yemen Walks Tightrope in Terrorism Stance," *The Washington Post*, 29 September 2001.

3. Ian Fisher, "Hate of the West Finds Fertile Soil in Yemen. But Does Al Qaeda?" *The New York Times*, 9 January 2003.

4. "Yemen: Economy," CIA *World Factbook 2004*, 10 February 2004, <http://www.cia.gov>.

5. "Yemen: Country Reports on Human Rights Practices 2003," Bureau of Democracy, Human Rights, and Labor, U.S. Department of State, 25 February 2003, <http://www.state.gov>.

6. "Yemen Economy Reliance on Oil Deplored," UPI, Softcom, 7 December 2004, <http://www.softcom.net>.

7. Christopher Ward, "Yemen's Water Crisis," The British-Yemeni Society, July 2001, <http://www.al-bab.com>.

8. "Yemen: Economy."

9. "Yemen: Commitment to Education," *Human Development Indicators 2003*, Human Development Reports, UN Development Programme, 2003, <http://hdr.undp.org>.

10. "Democracy, Human Rights and Women's Issues," Embassy of the Republic of Yemen, Washington DC, 2004, <http://www.yemenembassy.org>.

11. T. I. Farag and A. S. Toughan, "1001 Nights in Old and Modern Yemen, Part 4," *The Ambassadors, Online Magazine* (Canada) 6, no. 1, January 2003, <http://www.ambassadors.net>.

Kuwait

1. "Kuwait," *Freedom in the World*, Freedom House, 2004, <http://www.freedomhouse.org>.

2. "Kuwait, Elections and Parliament," European Institute for Research on Mediterranean and Euro-Arab Cooperation (MEDEA), July 2003, <http://www.medea.com>.

3. Peter Mansfield, *The New Arabians* (New York: Doubleday, 1981), 112.

4. "Water Quality," *Arab News*, 2002, <http://www.arabnews.com>.

5. "Kuwait Way of Life," Embassy of the State of Kuwait, 2000, <http://www.Kuwait-embassy.or.jp>.

6. Nirmala Janssen "7.3pc More Kuwaiti Women Join Workforce This Year," *Aman Daily News*, Aman News Center (Jordan), 18 August 2004, <http://www.amanjordan.org>.

7. Hassan M. Fattah, "Kuwait Grants Political Rights to Its Women," *The New York Times*, 17 May 2005.

Bahrain

1. "Background Note: Bahrain," Bureau of Near Eastern Affairs, U.S. Department of State, November 2004, <http://www.state.gov>.

2. "Bahrain Holds Elections, and Women Are Included," *The Washington Post*, 10 May 2002.

3. Nora Boustany, "In Bahrain Doubts about Reform," *The Washington Post*, 24 June 2005.

Qatar

1. "Islam by Country: Qatar," ReligionFacts, 2004, <http://www.religionfacts.com>.

2. "Qatar: Economy," *Encarta: Online Encyclopedia*, Microsoft Corp., 2005, <http://www.encarta.msn.com>.

3. "Qatar: Country Profile," *Emerging Markets Series*, Oxford Business Group, 2005, <http://www.oxfordbusinessgroup.com>.

4. "Qatar," *International Religious Freedom Report 2004*, U.S. Department of State, 2004, <http://www.state.gov>.

5. "Arab Constitutions: Qatar," POGAR, Programme on Governance of the Arab Region, U.N. Development Programme, 2005 <http://www.pogar.org>.

6. Dilip Hiro, "Allah and Democracy Can Get Along Fine," *The New York Times*, 1 March 2005.

7. "Qatar: Country Profile."

8. "Nation and Citizens," The Qatar Foundation, Qatari Ministry of Foreign Affairs, 13 February 2005, <http://english.mofa.gov.qa>.

9. Hiro, "Allah and Democracy."

United Arab Emirates

1. "UAE Population Topped Four Million in 2003," *Middle East Online*, 13 April 2004, <http://www.middle-east-online.com>.

2. "Financial Management: United Arab Emirates," POGAR, Programme on Governance of the Arab Region, U.N. Development Programme, 2004, <http://www.pogar.org>.

3. Ibid.

4. "Universities," The Emirates Network, 2005, <http://www.theemiratesnetwork.com>.

5. Nadim Kawach, "UAE Citizens Emerge Top Spenders in Arab World," *Gulf News*, 2 February 2004, <http://www.gulfnews.com>.

Oman

1. "Oman: Population," *Infoplease*, 2004, <http://www.infoplease.com>.

2. John Daniszewski, "The Sultanate's Arabian Knight," *Los Angeles Times*, 15 December 1999.

3. "Oman's Leader Extends Voting Rights to All Adults," *The Washington Post*, 28 November 2002.

4. Arif Ali, "Oman's Appointment of Another Woman Minster Welcomed," *Al-Jazeera*, *Arab News*, 22 October 2004, <http://www.arabnews. com>.

Appendix: The Arabic Language

1. Jon Mandeville, "Impressions from a Writer's Notebook—At Home in Yemen," *Aramco World* 32, no. 3, May/June 1981:30.

Bibliography
and References

"1999 Revision: Key Findings." *World Urbanization Prospects, World Global Trends.* 1999. <http://www.t21.ca>.

"A Conservative Christian Group Sues the U.N.C. for Assigning Book on Islam." Democracy Now. 8 August 2002. <http://www.democracynow.org>.

"A Year after Iraq War." The Pew Research Center. 16 March 2004. <http://www.people-press.org>.

Abdallah, Abdel Mahdi. "Causes of Anti-Americanism in the Arab World: A Socio-Political Perspective." *Middle East Review of International Affairs* 7, no. 4. December 2003.

Abdel-Halim, Mustafa. 2004. "Denmark Imposes Restrictions on Imams." IslamOnline. 18 February 2004. <http://www.islamonline.net>.

Abul Einein, Tamer and Ahmed Al-Matboli. "Austrian Muslims Score Big in 2004." *American Muslim Perspective*, Islam Online. 4 January 2005. <http://www.islamonline.net>.

Ajami, Fouad. "Bush Country." *The Daily Star* (Beirut), 23 May 2005. <http://www.dailystar.com.lb>.

Ajami, Fouad. "The Meaning of Lebanon." The Foundation for the Defense of Democracy, 1 May 2005. <http://www.defenddemocracy.com>.

Alam, M. Shahid. "The Clash Thesis: A Failing Ideology?" Common Dreams News Center. 2004. <http://www.commondreams.org>.

Al-Ajmi, Nassir M. "Heart to Heart Talk—A Friend to Friend Discussion." The Ladah Foundation. 23 October 2003. <http://www.ladah.org>.

Al-Attas, S.N., ed. *Aims and Objectives of Islamic Education.* Jeddah: King Abdulaziz University, 1979.

Al-Ba'albaki, Munir. "English Words of Arabic Origin." *In Al-Mawrid, A Modern English-Arabic Dictionary*, 101–12. Beirut: Dar El-Ilm Lil-Malayen, 1982.

Al-Helwa, Muhammad Ibrahim. "Creating Civil Society: An Insider's View." *Al-Sharq Al-Awsat* (London). 9 December 2003. <http://www.asharqalawsat.com>.

Al-Khalidi, Sulaiman. "Iraqi Economic Recovery Seen in 2005," World Bank. Global Policy. 6 December 2004. <http://www.globalpolicy.org>.

Al-Krenawi, Alean. "Principles of Social Work Practice in the Muslim Arab World." *Arab Studies Quarterly* (Fall 2003).

"Algeria: Agri-Food Country Profile." Agri-Food Trade Service (Canada). July 2004. <http://atnriae.agr.ca>.

"Algeria Election: Reluctant Youth." *Arab-American Journal.* 23 December 2004. <http://www.arabamerican.com>.

Ali, Arif. "Oman's Appointment of Another Woman Minster Welcomed." *Al-Jazeera, Arab News.* 22 October 2004. <http://www.arabnews.com>.

Allaf, Rime. "Dangerous Delusions." *The Daily Star* (Beirut). 3 October 2001. In *World Press Review*, December 2001. <http://www.worldpress.org>.

Allen, J. A. *Libya: The Experience of Oil.* Boulder, CO: Westview Press, 1981.

Al-Tohami, Mahmoud. "The Reasons for the Enmity and Hatred." *Alam-al-Youm* (Egypt). In *World Press Review.* 1 September 2002. <http://www.worldpress.org>.

Andalusi, Al-Amin. "Spanish Muslims Renew Anti-Terror Stand." Islam Online. 9 March 2005. <http://www.islamonline.net>.

Annan, Kofi. "Confronting Islamophobia: Education for Tolerance and Understanding." *Address to the PDI Seminar.* Document SG/SM/ 9637. 7 December 2004. <http://www.un.org>.

"Anti-Americanism: What's New, What's Next?" (quoting Ussama Makdisi). *World Economic Forum.* 2002. <http://www.weforum .org>.

"Anti-Muslim Bias Spreads in EU." *BBC News.* 7 March 2005. <http:// www.bbc.co.uk>.

"Arab Constitutions: Qatar." *POGAR, Programme on Governance of the Arab Region.* U.N. Development Programme. 2005. <http:// www.pogar.org>.

"Arab Democracy." *Outpost.* July/August 2003. Americans for a Safe Israel. <http://www.afsi.org>.

Arberry, A. J. *The Koran Interpreted.* New York: MacMillian, 1955.

Armas, Genaro. "Census Bureau Says People of Arab Descent Doing Well in the United States." *Detroit Free Press.* 9 March 2005.

Armstrong, Karen. *Muhammad, A Biography of a Prophet.* San Francisco: HarperSanFrancisco, 1992.

Asim, Thabet. "The Muslim Science Wars: Modern Muslim Discussion on Science." *Muslims Under Progress* (UK). 2005. <http://www. underprogress.blogs.com>.

Atiyeh, George N. *Arab and American Cultures.* Washington DC: American Enterprise Institute for Public Policy Research, 1977.

"Background Note: Bahrain." *Bureau of Near Eastern Affairs.* U.S. Department of State. November 2004.

"Background on Women's Status in Iraq Prior to the Fall of the Saddam Hussein Government." *Human Rights Watch Briefing Paper.* Human Rights Watch. November 2003. <http://hrw.org>.

Bagby, Ihsan, Paul Perl, and Bryan Froehle. "The Mosque in America: A National Portrait." Washington, DC: Council of American Islamic Relations. 2001. <http://www.cair-net.org>.

"Bahrain Holds Elections, and Women Are Included." *The Washington Post.* 10 May 2002.

Bakar, Osman. *The History and Philosophy of Islamic Science.* Cambridge, England: Islamic Texts Society, 1999.

Barakat, Halim. *The Arab World: Society, Culture, and the State.* Berkeley: University of California Press, 1993.

Barber, Mike. "Muslims in the U.S. Military Are as Loyal as Any, Chaplain Says." *Seattle Post-Intelligencer.* 20 October 2001. <http://www.seattlepi.newssource.com>.

Barsamian, David. "*The Progressive* Interview: Robert Fisk." *The Progressive*, 39–43. June 2005.

Bashir, Abdul Wahab. "Scholars Define Terrorism, Call for Joint Action to Defend Islam." *Arab News.* 12 January 2002. <http://www.arabnews.com>.

Bassoul, Joelle. "Iraqi Women Poised For Parliament." *The Monday Phenomenon.* 15 February 2005. <http://www.iafrica.com>.

Bayoumi, Alaa. "Integrating European Muslims: Europe's Fearful Bid." IslamOnline. 17 March 2004. <http://www.islamonline.net>.

Bazzi, Mohamed. "After a Period During Which Change Seemed Impossible, Saudi Family Tightens Grip." *Newsday.* 26 October 2004. <http://www.newsday.com>.

"Belgium Bans Popular Racist Party." *Dhimmi Watch.* November 2004. <http://www.jihadwatch.org/dhimmiwatch>.

Bell, Richard. *Introduction to the Qur'an.* Edinburgh: University Press, 1953.

"Berber Languages." *Columbia Encyclopedia.* 6th ed. 2005. <http://www.bartleby.com>.

"Berber Languages." *Wikipedia.* 2004. <http://www.en.wikipedia.org>.

Bergstrom, Theodore. "On the Economics of Polygyny." *Centre on Economics Learning and Social Evolution* (ELSE). 1994. <http://www.netec.mcc.ac.uk>.

Bhutto, Benazir. "Politics and the Modern Woman." In *Liberal Islam, A Sourcebook*, edited by Charles Kurzman. New York: Oxford University Press, 1998.

Bilefsky, Dan. "In Netherlands, Some Muslims Work to Convince Voters Islam Is Tolerant." *The Wall Street Journal.* 23 May 2002.

Blank, Johan. "The Muslim Mainstream." *U.S. News and World Report.* 20 July 1998.

Blythe, Gilbert P. "We Are All Jews Now." *The Last Ditch, WTM Enterprises.* 19 October 2003. <http://www.thornwalker.com>.

Boehlert, Eric. "Terrorists under the Bed." *Salon.com.* 5 March 2002. <http://www.salon.com>.

Boustany, Nora. "In Bahrain, Doubts about Reform." *The Washington Post.* 24 June 2005.

Bowen, Donna Lee, and Evelyn A. Early, eds. *Everyday Life in the Muslim Middle East.* Bloomington: Indiana University Press, 1993.

Brandon, James. "Koranic Duels Ease Terror." *Christian Science Monitor.* 4 February 2005.

Bremmer, Charles. "Stoned to Death: Why Europe Is Starting to Lose Its Faith in Islam." *Times Online* (UK). 4 April 2004. <http://www.timesonline.co.uk>.

Bukay, David. "Islamic Fundamentalism and the Arabic Political Culture." *NATIV Online,* no. 3. April 2005. <http://www.acpr.org.ilenglish-nativ/index.htm>.

Buruma, Ian. "Lost in Translation." *The New Yorker.* 184–191. 14–21 June 2004.

Caldwell, Christopher. "Allah Mode: France's Islam Problem." *The Weekly Standard* vol. 7, no. 42. 15 July 2002. <http://www.weekly-standard.com>.

Caldwell, Deborah. "'Something Major Is Happening': Are We Witnessing the Beginnings of an Islamic Reformation?" *Beliefnet.* December 2001. <http://www.beliefnet.com>.

Carter, Tom. "Tolerance Tested in Holland." *The Washington Times.* 20 December 2004.

Casciani, Dominic. "Rise in Muslim Discrimination." *Community Affairs, BBC News.* 16 December 2004. <http://www.bbc.co.uk>.

_____. "Islamophobia Pervades UK—Report." *Community Affairs, BBC News.* 2 June 2004. <http://www.news.bbc.co.uk>.

"Census 2000: Portrait of the Nation." *The Washington Post.* 5 June 2002.

Cesari, Jocelyne. "Islam in France: The Shaping of a Religious Minority." *In Muslims in the West: From Sojourners to Citizens,* edited by Yvonne Haddad. New York: Oxford University Press, 2002.

Cheney, Elizabeth. "U.S. Supports Democracy in Every Nation, Culture." U.S. Department of State. 14 June 2005. <http://usinfo.state.gov>.

Choucair, Julia. "Dates of Women's Suffrage and Current Ministerial Positions Held By Women in Arab Countries." *Carnegie Endowment for International Peace, Human Development Report.* 2004. <http://www.ceip.org>.

_____. "Women in Parliament in the Arab World." Carnegie Endowment For International Peace. 2004. <http://www.ceip.org>.

Chu, Jeff, and Nadia Mustafa. "Her Turn to Pray." *Time,* 28 March 2005.

"CIA Insider: The Threat We Refuse to Get." *The Washington Post.* 11 July 2004.

Clark, Nick. "Education in Libya." *World Education News and Reviews.* July/August 2004. <http://www.wes.org>.

Clayton, Mark. "How Are Mosques Fighting Terror?" *Christian Science Monitor.* 12 August 2004.

Cohn, D'Vera. "Statistics Portray Settled, Affluent Mideast Community." *The Washington Post.* 20 November 2001.

Collelo, Thomas, ed. *Syria: A Country Study,* 3d ed. Washington, DC: Department of the Army, 1988.

"Complete Text of President Bush's National Address." *Globe and Mail* (Canada). 12 September 2002. <http://www.theglobeandmail.com>.

Cooperman, Alan. "September 11 Backlash Murders and the State of Hate." *The Washington Post.* 20 January 2002.

"Countries in Order of People Per Doctor." *World Development Indicators.* 2001. <http://www.worldbank.org>.

Culver, Virginia. "Many American Muslims Well Off, College Educated, Poll Shows." *Denver Post.* 18 January 2002.

"Current Religious Affairs Consultation Meeting, Final Communique." Higher Council of Religious Affairs. 18 May 2002. <http://www .turkishpolicy.com>.

Daniszewki, John. "The Sultanate's Arabian Knight." *Los Angeles Times*. 15 December 1999.

_____. "A Ray of Hope in a War-Torn Sudan." *The New York Times*. 18 October 1997.

Dawood, Khaled. "Arab Opinions." *Al-Ahram Weekly*. 30 July 2004. <http://www.ahram.org.eg>.

DeBendern, Paul. "Algeria to Press Ahead with Women's Rights Bill," *Jordan Times*. 16 September 2004. <http://www.jordantimes.com>.

"Democracy, Human Rights and Women's Issues." Embassy of the Republic of Yemen, Washington DC. 2004. <http://www. yemenembassy.org>.

"Denmark Rejects Headscarf Plea." *BBC News Europe*. 21 January 2005. <http://www.bbc.co.uk>.

DeYoung, Karin. "Poll Finds Arabs Dislike U.S. Based on Policies It Pursues." *The Washington Post*. 7 October 2002.

"Distribution of the Islamic Ruling on Smoking in 53,000 Mosques across Egypt." *Tobacco Free Initiative*, World Health Organization. 2005. <http://www.enro.who.int>.

Djerejian, Edward (Chairman). "Changing Minds, Winning Peace." (Submitted to the Committee on Appropriations, U.S. House of Representatives). 1 October 2003.

Dobbs, Michael. "Arab Hostility toward U.S. Growing, Poll Finds." *The Washington Post*. 4 June 2003.

Donovan, Patricia. "'The Illegitimacy Bonus' and State Efforts to Reduce Out-of-Wedlock Births." *Family Planning Perspectives* 31, no. 2. March/April 1999. <http://www.agi-usa.org>.

Douglas, Marian. "U.S. Support of Saudi Arabia? Mideast, Oil, Terror." *The Guardian* (UK). 5 June 2004. <http://www.guardian.co.uk>.

Douthat, Ross. "A Muslim Europe?" *The Atlantic Monthly.* January/February 2005.

Dover, Hanan. "Siege Mentality: Current Australian Muslim Response." *Forum on Australia's Islamic Relations* (FAIR). 2 November 2003. <http://www.fair.org.au>.

"Economy: Jordan." *CIA World Factbook.* 2004. <http://www.cia.gov>.

"Egypt." *Encarta Online Encyclopedia,* Microsoft Corp. 2005. <http://www.encarta.msn.com>.

Emerson, Steven. *American Jihad, The Terrorists Living Among Us.* New York: Free Press, 2002.

"Enhancing Women's Political Participation Through Social Measures in the Arab Region." International IDEA. National Council for Women (Egypt). UN Development Programme. 2005. <http://www.hdr.undp.org>.

"EU Laments Growing Hostility to Muslims since 9/11." *EU Business.* 22 May 2003. <http://www.eubsiness.com>.

"EU Opens Debate on Economic Migration." *EurActiv.* 14 January 2005. <http://www.euractiv.com>.

Ezzat, Dina. "Rewriting the Textbooks." *Al-Ahram Weekly,* 16–22 December 2004. <http://www.weeklyahram.org.eg>.

_____. "Fortifying Women's Rights." *Al-Ahram Weekly.* 17–23 June 2004. <http://www.weeklyahram.org.eg>.

Farag, T. I., and A. S. Toughan. "1001 Nights in Old and Modern Yemen, Part 4." *The Ambassadors, Online Magazine* (Canada) 6, no. 1. January 2003. <http://www.ambassadors.net>.

"Fatima Urges Protection of Arab Family." *UAE Interact, Ministry of Information and Culture.* 1999. <http://www.uaeinteract.com>.

Fattah, Hassan M. "Kuwait Grants Political Rights to Its Women." *The New York Times.* 17 May 2005.

Fernea, Elizabeth. "Islamic Feminism Finds a Different Voice." *Foreign Service Journal,* 24–31. May 2000.

"Financial Management: United Arab Emirates." POGAR, Programme on Governance of the Arab Region. U.N. Development Programme. 2004. <http://www.pogar.org>.

Finnegan, William. "The Invisible War." *The New Yorker*. 25 January 1999.

Fisher, Ian. "Hate of the West Finds Fertile Soil in Yemen. But Does Al Qaeda?" *The New York Times*. 9 January 2003.

Fleischman, Jeffrey. "Minarets Rise in Germany." *Los Angeles Times*. 17 March 2004.

Ford, Peter. "What Place for God in Europe?" *Christian Science Monitor*. 22 February 2005.

"France Pledges Protection for Mosques." IslamOnline. 9 March 2004. <http://www.islamonline.net>.

Fromkin, David. *A Peace to End All Peace*. New York: Henry Holt, 1989.

Furlong, Ray. "Germans Argue over Integration." *BBC News*. 30 November 2004. <http://www.bbc.co.uk>.

"Gender: Lebanon." POGAR, Programme on Governance in the Arab Region. UN Development Programme. 2004. <http://www.pagar .org>.

"Germans Have Negative View of Islam." *BUPA International, Expatica*. 16 September 2004. <http://www.expatica.com>.

Graham, Franklin. "My View of Islam." *Covenant News*. 9 December 2001. <http://www.covenantnews.com>.

"Great Hopes Pinned on Syria's Women and Education Forum." *Aman Daily News* (Jordan). 2 February 2003. <http://www.amanjordan.org>.

Greenburg, Irving and Jerome Shestack. "Carnage in Sudan." *The Washington Post*. 31 October 2000.

Grimsley, Kerstin. "More Arabs, Muslims Allege Bias on the Job." *The Washington Post*. 12 February 2001.

"Growing Urbanization." *Human Development Report*. UN Development Programme. 1999. <http://www.hdr.undp.org>.

Haddad, Yvonne, and Jane Smith, eds. "Introduction" in *Muslim Minorities in the West: Visible and Invisible*. New York: Altamira Press, 2002.

Haddad, Yvonne, ed. *Muslims in the West, From Sojourners to Citizens*. New York: Oxford University Press, 2002.

Hadidi, Subhi. "Can Saudi Arabia Save Itself?" *Al-Quds Al-Arabi* (London). 28 November 2003. Reprinted in *World Press Review.* February 2004. <http://www.worldpress.org>.

"Half Million Child Deaths 1991–1998." Global Policy Forum. United Nations. 2000. <http://www.globalpolicy.org>.

Hall, Edward T. *The Hidden Dimension.* New York: Doubleday, 1966.

Hamady, Sania. *Temperament and Character of the Arabs.* New York: Twayne, 1960.

Hamamy, Hanan. "Consanguineous Marriages in the Arab World." National Centre for Diabetes, Endocrinology and Genetics, Amman, Jordan. *The Ambassadors.* Online Magazine (Canada), 3, no. 7. July 2003. <http://www.ambassadors.net>.

Hanania, Ray. "Failure to Understand Arab-Muslim Issues Exposes Nation To Attacks." 11 March 2005. <http://www.hananiacreators. blogspot.com>.

Harrington, Kimberley. "Microfund for Women: Building a Better Future for Women in Jordan." *Jordan Times.* 7 December 2001.

Hasan, Aida. "Arab Culture and Identity—Arab Food and Hospitality." Suite University Online. 1999. <http://www.suite101.com>.

"Healing the Nation: Arab American Response to September 11 Attacks." Arab American Institute. 2001. <http://www.aaiusa.org>.

"Health Situation in Iraq." World Health Organization, United Nations. 2003. <http://www.who.int>.

"Healthcare in Saudi Arabia." *Mediwales.* 25 May 2004. <http://www. mediwales.com>.

Hiro, Dilip. "Allah and Democracy Can Get Along Fine." *The New York Times.* 1 March 2005.

Hirst, David. "Syria's Unpredictable Storm." *Los Angeles Times.* 7 June 2005.

"Historical Ties Leave Trying Legacy." *Christian Science Monitor.* 27 January 1993.

Hoagland, Jim. "The Unheralded Revolution." *The Washington Post.* 24 February 2005.

_____. "In Europe, The Enemy Within." *The Washington Post.* 26 February 2004.

_____. "The Word in Paris." *The Washington Post*. 21 July 2002.

Holtzman, Michael. "Washington's Sour Sales Pitch." *The New York Times*. 4 October 2003.

"How Many Muslims Are in the U.S. and the Rest of the World?" Ontario Consultants on Religious Tolerance. 2002. <http://www.religioustolerance.org>.

"Hughes's Role to Be Outreach to Muslims." *The Washington Post*. 15 March 2005.

"Human Trafficking in Libya." *The Villager* 74, no. 34. December/January 2004. <http://www.thevillager.com>.

Huntington, Samuel P. "The Clash of Civilizations" *Foreign Affairs* 72, no. 3 (Summer 1993).

_____. *The Clash of Civilizations and the Remaking of World Order*. New York: Simon and Schuster, 1996.

"Internet Users Per 1,000 People." *Human Development Report 2004*. U.N. Development Programme. 2004. <http://www.hdr.undp.org>.

"Intolerance and Discrimination against Muslims in the E.U.—Developments since September 11." International Helsinki Federation for Human Rights. March 2005. <http://www.ihf-hr.org>.

"Iraq: Briefing Paper on Health." Office for Coordination of Humanitarian Affairs, United Nations. 18 May 2002. <http://www.ochaonline.un.org>.

"Iraqi Women and Children's Liberation Act of 2004." S 2519, U.S. Congress. *The Orator*. 15 June 2004. <http://www.theorator.com>.

"Islam by Country: Qatar." *ReligionFacts*. 2004. <http://www.religionfacts.com>.

"Islam Is Love." *Bush on Muslims*. 5 January 2002. <http://www.muslimsforbush.com>.

"Islam Is Violent." *Jesus Is Lord*. <http://www.jesus-is-lord.com>.

"Islam, Jihad and Terrorism." Institute of Islamic Information and Education. 14 October 2004. <http://www.iiie.net>.

Islam, Shada. "The Plot Thickens: Testing European Tolerance." *Yale Global Online*. 17 November 2004. <http://www.yaleglobal.yale.edu>.

Jacoby, Susan. "*Sharia*: Iraq's Dark Cloud." *Los Angeles Times*. 21 March 2005.

Janssen, Nirmala. "7.3pc More Kuwaiti Women Join Workforce This Year." Aman News Center. 18 August 2004. <http://www.amanjordan.org>.

Jawdat, Ridwaan. "Islam Fastest Growing Faith in Australia." *Arab News*. 25 October 2004. <http://www.arabnews.com>.

Johnson, Larry. "Commentary." *Seattle Post Intelligencer*, 20 June 2004. <http://www.seattlepi.nwssource.com>.

Jun, Jan. "U.K.: Report Says Britain's Muslims Most Underprivileged Religious Group." Muslim Public Affairs Committee (U.K.). 25 October 2004. <http://www.mpacuk.org>.

Kaiser, Robert. "Enormous Wealth Spilled into American Coffers." *The Washington Post*. 11 February 2002.

Kaplan, David. "Of Bedouins and Bombings." *U.S. News and World Report*. 24 November 2004.

Karmi, Ghada. *In Search of Fatima, A Palestinian Story*. London: Verso, 2002.

Katulis, Brian. "*Women's Rights in Focus: Egypt*." Freedom House, The Communication Initiative. 19 October 2004. <http://www.comminit.com>.

Kawach, Nadim. "UAE Citizens Emerge Top Spenders in Arab World." *Gulf News*. 2 February 2004. <http://www.gulfnews.com>.

Kennicott, Philip. "An About-Face on America." *The Washington Post*. 24 August 2004.

Khalidi, Rashid. *Resurrecting Empire: Western Footprints and America's Perilous Path in the Middle East*. Boston: Beacon Press, 2004.

Khan, M. A. Muqtedar. "American Muslims Push for Role in Policy Planning." The Brookings Institution. *Daily Times*. 25 December 2004. <http://www.brookings.edu>.

Kharoufi, Mostafa. "Urbanization and Urban Research in the Arab World." *UNESCO*. 1996. <http://www.unesco.org>.

Khouri, Rami. "For Arabs, A Cruel Echo of History." *The Daily Star* (Beirut). 21 March 2003. <http://www.dailystar.com.lb>

Kole, William J. "Hostility and Discrimination toward Muslims Widespread in EU." *Al-Jazeerah.* 14 September 2004. <http://www.aljazeerah.info.>.

Krauthammer, Charles. "Syria and the New Axis of Evil." *The Washington Post.* 1 April 2005.

_____. "What's Left? Shame." *The Washington Post.* 18 March 2005.

_____. "Why It Deserves The Hype." *Time,* 14 February 2005.

Kristof, Nicholas. "Bigotry in Islam and Here." *The New York Times.* 9 July 2002.

Kronemer, Alexander. "Understanding Muhammad." *Christian Science Monitor.* 9 December 2002.

"Kuwait." *Freedom in the World.* Freedom House. 2004. <http://www.freedomhouse.org>.

"Kuwait, Elections and Parliament." European Institute for Research on Mediterranean and Euro-Arab Cooperation (MEDEA). July 2003. <http://www.medea.com>.

"Kuwait Way of Life." Embassy of the State of Kuwait. 2000. <http://www.Kuwait-embassy.or.jp>.

Labidi, Kamel. "The Wrong Man to Promote Democracy." *Los Angeles Times.* 21 January 2004.

Lamb, David. "In a Region of Hate, Morocco is the Land of Harmony." *Los Angeles Times.* 25 October 1995.

Lampman, Jane. "Muslim in America." *Christian Science Monitor,* 10 January 2002.

Lawrence, T. E. *The Seven Pillars of Wisdom.* New York: Doubleday, 1926.

Levinson, Charles. "Egyptian Women See Divorce as Religious Right." *Women's e-News.* 9 January 2005. <http://www.womensenews.org>.

Lewis, Bernard. "Targeted by a History of Hatred." *The Washington Post.* 10 September 2002.

_____. "The Roots of Muslim Rage." *The Atlantic Monthly* 266, no. 3. September 1990.

"Libya: Economy." *CIA World Factbook 2004.* 2004. <http://www.cia.gov>.

"Libya: Economy." *ExxUN.* 2003. <http://www.exxun.com>.

Lippman, Thomas. *Understanding Islam, An Introduction to the Muslim World.* New York: Penguin Books, 1990.

Linzer, Dafna. "Poll Shows Growing Arab Rancor at U.S." *The Washington Post.* 23 July 2004.

Lynch, Colum. "Report Urges Arab Governments to Share Power." *The Washington Post.* 6 April 2005.

_____. "U.N. Panel Finds No Genocide in Darfur but Urges Tribunals." *The Washington Post.* 1 February 2005.

MacFarquhar, Neil. "Under Pressure to Change, Saudis Debate Their Future." *The New York Times.* 23 November 2003.

_____. "Syria Reaches Turning Point, But Which Way Will It Turn?" *The New York Times.* 12 March 2001.

"Majority of Europeans Unhappy with Muslims." Euro-Islam.Info, World Affairs Board. December 2004. <http://www.worldaffairsboard.com>.

Makdisi, Ussama. "Anti-Americanism in the Arab World: An Interpretation of a Brief History." *Journal of American History* 89, no. 2. September 2002.

Mandeville, Jon. "Impressions from a Writer's Notebook—At Home in Yemen." *Aramco World*, 32, no. 3. May/June 1981.

Mansfield, Peter. *The New Arabians.* New York: Doubleday, 1981.

Mansur, Yusuf. "Combating Poverty in Jordan." *Aman Daily News.* 14 February 2004. <http://www.amanjordan.org>.

Martin, Lee A. "Not a Prayer." *Harper's Magazine*, 77–79. June 2004.

McCain, John. "The Road to Baghdad." *Time*, 9 September 2002.

McConnell, Scott. "Why Many Arabs Hate America." Media Monitors Network. 12 September 2001. <http://www.mediamonitors.net>

McGrory, Mary. "Nuancing the Mideast Dilemma." *The Washington Post.* 14 April 2002.

McLoughlin, Leslie J. *Colloquial Arabic (Levantine)*. London: Routledge and Kegan Paul, 1982.

Merle, Renae. "Pentagon Funds Diplomacy Effort." *The Washington Post*. 11 June 2000.

Metz, Helen Chapin, ed. *Saudi Arabia: A Country Study*. 5th ed. Washington, DC: Library of Congress Federal Research Division, 1993.

"Middle East and North Africa, 2001." *Europa*, European Union. 2001. <http://www.curopa.edu.int>.

"Middle East Population Set to Double." *Popline*, Population Institute. 25 April 2005. <http://www.populationinstitute.org>.

Mitchell, Joshua. "Not all Yearn to Be Free." *The Washington Post*.10 August 2003.

Mitchell, Paul. "Egypt Reintroduces Food Vouchers as Poverty Worsens." *World Socialist Web Site*. 5 May 2004. <http://www.wsws.org>.

"Morocco: Country Reports on Human Rights Practices 2004." U.S. Department of State. 28 February 2005. <http://www.state.gov>.

"Morocco: Husbands and Wives Now Equal." *Cairo Times*. 26 January-11 February 2004. <http://www.cairotimes.com>.

Morrod, Tessa. "Too Little: The Vicious Circle of Drought in North Darfur." Intermediate Technology Development Group (UK). October 2003. <http://www.itdg.org>.

Mosa, Ali A. "Pressures in Saudi Arabia." Center for International Higher Education, Boston College. 2000. <http://www.bc.edu>.

Mousalli, Ahmad S. *Moderate and Radical Islamic Fundamentalism*. Gainesville: University Press of Florida, 1999.

Mujahid, Abdul Malik. "Profile of Muslims in Canada." TorontoMuslims.com. 20 April 2004. <http://www.torontomuslims.com>.

_____. "Muslims in America: Profile 2001." Soundvision.com. 2001. <http://www.soundvision.com>.

Murad, Abdal-Hakim. "Muslims and the European Right." The American Muslim. September/October 2000. <http://www.theamericanmuslim.org>.

Murphy, Caryle. "Distrust of Muslims Common in the U.S., Poll Finds." *The Washington Post*. 5 October 2004.

"Muslim Communities in Eastern Europe and Baltic Countries." IslamOnline. February 2005. <http://www.islamonline.net>.

"Nation and Citizens." *The Qatar Foundation.* Qatari Ministry of Foreign Affairs. 13 February 2005. <http://english.mofa.gov.qa>.

"New Polling Shows Deep Fractures among Lebanese." *Zogby International.* 7 March 2005. <http://www.zogby.com>.

"News From Italy: Immigrazione Pera." *Euro-Islam.info.* 29 December 2004. <http://64.207.171.242/pages/newsitaly.html>.

Ngawi, Rodrique. "Rwanda Turns to Islam after Genocide." *Times Daily.* 7 November 2002. <http://www.timesdaily.com>.

"Not at War against Islam." Bush on Muslims. 5 January 2002. <http://www.muslimsforbush.com>.

"Oman: Population." Infoplease. 2004. <http://www.infoplease.com>.

"Oman's Leader Extends Voting Rights to All Adults." *The Washington Post.* 28 November 2002.

Omestad, Thomas. "The Casbah Connection." *U.S. News and World Report.* 9 May 2005.

Ottaway, Marina. "Listen to Arab Voices." *The Washington Post.* 5 April 2005.

Oumimoun, Nabil. "Teaching Berber in the Moroccan Primary Schools." Amazigh World 2004. <http://www.amazighworld.net>.

Pakkiasamy, Divya. "Saudi Arabia's Plan for Changing Its Workforce." Migration Policy Institute. 1 November 2004. <http://www.migrationinformation.org>.

Patai, Raphael. *The Arab Mind.* 1973. Reprint, Long Island, NY: The Hatherleigh Press, 2002.

"Literacy." *CIA World Factbook 2004.* 2004. <http://www.cia.gov>.

Peters, Ralph. *Beyond Terror.* Mechanicsburg, PA: Stackpole Books, 2002.

"Physicians per 1000 Population." *Commitment to Heath, Human Development Report.* U.N. Development Programme. 2004. <http://www.hdr.undp.org/reports/global/2004>.

Pilger, John. "Squeezed to Death." *The Guardian (UK).* 4 March 2005. <http://www.guardian.co.uk>.

Pipes, Daniel. *Militant Islam Reaches America*. New York: W.W. Norton & Co, 2003.

"Polygyny." *Institute of Cultural Social Studies*. Leiden University, Netherlands. 10 March 2005. <http://www.eolss.net>.

Pope, Hugh. "For Saudi Women, Running a Business Is a Veiled Initiative." *The Wall Street Journal*. 2 January 2002.

"Population Growth." *Human Development Report*. U.N. Development Programme. 2005. <http://www.hdr.undp.org>.

"Primary School-Age Population." *Global Education Database*, U.S. Agency for International Development. Center for Development Information and Evaluation. 2001. <http://esdb.cdie.org>.

Pugh, Deborah. "Yemen's Remarkable Elections Are a First for Arabian Peninsula." *Christian Science Monitor*. 29 April 1993.

"Qatar." *International Religious Freedom Report 2004*. U.S. Department of State. 2004. <http://www.state.gov>.

"Qatar: Country Profile." *Emerging Markets Series*. Oxford Business Group. 2005. <http://www.oxfordbusinessgroup.com>.

"Qatar: Economy." *Encarta: Online Encyclopedia*. Microsoft Corp. 2005. <http://www.encarta.msn.com>.

"Qatar is the Richest Arab Nation, Among Top 20 in the World." Qatar National Bank. 2004. <http://www.qnb.com.qa>.

Qumsiyeh, Mazin. "100 Years of Anti-Arab and Anti-Muslim Stereotyping." *The Prism*, The American-Arab Anti-Discrimination Committee. January 1998. <http://www.ibiblio.org/prism>.

"Quotation of the Day." *New York Times*. 13 April 2005.

Qusti, Raid. "Our Female Problem." *The Washington Post*. 9 July 2002.

Ramadan, Tariq. *Western Muslims and the Future of Islam*. Oxford: Oxford University Press, 2004.

_____. "Muslims in Italy." In *Muslims in the West: From Sojourners to Citizens*, edited by Yvonne Haddad, 158–166. New York: Oxford University Press, 2002.

Rasmussem, Will. "LIA Chief Eager to Dabble an the Bigger Picture." *The Daily Star* (Beirut). 6 February 2005. <http://www.dailystar.com.lb>.

Rauf, Imam Faisal. *What's Right with Islam*. New York: Harper's San Francisco, 2004.

"Report Instances of Extremism or Support of Terrorism." Free Muslims Against Terrorism. 2005. <http:www.freemuslims.org>.

Richberg, Keith. "French President Urges Ban on Headscarves." *The Washington Post*. 17 March 2003.

Richman, Sheldon. "Another Frankenstein's Monster." Commentaries, *The Future of the Freedom Foundation*. 27 December 2002. <http://www.fff.org/comment>.

Roudi-Fahimi, Farazneh, and Valentine M. Moghadam. "Empowering Women, Developing Society: Female Education in the Middle East and North Africa." *Population Reference Bureau*. November 2003. <http://www.prg.org>.

Rubin, Barry. "The Real Roots of Arab Anti-Americanism." *Foreign Affairs*, (November/December 2002): 73–85.

Rumsfeld, Donald. "Rumsfeld on Message of 9–11." *International Broadcasting Bureau*, U.S. Government. 11 September 2002. <www.ibb.gov>.

Sachs, Susan. "Where Muslim Traditions Meet Modernity." *The New York Times*. 17 December 2001.

Saloojie, Riad. "The Nature of Islam." *The Globe and Mail* (Canada). 16 January 2000.

Samhan, Helen. "Arab Americans." Arab American Institute. 2001. <http://www.aaiusa.org>.

Sardar, Ziauddin. *Introducing Muhammad*. New York: Totem Books, 1994.

"Saudi Arabia." *Country Analysis Briefs*. U.S. Department of Energy. January 2005. <http://www.eia.doe.gov>.

"Saudi Arabia: Education." *MapZones*. 2002. <http://www.mapzones .com>.

"Saudi Arabia, International Religious Freedom Report 2004." Bureau of Democracy, Human Rights, and Labor. U.S. Department of State. November 15 2004. <http://www.state.gov>.

"Saudi Arabia: Population, Health and Well-Being." *EarthTrends* 2002. <http://www.earthtrends.wri.org>.

"Saudi Arabia Ends Ban Limiting Female Employment." *U.N. Wire.* U.N. Foundation. 11 June 2004. <http://www.unwire.org>.

"Saudi Arabia's Foreign Workforce." *BBC News World Edition.* 13 May 2003. <http://news.bbc.co.uk>.

Schell, Jonathan. "Iraq's Unpredictable Politics." *The Nation.* 11 February 2005. <http://www.thenation.com>.

Sedgman, Jayne-Maree. "Discrimination Isolates Muslim Australians." *ABC News Online.* 17 June 2004. <http://www.abc.net.au>.

Shadid, Anthony. "Hussein's Baghdad Falls." *The Washington Post.* 10 April 2003.

————————. "Old Arab Friends Turn away from U.S." *The Washington Post.* 26 February 2003.

Sharabi, Hisham, and Mukhtar Ani. "Impact of Class and Culture on Social Behavior: the Feudal-Bourgeois Family in Arab Society." In *Psychological Dimensions of Near Eastern Studies,* edited by L. Carl Brown and Norman Itzkowitz. Princeton: Darwin Press, 1977.

Sheldon, Louise. "Reflections on the Status of Women in Islam." *Baltimore Chronicle and Sentinel.* 2 June 2004. <http://www.baltimorechronicle.com>.

Shepherd, Robin. "In Europe, Is it a Matter of Fear, or Loathing?" The *Washington Post.* 25 January 2004.

Sheridan, Mary Beth. "Sensitizing Police toward Muslims." *The Washington Post.* 6 October 2003.

"Shi'i [Shia] in Saudi Arabia." *Minorities at Risk Project.* Center for International Development and Conflict Management. University of Maryland. 15 July 2004. <http://www.cidcm.umd.edu>.

Shipler, David K. *Arab and Jew, Wounded Spirits in a Promised Land.* New York: Penguin Books, 1986.

Simmons, Erica. "A Passion for Justice." *New Internationalist,* no. 210. 9 August 1990.

"Situation of Muslims in Denmark a Major Part of LWF Inter-religious Study on Conflict." *Lutheran World Federation.* 11 December 2003. <http://www.lutheranworld.org>.

Slade, Shelley. "The Image of the Arab in America: Analysis of a Poll of American Attitudes." *Middle East Journal* 35, no. 2. Spring 1981.

Smith, Craig. "Voices of the Dead Echo Across Algeria." *The New York Times*. 18 April 2004.

Smith, Lee. "Democracy Inaction: Understanding Arab Anti-Americanism." *Slate*. 23 April 2004. <http://www.slate.msn.com>.

_____. "Egypt's Islamist Dilemma." *The Nation*, 227, no. 18. 1 December 2003.

"Spanish Muslims Issue Fatwa against Usama." *U.S. and World, Fox News.com*. 11 March 2005. <http://www.foxnews.com>.

Spencer, Robert. "Death Knell of the West." *FrontPageMagazine.com*. 22 December 2004. <hhtp://www.frontpagemag.com>

Spinner, Jackie. "An Attack Burns Anguish into Kurdish Region." *The Washington Post*. 6 February 2005.

Stack, Megan. "The Many Layers of the Veil." *Los Angeles Times*. 12 January 2005.

"Statistics and Indicators on Men and Women." U.N. Statistics Division, Demographic. 2005. <http://www.unstats.un.org>.

Steele, Jonathan. "Terrorism Is Not an Enemy State That Can Be Defeated." *The Guardian* (UK). 23 November 2003.

Stewart, Desmond. *The Arab World*. New York: Time Life Books, 1972.

"Study Shows What Germans Think about Islam." *Deutsche Welle* (Broadcaster). 27 July 2003. <http://www.dw-world.de>.

"Sudan: Population." *Encyclopedia Britannica Online*. 13 February 2005. <http://www.britannica.com>.

"Syria." *Columbia Encyclopedia*, The Free Dictionary.com. 2005. <http://columbia.thefreedictionary.com>.

"Syria, International Religious Freedom Report 2004." Bureau of Democracy, Human Rights, and Labor. U.S. Department of State. 15 September 2004. <http://www.state.gov>.

Taspinar, Omer. "Europe's Muslim Street." *Foreign Policy* 135. March/ April 2003.

"Tasks and Challenges of the Reconstruction of Iraq." Baghdad Economic Research Center. Center for International Private Enterprise. 2001. <http://www.cipe.org>.

Taylor, Catherine. "Fundamentals of Democracy." *The Australian.* 1 December 2003. <http://www.theaustralian.news.com>.

Telhami, Shibley. *The Stakes.* Boulder, CO: Westview Press, 2002.

"Tertiary Gross Enrollment Ration." *Global Education Database.* U.S. Agency for International Development, Center for Development Information and Evaluation. 2002. <http://esdb.cdie.org>.

"The Business Outlook for Arab Women." *AME Info Middle East Finance and Economy.* 6 October 2003. <http://www.ameinfo.com>.

"The Forgotten: Palestinian Refugees in Lebanon." Ockenden International (UK). 6 February 2005. <http://www.ockenden.org.uk>.

"The World's Women 2004, Trends and Statistics." U.N. Statistics Division, Demographic. 2004. <http://www.unstats.un.org>

"Total Secondary Enrollment." *Global Education Database.* U.S. Agency for International Development, Center for Development Information and Evaluation. 2001. <http://esdb.cdie.org>.

"Tunisia." *World Report*, Human Rights Watch. 2004. <http://www.hrw.org>.

"Tunisia: Economy." Travel Document Systems. 2005. <http://www.traveldocs.com>.

"Tunisia: Education." Tunisia Online. 2001. <http://www.tunisiaonline.com>.

"Tunisia: International Religious Freedom Report 2003." Bureau of Democracy, Human Rights and Labor. U.S. Department of State. 18 December 2003. <http://www.state.gov>.

"Tunisia: Women and Civil Rights." Tunisia Online. 2001. <http://www.tunisiaonline.com>.

"UAE Population Topped Four Million in 2003." Middle East Online. 2004. <http://www.middle-east-online.com>.

"Universities." *The Emirates Network.* 2005. <http://www.theemirates-network.com>.

"UN Report: Most Arab Youth Want to Emigrate to Europe, U.S." *World Tribune.com.* 21 July 2002. <http://www.worldtribune.com>.

"Unprecedented Opportunity." The Center for Public Integrity. Interview with Rami Khoury. 16 March 2005. <http://www.publicintegrity.org>.

Usher, Sebastian. "The Berber Language Is Being Taught in Moroccan Schools for the First Time on Monday." *BBC News World Edition.* 15 September 2003. <http://www.bbc.co.uk>.

Vertovec, Steven, and Ceri Peach. "Introduction" in *Islam in Europe, The Politics of Religion and Community.* London: Macmillan, 1997.

"Views of a Changing World." *Pew Global Attitudes Project.* June 2003. <http://www.people-press.org>.

Vick, Karl. "Sudan, Newly Helpful, Remains Wary of U.S." *The Washington Post.* 10 December 2001.

_____. "Yemen Walks Tightrope in Terrorism Stance." *The Washington Post.* 29 September 2001.

Ward, Christopher. "Yemen's Water Crisis." *The British-Yemeni Society.* July 2001. <http://www.al-bab.com>.

"Water Quality." *Arab News.* 2002. <http://www.arabnews.com>.

Wax, Emily. "Jihad Is Taught as Struggle to Heal." *The Washington Post.* 23 September 2002.

Waxman, Sharon. "I Love You, Now Go Away" (quoting Farouk Hosny, Egyptian Minister of Culture). *The Washington Post.* 17 December 2001.

"When the Voiceless Speak." *Al-Ahram Weekly.* 1–7 April 2005. <http://www.weeklyahram.org.eg>.

"Where the North Meets the South, the Pollution Charges Fly." *The Christian Science Monitor.* 27 January 1993.

Whitaker, Brian. "Why the Rules of Racism Are Different for Arabs." *The Guardian* (UK). 18 August 2000. <http://www.guardian.co.uk>.

Whitlock, Craig. "Saudis Confront Extremist Ideologies." *The Washington Post.* 6 February 2005.

_____. "Moroccans Gain Prominence in Terror Groups." *The Washington Post*. 14 October 2004.

"Why the Islamic World Has Such Hate for the U.S." *Hardball with Chris Matthews, MSNBC*. 19 October 2001. <http://www.msnbc.msn.com>.

Wildman, Sarah. "Third Way Speaks to Europe's Young Muslims." *International Reporting Project. Johns Hopkins University School of Advanced International Studies*. Spring 2003. <http://www.journalismfellowships.org>.

Wilkinson, Tracy. "Promise of Mosque Unfulfilled in Athens." *The Washington Post*. 17 March 2004.

Williams, Daniel. "Egypt Reins in Opponents of Longtime Leader." *The Washington Post*. 2 January 2005.

_____. "Egyptian President Says He Will Push Multiparty Elections." *The Washington Post*. 26 February 2005.

_____. "Immigrants Keep Islam—Italian Style." *The Washington Post*. 24 July 2004.

_____. "Unveiling Islam: Author Challenges Orthodox Precepts." *The Washington Post*. 7 March 2005.

Williams, Peter. "Fighting Through Listening." *Al-Ahram Weekly*. 8–14 April 2004. <http://weeklyahram.org.eg>.

Willis, David K. "The Impact of Islam." *Christian Science Monitor, Weekly International Edition*. 18–24 August 1984.

Wilson, Scott. "Rallies Highlight Rifts in Lebanon." *The Washington Post*. 15 March 2005.

_____. "Religious Surge Alarms Secular Syrians." *The Washington Post*. 23 January 2005.

_____. "Saudi Men Cast Ballots in First Election Since '63." *The Washington Post*. 11 February 2005.

_____. "Shiites See an Opening in Saudi Arabia." *The Washington Post*. 28 February 2005.

_____. "Saudis Fight Militancy With Jobs." *The Washington Post*. 31 August 2004.

Wilson, Willow. "The Show-Me Sheikh." *The Atlantic Monthly*, 40–44 July/August 2005.

"Women in Parliament in the Arab World." Carnegie Endowment for International Peace. 2003. <http://www.ceip.org>.

"Working Conditions in Morocco." CCC, Spanish Clean Clothes Campaign. 2003. <http://www.cleanclothes.org>.

"Worldwide Suicide Rates." Suicide and Mental Health Association International. February 2005. <http://www.suicideandmental-healthassociationinternational.org>.

Wright, Robin. "In Mideast, Shiites May Be Unlikely U.S. Allies." *The Washington Post*. 16 March 2005.

_____. "U.S. Struggles to Win Hearts, Minds in the Muslim World." *The Washington Post*. 20 August 2004.

Yahmid, Hadi. "Belgium Recognizes Muslim Executive Body." Islam Online. 2003. <http://www.islamonline.net>.

"Yemen: Commitment to Education." *Human Development Indicators. Human Development Reports*. U.N. Development Programme. 2003. <http://www.hdr.undp.org>.

"Yemen: Country Reports on Human Rights Practices 2003." Bureau of Democracy, Human Rights, and Labor. U.S. Department of State. 25 February 2003. <http://www.state.gov>.

"Yemen: Economy." *CIA World Factbook 2004*. 10 February 2004. <http://www.state.gov>.

"Yemen Economy Reliance on Oil Deplored." *UPI, Softcom*. 7 December 2004. <http://www.softcom.net>.

Zogby, James J. *What Arabs Think*. Washington, DC: Zogby International, 2002.

Zogby, John. "American Muslim Poll, November-December 2001." Zogby International. 2001. <http://www.amperspective.com>.

Index

About the Author

Margaret K. Nydell is a widely respected scholar and professor of both Standard Arabic and many Arabic dialects. She is currently a visiting associate professor in the Department of Arabic at Georgetown University. She was an Arabic linguist for the Foreign Service Institute, U.S. Department of State, in Washington, D.C., and directed the advanced training school in Tunis, Tunisia. She has also headed several Arabic materials development projects and directed a summer Arabic program in Tangier, Morocco.

Dr. Nydell's publications include *Saudi Arabia Basic Course* (1975), *Arabic Dialect Identification Course* (1993), *Syrian Arabic through Video* (1995), and a six-book series *From Modern Standard Arabic to the* [regional Arabic] *Dialect*. Dialects in this series include Levantine, Egyptian, Iraqi, Gulf, Moroccan, and Libyan. Many of Dr. Nydell's language books are in use as textbooks.

On a consulting basis, Dr. Nydell has lectured on Arabic language and Arab cultural orientation since 1969 for numerous government agencies and private organizations.

Margaret Nydell holds a Ph.D. in Applied Linguistics from Georgetown University and a master's degree in Arabic. She has lived and worked in Morocco, Saudi Arabia, and Tunisia, and she completed postgraduate studies at the American University in Cairo. She is currently consulting with the Center for Advanced Study of Language on a project recording and analyzing Arabian Gulf dialects.